Saudi Arabia

Saudi Arabia's role in the international arena has become increasingly critical to global peace and stability. The fight against international terrorism, the security of the Gulf region and the crucial pricing of oil are all issues where Saudi Arabia stands at the centre of the world stage. This book is a timely guide to explaining the dynamics underlying political developments in Saudi Arabia. It covers the country's historical and religious background, its oil rentier economy and its international role, showing how they interact to create the dynamics of the contemporary Saudi state.

The development of the state is traced through three stages: the formative period to 1962, the centralisation of the state, and the initiation of intensive economic development, between 1962 and 1979 and the re-shaping of the state over the years since 1979. Emphasis is placed on the recent period, with particular attention given to the following areas:

- the economic and foreign policy problems which now confront the state,
- the linkages between Saudi Arabia and Islamic radicalism, with the relationship/conflicts involving al-Qa'ida traced through from events in Afghanistan in the 1980s,
- the impact of 9/11 and the 2003 Gulf War and
- the major problems facing the contemporary state and their solutions.

With the death of King Fahd and the succession of Prince Abdullah who is facing international pressure to undertake reforms, *Saudi Arabia* provides a unique and comprehensive understanding of this state at a crucial time. This book is essential reading for those with interests in Saudi Arabia and its role in Middle Eastern politics and on the international stage.

Tim Niblock is Professor of Arab Gulf Studies at the University of Exeter. He has served as Director of the Institute of Arab and Islamic Studies at Exeter, and formerly as Director of the Centre for Middle Eastern Studies at the University of Durham.

The Contemporary Middle East
Edited by Professor Anoushiravan Ehteshami
Institute for Middle Eastern and Islamic Studies, University of Durham

For well over a century now the Middle East and North Africa countries have formed a central plank of the international system. **The Contemporary Middle East Series** provides the first systematic attempt at studying the key actors of this dynamic, complex and strategically important region. Using an innovative common format – which in each case study provides an easily digestible analysis of the origins of the state, its contemporary politics, economics and international relations – prominent Middle East experts have been brought together to write definitive studies of the MENA (Middle East and North Africa) region's key countries.

Jordan
A Hashemite legacy
Beverley Milton-Edwards and Peter Hinchcliffe

Syria
Revolution from above
Raymond Hinnebusch

Israel
Challenges to identity democracy and the state
Clive Jones and Emma C Murphy

Turkey
Challenges of continuity and change
Meliha Benli Altunişik and Özlem Tür Kavli

Sudan
Abdel Salam Sidahmed and Alsir Sidahmed

Saudi Arabia
Power, legitimacy and survival
Tim Niblock

Saudi Arabia

Power, legitimacy and survival

Tim Niblock

WITHDRAWN
UTSA Libraries

Routledge
Taylor & Francis Group

LONDON AND NEW YORK

First published 2006
by Routledge
2 Park Square, Milton Park, Abingdon, Oxon OX14 4RN

Simultaneously published in the USA and Canada
by Routledge
270 Madison Ave, New York, NY 10016

Routledge is an imprint of the Taylor & Francis Group

© 2006 Tim Niblock

Typeset in Times New Roman by
Newgen Imaging Systems (P) Ltd, Chennai, India
Printed and bound in Great Britain by
TJ International Ltd, Padstow, Cornwall

British Library Cataloguing in Publication Data
A catalogue record for this book is available
from the British Library

Library of Congress Cataloging in Publication Data
A catalog record for this book has been requested

ISBN10: 0–415–27419–2 (hbk)
ISBN10: 0–415–30310–9 (pbk)
ISBN10: 0–203–57235–1 (ebk)

ISBN13: 978–0–415–27419–7 (hbk)
ISBN13: 978–0–415–30310–1 (pbk)
ISBN13: 978–0–203–57235–1 (ebk)

Contents

Acknowledgements

I am indebted to the many people who have generously shared with me their information, advice and views on developments in Saudi Arabia. It would be impossible to name them all, but I must make particular mention of the PhD students of mine who have worked on Saudi Arabia over the years. As so often in PhD supervision, I have felt that I have learnt more from them, than them from me. My colleagues at Exeter, and previously in Durham, have also helped me considerably with their comments and insights.

Some of the material in Chapter 5 also appears in a chapter which I wrote with Dr Monica Malik, in Paul Aarts and Gerd Nonneman, eds, *Saudi Arabia in the Balance: Political Economy, Society, Foreign Relations* (London: Hurst). I must thank Monica for her help with this part of the work. Some of the editing needed to bring the final text to completion was undertaken by Rebecca Niblock, to whom I also extend my thanks.

At a personal level, I have benefited from the help and patience of family members over the time while I am been working on the book. I am grateful to Sally and Stuart, Kate and Dom, and Becky and William for all their support.

A note on transliteration and use of names

It has not been easy to find ways of transliterating Arabic words and names for this book which is both linguistically consistent and enables the words/names to be recognisable and manageable for the lay reader. In practice, I have opted for a measure of inconsistency. Where an Arabic name tends to have an accepted form of spelling in most English-language writing, I have used that. While I refer to the royal family in the linguistically correct form of Al Su'ud, for example, any reference to the country or its people uses the form 'Saudi'. Rather than 'Al-Qa'idah' I write 'Al-Qa'ida'. Similarly, there is the issue of which of a person's names to use as a short-form reference to the individual. Whereas Jamal 'Abd al-Nasir is usually known as Nasir (or Nasser), 'Usama bin Ladin is usually known as 'Usama. I therefore have chosen, albeit inconsistently, to refer to each of them by the name usually associated with them: Nasir and 'Usama.

Chronology

1744	Alliance formed between Muhammed ibn 'Abd al-Wahhab and Muhammad ibn Su'ud.
1765	Ibn Su'ud dies and is succeeded by 'Abd al-'Aziz.
1773	Ibn 'Abd al-Wahhab abandons the position of *imam*. The spread of Saudi political control over the whole of southern and central Najd is completed.
Late 1780s	Northern Najd incorporated into the Saudi emirate.
1792	Al-Hasa falls under Saudi control.
1793	Ibn 'Abd al-Wahhab dies.
1797	Qatar and Bahrain come under Saudi suzerainty.
1801	Raids launched into Mesopotamia.
1802	Saudi emirate gains control of Ta'if.
1803	Sacking of holy city of Karbala. 'Abd al-'Aziz assassinated, succeeded by his son Su'ud. Saudi emirate gains control of Makkah.
1804	Saudi emirate gains control of Madina.
1811	Egyptian forces, at the request of the Ottoman Sultan, land on the Arabian peninsula and are driven back to the sea by Su'ud's son, 'Abdallah. More Egyptian troops arrive.
1812	Egyptian forces take Madina.
1813	Egyptian forces take Makkah and Ta'if.
1814	Su'ud dies and is succeeded by 'Abdallah.
1818	End of the first Saudi state.
1824	Second Saudi state created under Turki ibn 'Abdallah Al Su'ud.
1843	Most successful stage of the second Saudi state begins under the rule of Faisal ibn Turki.
1871	Ottomans occupy al-Hasa and 'Asir.
1887	Ibn Rashid, ruler of Ha'il, captures al-Riyadh. 'Abd al-Rahman ibn Faisal, the main claimant to the leadership of the Al-Su'ud, flees to Kuwait.

1902 'Abd al-'Aziz recaptures al-Riyadh. Creation of third Saudi state.

1906 Most of Najd brought under control of 'Abd al-'Aziz.

1913 Al-Hasa falls to 'Abd al-'Aziz.

1914 First World War breaks out, leading to the end of Turkish influence in the Arabian peninsula.

1915 Signing of Saudi–British treaty of alliance (December).

1920 Most of the 'Asir region brought under Saudi control.

1926 Last vestiges of the Hashimite presence in the Hijaz swept away. First royalties for oil exploration paid. Britain recognises 'Abd al-'Aziz as 'King of Hijaz, Sultan of Najd and its Dependencies'.

1927 Saudi-British Treaty of Jeddah, recognises the absolute independence of the dominions of 'Abd al-'Aziz.

1928 'Abd al-'Aziz asks the United States to extend recognition to Saudi Arabia. Parts of the *Ikhwan* movement revolt against 'Abd al-'Aziz.

1930 'Abd al-'Aziz defeats rebellious elements of the *Ikhwan*. Saudi–British exchange of ambassadors.

1931 The United States gives diplomatic recognition to Saudi Arabia. Ministry of Foreign Affairs established.

1932 Formal adoption of the name Kingdom of Saudi Arabia. Ministry of Finance established.

1933 Oil concession agreement concluded with SOCAL. Saudi–US agreement on consular recognition.

1934 Saudi–Yemeni war; some formerly Yemeni territory added to the Saudi state.

1936 Palestinian uprising. Saudi government position in support of the rights of the Palestinian Arab population begins to develop.

1937 'Abd al-'Aziz persuades Palestinian representatives to attend conference on the future of Palestine.

1938 Discovery of oil in commercial quantities. Development of oil production begins.

1939 US representation is upgraded to ambassadorial level.

1942 The United States begins to give aid to Saudi Arabia.

1943 Roosevelt issues an executive order stating that 'the defence of Saudi Arabia is vital to the defence of the United States.'

1944 Arab League formed, with Saudi Arabia a founding member. Ministry of Defence established.

1945 Saudi Arabia becomes a founder member of the United Nations. 'Abd al-'Aziz meets with Roosevelt and Churchill. Military links with the United States created; the United States establishes an air base for its own use.

1948 Initiation of substantial oil exports.

1951   Commencement of Point Four military assistance agreement with the United States.

1953   Council of Ministers brought into being. Ministries of Agriculture and Water, Education, and Communications established.
'Abd al-'Aziz dies, and is succeeded by Su'ud ibn 'Abd al-'Aziz. ARAMCO strike.

1954   Ministry of Commerce and Industry and Ministry of Health established. Termination of Point Four military assistance agreement with the United States. Faisal is made Prime Minister.

1955   Army officers coup plot discovered.

1956   Suez war: Saudi Arabia supports Egypt and breaks off diplomatic relations with Britain and France. ARAMCO strike. Execution of army officers accused of plotting.

1957   Su'ud gives support to the Eisenhower doctrine. Breakdown of relations between Saudi Arabia and Nasir's Egypt.

1958   Su'ud provides finance for an attempted assassination of Nasir. Saudi government requests a loan from the International Monetary Fund (IMF). Establishment of the United Arab Republic. Overthrow of the Hashimite monarchy in Iraq. Meeting of senior princes, religious and tribal leaders held; all governmental responsibility transferred to Faisal.

1960   Su'ud regains control of the government. Faisal ceases to exercise governmental functions. Talal puts forward his programme of political reform.

1961   Supreme Planning Board brought into existence. Talal criticises the Saudi regime in Beirut. He and two other liberal princes are subsequently dismissed (August). Faisal resumes some government functions (October). Su'ud refuses to sign Faisal's national budget (December). Faisal then ceases to exercise his powers. Su'ud appoints himself Prime Minister. Radio Makkah announces that the Council of Ministers has approved the draft for a national assembly. Three days later, the story is denied.

1962   Faisal and Su'ud agree to share governmental powers (March). Talal leaves Saudi Arabia and restates his demands in Beirut (July). Overthrow of the Hamid al-Din dynasty in Yemen (September), leading to intense Saudi – Egyptian rivalry in the ensuing civil war. Faisal regains full governmental powers and the 'Ten Point Programme' is issued (October). Slavery abolished (November).

1963   Ministry of Information established. Reorganisation of local administration by royal decree.

1964 Su'ud tries to regain governmental control. Su'ud is deposed, Faisal becomes King.

1965 Central Planning Organisation (CPO) established.

1966 Su'ud begins final unsuccessful attempt to regain crown, from Cairo.

1967 Arab–Israeli war. Major financial support for Egypt and Jordan begins.

1968 Public Land Distribution Ordinance passed. Britain announces its decision to withdraw from the Gulf area (January). Ba'thist regime comes to power in Iraq (July).

1969 Labour legislation introduced. Financial support to Palestinian movements begins. Su'ud dies in Cairo. Hundred and fifty people arrested on suspicion of plotting to overthrow the government.

1970 Ministry of Justice established. Faisal makes agreement with North Yemen, ending support for the royalists.

1971 Britain completes its withdrawal from the Gulf (November), with Saudi Arabia now emerging as one of the 'Twin Pillars' of Gulf Security.

1973 October 1973 War. Saudi Arabia orchestrates the oil embargo. Major increase in oil prices.

1974 Lifting of the oil embargo. First Egyptian–Israeli disengagement agreement.

1975 Second Egyptian–Israeli disengagement agreement. Civil War breaks out in Lebanon. Ministries of Higher Education, Municipal and Rural Affairs, Planning (formerly CPO), Public Works and Housing, Commerce, Industry and Electricity, and Posts, Telegraphs and Telecommunications established. Supreme Judicial Council created. Royal Commission for Jubail and Yanbu established. Faisal assassinated, Khalid becomes King (July).

1976 Egyptian government renounces treaty of friendship with the Soviet Union. Saudi Arabian Basic Industries Corporation established.

1977 Sadat announces intention to visit Jerusalem.

1978 Signature of the Camp David agreements. Saudi government offers economic assistance if Egypt reneges on the agreements.

1979 Overthrow of the Shah of Iran (January). Soviet military occupation of Afghanistan (December) Seizure of the Great Mosque in Makkah by Juhayman al-Otaibi and his associated group (November). Shiite demonstrations in the Eastern Province (November).

1980 Outbreak of the Iran–Iraq war (September).

1981   Gulf Cooperation Council (GCC) established.

1982   Khalid dies, Fahd becomes King.

1987   Iranian pilgrims organise a major demonstration in Makkah and Madina.

1988   Iran–Iraq war ends.

1990   Iraqi troops enter Kuwait (August), leading to the Saudi government's invitation for the United States to send troops to Saudi Arabia, and to Saudi participation in the First Gulf War. Saudi women demonstrate for their right to drive (November).

1991   Iraq attacks the Saudi town of al-Khafji (January). Liberals present the King with a petition on political reform (January). First Gulf War (February). Reformists (mainly Islamists) submit a petition, the Letter of Demands, to the Government (May).

1992   Fahd announces reforms (March 1992). Basic Law and Law of the Provinces adopted. Memorandum of Advice presented to the government (July).

1993   Committee for the Defence of Legitimate Rights formed (May). Subsequently some of the prominent members, led by Muhammad al-Mas'ari, leave Saudi Arabia and base themselves in London. *Majlis al-Shurah* begins to operate.

1994   Leaders of the Islamist reformist grouping arrested and imprisoned. 'Usama bin Ladin stripped of Saudi nationality.

1995   'Abdallah takes charge of government, after Fahd's medical incapacitation.

1996   Bombing of the US facility in al-Khobar. Agreement between the Shiite-based Reform Movement and the Saudi government.

1998   Bombing of the US embassies in East Africa, linked to 'Usama bin Ladin.

2001   9/11. Saudi Arabia comes under pressure, due to 15 of the 19 hijackers being of Saudi nationality. Indirect Saudi support for the US military action against Afghanistan (November).

2003   Liberals present petition to the government. National Dialogue started.
       Second Gulf War. Saudi Arabia does not participate.

2004   Trial of academics organising movement for political reform (September).

2005   Municipal elections. Death of Fahd. 'Abdallah becomes King (August).

Abbreviations

AWACS	Airborne warning and control system
b/d	barrels per day
CDLR	Committee for the Defence of Legitimate Rights
CPO	Central Planning Organisation
CRS	Congressional Research Service
EIU	Economist Intelligence Unit
FT	*Financial Times*
GATT	General Agreement on Tariffs and Trade
GCC	Gulf Cooperation Council
GDP	Gross Domestic Product
GOSI	General Organisation for Social Insurance
IFC	International Finance Corporation
IMF	International Monetary Fund
ISI	Inter-Services Intelligence (Pakistani military intelligence)
KSA-CDS	Kingdom of Saudi Arabia, Central Department of Statistics
KSA-CM	Kingdom of Saudi Arabia, Council of Ministers
KSA-MP	Kingdom of Saudi Arabia, Ministry of Planning
KSA-SCPM	Kingdom of Saudi Arabia, Supreme Council for Petroleum and Minerals
KSA-SCT	Kingdom of Saudi Arabia, Supreme Council of Tourism
KSA-SEC	Kingdom of Saudi Arabia, Supreme Economic Council
MAADEN	Saudi Arabian Mining Company
MEED	Middle East Economic Digest
MEES	Middle East Economic Survey
MENA	Middle East and North Africa
MIRA	Movement for Islamic Reform in Saudi Arabia
NCB	National Commercial Bank
NCCI	National Company for Co-operative Insurance
NYT	*New York Times*
OECD	Organisation for Economic Cooperation and Development

OPEC	Organisation of the Petroleum Exporting Countries
PDFLP	Popular Democratic Front for the Liberation of Palestine
PDRY	People's Democratic Republic of Yemen
PFLP	Popular Front for the Liberation of Palestine
PIF	Public Investment Fund
PLO	Palestine Liberation Organisation
RPD	Retirement Pension Directorate
SABIC	Saudi Arabian Basic Industries Corporation
SACMA	Saudi Arabian Capital Markets Authority
SAGIA	Saudi Arabian General Investment Authority
SA-IR	Saudi Arabia Information Resource
SAMA	Saudi Arabian Monetary Agency
SAMBA	Saudi-American Bank
SASE	Saudi Arabian Stock Exchange
SAUDIA	Saudi Arabian Airlines
SCCSRA	Saudi Constitutional and Civil Society Reform Advocates
SCPM	Supreme Council for Petroleum and Minerals
SEC	Saudi Electricity Company
SGI	Saudi Integrated Gas Initiative
SIDF	Saudi Industrial Development Fund
SOCAL	Standard Oil Company of California
SR	Saudi Riyal. For most of the 1970s, 1980s and 1990s, trading at between $1 = SR3 and $1 = SR4
STC	Saudi Telecommunications Company
TI	Transparency International
TRIPS	WTO Agreement on Trade Related Aspects of Intellectual Property Rights
UAE	United Arab Emirates
UNCTAD	United Nations Conference on Trade and Development
UPAP	Union of Peoples of the Arabian Peninsula
UPI	United Press International
US-CB	US Census Bureau
US-CIA	US Central Intelligence Agency
US-DOS	US Department of State
US-EIA	US Energy Information Administration
US-NC	United States National Commission on Terrorist Attacks upon the United States
US-TRO	United States Trade Representative Office
VAT	Value-added tax
WHO	World Health Organisation
WMO	World Migration Organisation
WTO	World Trade Organisation

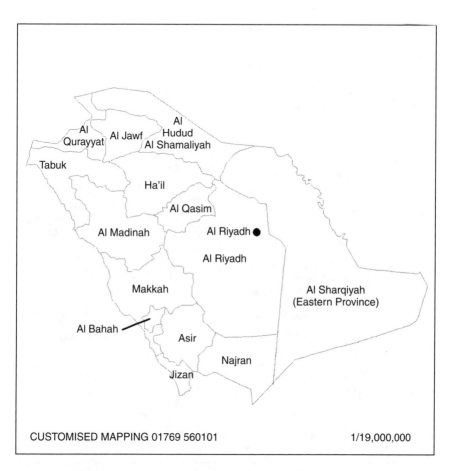

Map 1 Administrative divisions of Saudi Arabia.

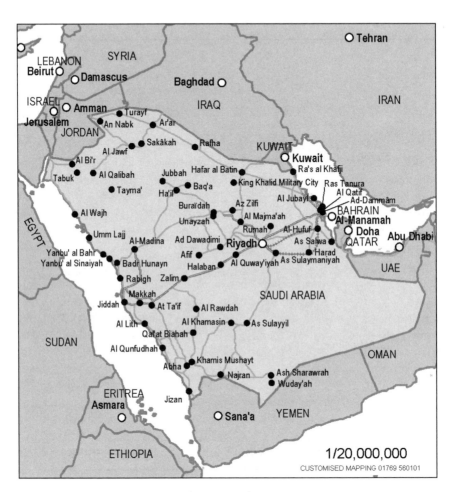

Map 2 Towns and communications of Saudi Arabia.

1 Introduction

The contemporary interest

Saudi Arabia stands at the centre of many of the critical issues and crises which are confronting the Middle East, the Islamic world and the wider global order today. Developments within the country will, therefore, be of crucial importance to the pattern of international relations prevailing in the twenty-first century. There is clearly an urgent need for a good understanding of the dynamics which have shaped, and will continue to shape, the development of the country. There are three main strands to the country's significance: global dependence on Saudi Arabian oil and gas, its critical role on issues of radical Islamism and international terrorism, and its impact on security issues in the Gulf and the wider Middle East. The latter constitute some of the most crucial problems in global security today.

Global dependence on Saudi Arabian oil and gas

Saudi Arabia's production of these hydrocarbon fuels is critical to the international political economy. The level of production and pricing of oil and gas exerts an influence on every aspect of the global economy. No country exerts a stronger impact on the production and pricing of these fuels than Saudi Arabia. Living conditions throughout the world will be critically affected by the ability of the Kingdom to continue a high level of oil production. This, in turn, is dependent on the existence of political stability within the Kingdom and on the strategy which the Saudi government chooses to pursue with regard to pricing, marketing and production. All projections of oil availability and pricing over the coming decades are crucially dependent on how the development of Saudi oil exports is evaluated. Domestic Saudi politics, interacting no doubt with international and global factors, will thus be critical in determining the pattern of world oil production and pricing, and through that the pattern and pace of international economic development.

Saudi Arabia currently holds some 25 per cent of the remaining proven oil reserves in the world. Total worldwide proven oil reserves are estimated (2002 figures) at 1,050 billion barrels, of which 65 per cent (686 billion) is situated in the Middle East. Saudi proven reserves are approximately 260 billion. At the 2004 rate of production these reserves would last about 75 years. Above the proven reserves, Saudi Arabia has an estimated 100 billion 'possible and probable' reserves, and 'contingent reserves' of 240 billion. Oil production in Saudi Arabia, moreover, is cheap relative to elsewhere, increasing its attraction to the global market. Whereas the finding and development costs of oil production in Saudi Arabia come to $0.50 per barrel, the global average is $4–5 per barrel, with the costs in Russia running at $8, in the North Sea at $10.50 and in the US Gulf of Mexico sector at $14.50 (*Saudi ARAMCO Dimensions*: Summer 2004).

The supply side of the global oil market over the coming decades is not likely to see substantial expansion. Despite recent discoveries of new oil fields in Central Asia, Russia, the Falklands and elsewhere, the Saudi share of remaining global oil reserves has risen over the past quarter-century. In 1978 the proportion of global proven reserves made up by Saudi Arabia came to 17.5 per cent (Stevens 1981: 215), as against the 25 per cent figure today. Globally, then, the discovery of new fields in different parts of the world has not even balanced the increase in the estimates of Saudi Arabia's own reserves and the exhaustion of existing fields elsewhere. Although global oil production has continued to rise, some analysts have predicted that the level of production reached in 2004 – 82 million barrels a day – may represent a peak, with production declining thereafter (Deffeyes 2001). Others dispute this prediction, but their perspectives are often based on Saudi Arabia being prepared to produce oil up to its capacity (perhaps 50 per cent above its existing level of production). This would shorten the period through to the exhaustion of its supplies. The decline of production in some of the world's established oil fields, especially those in the North Sea and the United States, will clearly increase further the dependence on the supply of oil from Saudi Arabia. The massive size of the Saudi reserves will thus become of yet greater significance as the twenty-first century progresses.

While the supply side appears to be straining at its limits, the demand side of the global oil market is expanding exponentially. Current estimates are that world energy consumption will rise by 54 per cent over the 2001–2025 period. The main factor here is the rapid industrialisation which China and India have been undergoing, together with that of the wider Asian grouping of developing countries. Developing Asia is expected to grow at an annual rate of 5.1 per cent over the period, as against a global rate of 3.0 per cent. China and India are expected to account for 40 per cent of the increase in world energy consumption. Within the overall energy consumption market, the proportion made up by demand for oil is expected to rise a little, from 38 per cent to 40 per cent, and overall demand for oil is predicted to rise from 77 million barrels a day in 2001 to some 121 billion in 2025. Demand for oil is expected to continue growing after 2025, perhaps reaching some 152 million barrels per day (b/d) per annum in 2050. A portent of the future was the rapid rise in oil prices during 2004 and 2005, with the oil price reaching $60 per barrel for the first time in June 2005. While the price was not expected to remain at that level, the International Monetary Fund (IMF) 2004 World Economic Outlook published in September 2004 predicted that oil prices would remain high over the ten years ahead.

The development of alternative energy supplies will, in due course, reduce the significance of Saudi (and other) oil production. The priority which developed nations give to diversifying their energy sources, spurred on by environmental as well as political concerns, will therefore exert considerable influence on the role and pricing of oil. Energy diversification, however, is a long-term process. The exploitation of energy from renewable sources (wind, wave, sun, hydroelectricity etc.) is developing gradually, and further development can no doubt raise the percentage of energy coming from these sources. In most developed countries, however, these sources currently only account for a small proportion of energy supplies, and change can only come slowly. The United States is the largest consumer of energy in the world (about 33 per cent of the total), and only 7 per cent of US energy consumption comes from this sector, about half of which is from hydroelectric sources (Heinberg 2003: 140). Nuclear energy could be increased significantly, but environmental concerns have in recent years restrained such an increase. Technologies of nuclear fusion and the possibility of cold fusion promise limitless quantities of cheap and environmentally friendly energy, but the horizon when such a development becomes scientifically feasible and practically deliverable tends to recede into the future. The estimated time-line today stands at around 30 years, just as it was 30 years ago. Even when alternative sources of energy become available, moreover, the demand for hydrocarbon fuels will not disappear overnight. Conversion of existing equipment to alternative energy sources will take time. When hydrocarbons are no longer needed for energy, moreover, there will remain a need for them in the production of petrochemicals.

It is probable, therefore, that Saudi oil will be of increasing importance to the global economy in the first half of the twenty-first century, and that no major collapse in the price of oil will occur.

Radical Islamism and the issue of international terrorism

The second dimension to Saudi Arabia's significance relates to its impact and influence on international Islam. Holding the two most holy sites in Islam, attracting many millions of pilgrims every year, Saudi Arabia will always occupy a special position of influence in the Islamic world. Any government of the country, whatever its complexion, would have to emphasise its role as protector of the holy sites, guaranteeing the well-being of pilgrims and perhaps claiming on this ground some right to global Islamic leadership.

The role of Saudi Arabia in international Islam, however, goes beyond this simple reality. The brand of Islam with which the House of Su'ud has always identified itself, and has promoted internationally, carries with it a missionary militancy framed around its puritanical 'return to the foundations' ideology. The call for a return to the foundational texts and to the practices of the *salaf al-salih* (the 'pious forefathers', comprising the prophet's companions and the first three generations of leaders of the Muslim *ummah* [community]) is not in itself a basis either for conservative social practices or for extremism. On the contrary, some of the great Islamic reformers in the late nineteenth and early twentieth century, who were seeking to re-fashion Islamic ideas to respond to the impact of the West, adopted this approach. Muhammad 'Abduh and Rashid Rida both saw themselves as *salafi*s, returning to the foundations of Islam to seek a source for the re-invigoration of Islam – and downplaying the traditions which had built up around Islamic practice over the intervening centuries. Salafism (the term now applied to the religious trends which call for such a return to the foundations), therefore, can be a channel through which the Islamic basis is re-interpreted so as to make clear its relevance to and compatibility with modern conditions. Some of the intellectuals who adopt that approach today are clearly pursuing this agenda. Nonetheless, there has been a prolonged tendency for Saudi Salafism both to be regressive socially and to inspire forms of political Islam which do not co-exist easily with established regimes and with the norms of civil society as perceived in the Western world.

To understand the dynamic of the problem posed by Saudi Salafism it is not sufficient simply to point to the religious ideas on which it is founded – the Islamic interpretations of Muhammad ibn 'Abd al-Wahhab, the religious leader who set the framework of Saudi Salafism in the mid-eighteenth century. As will be shown in Chapter 2, ibn 'Abd al-Wahhab's thoughts may not have been as narrow and dogmatic as they have often been portrayed. The form taken by Saudi Salafism, and the exceptional dynamism which has characterised it, has stemmed from the interaction between the religious basis, the relationship which Saudi *salafi*s have had with the state, and the social and economic context in which it has operated (including in recent times access to funding for spreading its message internationally). The interaction has thrown up dynamics which have both provided the crucial underpinning of the Saudi state and its global influence, and have at times created trends which have challenged Saudi policy internationally and threatened the stability of the state domestically. At a number of times in history, which includes the contemporary period, *salafi*s have challenged the House of Saud, deeming the royal family to have failed to establish or practice the puritanical norms which they believe to be warranted.

It has, however, been the international level which has, not unnaturally, attracted the most attention and has appeared to constitute the greatest threat to global stability. 'Usama bin Ladin was born a Saudi citizen and his ideas and those of his al-Qa'ida associates developed within the ambit of extremist trends in Saudi Salafism. As has been widely observed, 15 of the 19 hijackers who took part in the 11 September 2001 attacks in New York and Washington were Saudi citizens. Even those of the hijackers who were not Saudi citizens, moreover, adhered to a radical Islamist approach associated with extremist Saudi Salafism. This could be said, for example, of the Egyptian leader of the group, Muhammad al-Atta. The dividing line between the official Salafism promoted by the Saudi state and the extremist elements spawned by the movement, moreover, has not always been clear-cut. The trend towards Muslims taking more rigorous interpretations of the requirements of the Islamic *shari'ah*, rejecting the compromises which many Muslims have made to integrate into societies which are not exclusively Muslim in custom or practice, has certainly been given strength and backing from the religious hierarchy in Saudi Arabia.

Developments within Saudi Arabia, therefore, will be crucial in influencing how the Islamic world relates to the wider world and in particular how the forces of radical Islamism are controlled or accommodated within the global system. The Saudi government's ability to develop its own domestic political arena in an effective way, satisfying the interests of key groups and preventing extremists from using Saudi territory and economic resources as their home base, will greatly affect the resolution of the international terrorism dilemma. Much depends on whether the Saudi political leadership can regain the ideological initiative, defusing the radicalism which has been spawned within the country and re-directing it into channels which are less threatening to the stability of the international system. Saudi Arabia is, therefore, key to what President George Bush refers to as the 'war on terrorism'.

Security in the Gulf and the wider Middle East

The third dimension is Saudi Arabia's strategic position and influence on regional issues in the Gulf and the wider Middle Eastern and Indian Ocean regions. The Gulf has been the site of the three major inter-state wars which have occurred in the course of the last quarter-century. The wider Middle East has witnessed a continuing array of smaller conflicts and problem-areas, most notably in Palestine-Israel. Given that there are so many issues of development, identity, external penetration, political oppression and military occupation which remain live and unresolved, the likelihood is that the Middle East will in the coming decade (and perhaps more) continue to experience upheaval and unrest. Outside of the core Middle East, moreover, a new 'arc of crisis' has been forming, at least in the minds of US policy-makers, with developments from Afghanistan, through Iran, Central Asia and the Caucusus to North Africa, posing a challenge to the US-dominated global order. Whereas the Soviet Union was seen as the pivot orchestrating the arc of crisis of the late 1970s, putting it in a position where it could threaten Western oil supplies, now the challenge comes from movements and governments associated with – or reacting to – radical Islam.

Many of the strategic security issues link in with the two previously-mentioned dimensions, played out on the regional stage. Saudi Arabia's involvement in these regional issues clearly stems in part from it sharing with the wider region the same dilemmas posed by radical Islamism and the socio-economic and strategic impact of oil production. The political and strategic weight of the Kingdom, moreover, gives it a natural influence on developments in the region. The country's geographical contiguity or propinquity to the flashpoints of the region – in particular Iraq, Iran and Palestine/Israel – adds a further strand to the inevitable intertwining of Saudi interests with the outcome of regional struggles for power, liberation and ideological hegemony.

While Iraq, Iran and Palestine/Israel have in recent times constituted the foci of Middle Eastern political struggles, future conflict may not be restricted to these areas. The structural impact of oil production (even on non-oil producing countries), the direct access of populations to the international media through satellite television and the internet, the spread of Western cultural norms and tastes among elites, global Islam, pressures for democratisation, and external penetration of political systems, exert an influence on all countries in the region. The ability of governments to cope with the problems facing them is coming under increasing strain. Yemen, on Saudi Arabia's south-western borders, and Sudan and Egypt on the other side of the Red Sea, confront the problems acutely. The governments concerned are seeking to achieve economic and political development while confronting acute social tensions, keen to put forward an appearance of democracy while unwilling to risk their futures to electoral processes. If these issues are not well-handled, whether through the failures of political elites or ill-considered intervention by external powers or movements, the Red Sea region could become an area of conflict.

Population growth, moreover, is likely to change the balances of power and influence in the region. Yemen in 2002 had the highest population growth rate in the world, in excess of 4 per cent per annum, and the US-based Population Reference Bureau's estimates were that its population would reach some 71 million by 2050 (as against 20 million in 2004). The Bureau estimated that Egypt would have a population of 127.5 million (as against 73.5 million in 2004), and Sudan a population of 84 million (as against 39 million in 2004). The population of Saudi Arabia was expected to reach 55 million (as against 25 million in 2004). The changing balance comes out clearly through comparing the Saudi and Yemeni populations. Yemen's population is currently less than that of Saudi Arabia, but by 2050 will be approximately equal to the population of the rest of the Arabian peninsula combined. Among the non-Arab countries of the Red Sea, population increase in Ethiopia is expected to be particularly prominent, rising from 62.5 million in 2000 to 121 million in 2050 (all figures from the Population Reference Bureau). The population distribution around the Red Sea region, therefore, will be substantially different from what it is today, and Saudi Arabia's response to the resulting security and strategic problems is likely to be critical to the stability of the region.

There can be little doubt, therefore, that developments in Saudi Arabia will have a substantial impact on the shaping of the regional and global orders over the coming decades. Whether the impact will be positive or negative depends on the character of those developments. To create a positive impact the Saudi regime will need to pursue patterns of economic and political development which satisfy the needs and wishes of its own population and feed stabilising influences into the regional and international systems. Economic development needs to cover not only adequate economic growth but also a substantial measure of equity and justice in the division of wealth. Political development must enable the populations to determine their own futures, within a framework which coheres with their values.

The need for a new approach: devising an explanatory model of the dynamics of Saudi Arabian politics

There has in recent years come to be a rich and extensive literature on Saudi Arabia, providing valuable information on the country's history and contemporary social, political and economic conditions. Saudi Arabia's foreign relations have also been extensively covered, often within the context of Gulf security. The bibliography of this book provides ample evidence of the wealth of the literature.

What have been lacking, however, are analyses which focus on the dynamics shaping political developments in the country. It is the objective of this book to fill that gap. The task is to identify the underlying bases of political events and outcomes in Saudi Arabia, which are constituted by a range of specific economic, political, social, cultural and historical conditions. By showing how these conditions interact with one another, the dynamics shaping the country's political development in different time-periods are explained. The stress throughout is on understanding why events have taken the shape they have. Recommendations for the Kingdom's future must be based on a recognition of the close interweaving and interaction of the different factors.

Inevitably, a major concern of the book is with explaining what has enabled the monarchical system, with a monarch drawn from the Al Su'ud (House of Su'ud), to remain in power since the formation of the contemporary state, and what the likelihood is that this system of government will survive in the future. The death of King Fahd, and the ascension to the throne of King 'Abdallah, gives particular salience to these issues.

In view of the emphasis given to the dynamics shaping events, it is important to present a model of the elements which form part of the web of interactions. This is depicted in Figure 1. All of the elements in the model are conceived as interacting and moulding each other and in the process determining the direction of events. No part of the interacting system is deemed immutable to influence or change, and the challenge is to understand how each element is shaped by the others. Through building an analytical model of the country's dynamics in this way, it becomes possible to suggest how events may move in the future – or at least to identify the critical processes on which Saudi Arabia's future development depends.

Some explanation of the concepts behind the model is required. The elements in the model are of two kinds. First, there are the 'conditioning factors', which explain the character and nature of the political leadership and why it operates in the manner it does. These comprise the sources of legitimacy on which the leadership depends in claiming its right to rule, and the circles of cooperation (or bases of support) which underpin and surround the leadership. The two sets of factors are inevitably linked; the circles of cooperation close to the political leadership will come from those groupings which share the government's perception of its own legitimacy. In the figure, therefore, the sources of legitimacy and the circles of cooperation are connected by interacting arrows.

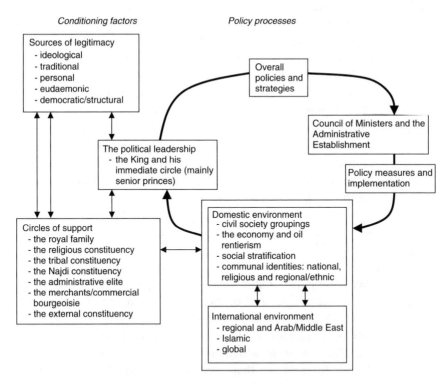

Conditioning factors   Policy processes

Figure 1 The dynamics of Saudi Arabian politics: a model.

Second are the 'policy processes' in the political system: how the political leadership conducts its policies and how this affects the country's development. The critical factors here, besides the leadership itself, are the policies and strategies pursued, the executive/administrative structures through which these are put into effect and the character of the domestic and international environments. Domestic and international developments naturally feed back into the leadership's policy-making. The term 'regime' is used in this book to indicate the political leadership and the channels through which it exerts authority.

In what follows in this chapter, the application of the model to Saudi Arabia will be explained. The ways in which the elements interact constitutes the theme underlying all of the subsequent chapters.

Sources of regime legitimacy

Legitimacy refers to 'the capacity of the system to engender and maintain belief that the existing political institutions are the most appropriate ones for the society' (Lipset 1960: 77). The prominent position given to it in the model requires some explanation. There has been a tendency in recent times for Western observers of Arab politics to neglect legitimacy considerations. To such observers, the role of the military and security services provides the key to understanding how regimes stay in power. Yet the reliance on military and police force for regime survival applies, ultimately, to all political systems. It does not prove the irrelevance of legitimacy considerations. Few regimes, if any, can depend on force alone. They need an acceptance of their right to rule (or at least an acquiescence to their governing) by some parts of the population. The more widespread the belief in the government's right to rule, the less force has to be used in the process of government. An important task, therefore, is to identify how important legitimacy and support groups are, relative to the use of force, in a political system. The claims which a regime makes to legitimacy indicate how the regime seeks to relate to the population and which parts of the population it will turn to for support.

This applies to Saudi Arabia as much as to any other country: the intelligence services, the police and the various divisions of the armed forces all ensure the immediate survival of the regime. Yet the regime could not survive for long on this basis alone. The sections which follow cover five possible bases of legitimacy, each of which has some relevance to the Saudi system. The manner in which each applies, and the strengths and limitations which follow from that, are all examined. The categories of legitimacy used in the analysis are: ideological, traditional, personal, eudaemonic, and democratic/structural.

Ideological legitimacy

This concept refers to a political system enjoying popular acceptance by virtue of articulating, promoting and defending a particular belief-system relevant to how society is organised.

In the Saudi case, the ideology takes the form of a religious-based perception of how society should be organised. The monarchy has always projected itself as protector of the Islamic faith, promoting the implementation of Islamic practices in the Kingdom and helping to propagate the faith in other parts of the world. While the claim to legitimacy is usually conveyed in terms of Islam in general, where the holy places act as symbols of Islam in all of its diverse manifestations, in practice the Islamic dimension is tied to the Islamic tradition initiated by Muhammad ibn 'Abd al-Wahhab and generally known as Wahhabi Islam. The concept, therefore, is generally implemented in terms of the propagation of Wahhabi-inspired Islam. [The term Wahhabism will be used in this book, despite some objections to the term. In practice there is no other term which describes this particular variant of *salafi* Islam.]

While there are very few Saudi citizens who would acknowledge being non-Muslim, there are significant numbers who do not subscribe to the Wahhabi tradition. Historically, Wahhabism has been strongest in central Arabia (Najd), while most of the inhabitants of al-Hasa in the east of the peninsula have been Shiites, the Hijaz has hosted a wide range of Sufi sects and non-Wahhabi Sunni trends, and 'Asir has had religious influences coming from the Zaidis of Yemen. The claim to legitimacy as promoters and protectors of the Islamic faith may be expected to cover all, in practice the link with Wahhabism provides a narrower basis.

Traditional legitimacy

This refers to a ruler enjoying acceptance on grounds of inheritance, where this inheritance links him to an established line deemed to hold the right to rule.

In the case of Saudi Arabia, traditional legitimacy stems from the Al Su'ud having ruled areas of the Arabian peninsula since the early part of the eighteenth century. The force of this claim to legitimacy, however, rests on its projection as a process of unification. The simple fact of having ruled is not in itself significant, as many other families have ruled substantial parts of the peninsula at different times. The claim is projected in terms of the Al Su'ud having been instrumental in bringing the country together – a process which achieved some success in the eighteenth century, experienced both successes and setbacks in the nineteenth century and finally came to fruition in the twentieth century. In effect, then, the claim rests on the construction of the contemporary state of Saudi Arabia, with the royal family entitled on that ground to retain the rulership of the country in their own hands. Accompanying this there is the idea that the Al Su'ud still provides the common element which keeps the country together. The Al Su'ud are portrayed as adept in weaving the different strands of the country together, preventing it from disintegrating.

The appeal of the traditional claim to legitimacy is bound to be stronger among the Najdi population than among the peoples of the other regions. The recollection which the Shiites of al-Hasa, the urban population of the Hijaz with its rich cultural history, and the Yemen-influenced people of the 'Asir have of the process of unification may have a different colouring – however much they may have benefited subsequently.

Personal legitimacy

This applies when popular acceptance of a right to rule rests on the personal qualities of the leader, which are regarded as exceptional. The leader is likely, in such cases, to carry the aura of charismatic leadership.

In Saudi Arabia it is perhaps difficult to disentangle personal legitimacy from traditional or eudaemonic legitimacy (see the following section). All of the kings from 'Abd al-'Aziz have been the focus of organised praise for their characters, abilities and achievements, with an emphasis also on the fatherly relationship traditionally existing between the King and his people. In the case of two kings, however, the element of charisma does appear to have played a particular role: 'Abd al-'Aziz and Faisal. In the case of King Saud, the lack of charisma may have been a factor which weakened his ability to retain the crown.

Eudaemonic legitimacy

This stems from a regime delivering the policies, welfare and perfor- mance which the population seeks. The right to rule comes from the regime being deemed to constitute the best means for the population to fulfil its needs. The policies referred to here do not relate only to mater- ial welfare, but also to wider aspects of well-being. A foreign policy which satisfies a need for national dignity or national security, for example, would be included in this concept. Similar ideas are conveyed by the term 'populist', as has been applied to some Arab nationalist regimes in the Arab world.

Since the beginnings of oil production, but especially since the oil price rises of the 1970s, the Saudi regime has stressed its eudaemonic achieve- ments. While the link to legitimacy has not been made specific, the mes- sage of a right to rule on eudaemonic grounds is nonetheless conveyed. The building up of the infrastructure, the provision of modern educational and medical services to the population, the institution of welfare pro- grammes for the poorer elements of the population, and the modernization of the institutions of the state are projected as the achievements of an effective political leadership.

The limitations to claims to eudaemonic legitimacy arise when popu- lar needs are not being met. Where economic resources are not being equitably spread across the population, and corruption leads both to mismanagement and the acquisition of immense fortunes by those in a position to gain, the eudaemonic dimension becomes de-legitimising. This occurred among some parts of the population of Saudi Arabia during the 1980s and 1990s.

Democratic/structural legitimacy

This covers the right to rule which underpins most liberal democratic political systems. Legitimacy here stems from the will of the majority, as articulated through elections conducted within a constitutional framework.

Any claim to legitimacy on democratic/structural grounds has, of course, been very weak in the case of Saudi Arabia. In response to criticism, the Saudi regime has advanced three kinds of defence. The character of the arguments advanced provides insight into the regime's perceptions on legitimacy. First, the contention is made that Saudi Arabia maintains a structure of law and government which carries a higher legitimacy than that of democracy, based on the Qur'an and associated Islamic texts. Second, it is claimed that the *majalis* (informal councils) of the King and of senior members of the royal family act as a tribal form of democracy where any citizen can approach the ruler or those around him so as to press his case. In practice the *majalis* may be useful for enabling a citizen to solve an immediate and practical problem which he/she is facing, but do not constitute a channel of input into major policy issues. Third, the transition to a more democratic/structural form of government has (especially in recent times) been acknowledged as a long-term goal, but one whose implementation will take time and must not be hurried.

Circles of cooperation and bases of support

Around the political leadership, and associated with particular dimensions of regime legitimacy, are the circles of cooperation on which the regime depends. By virtue of the regime's dependence on them, they may also (depending on the period) constitute critical bases of support.

The dividing line between civil society and the state in Saudi Arabia is less clearly defined than in a developed democratic state. In the latter, it is usually easy to define what groups operate from outside the state (civil society groups and economic interest groups), seeking to influence it, and what organisations are part of the state infrastructure. In Saudi Arabia, as in many developing countries, the distinction is often blurred. The groupings mentioned below, except for the last two, operate in part as elements of civil society – outside of the realms of state control. Yet most of them have an access to state decision-making, and in some cases the implementation of policy, which complicates the view of them as constituent parts of civil society. The delicate interweaving of civil society, the private sector and the state is a characteristic of Saudi Arabia, and the task is to show as accurately as possible how each grouping straddles the civil society–governmental divide.

The royal family

This constitutes the most immediate circle of cooperation around the political leadership. The state dimension of the grouping is, of course, clear at the top-most level. The monarch is drawn from the royal family, whose senior members can influence and sometimes determine who holds the crown. These senior princes, moreover, hold direct responsibility for decision-making in key areas, as well as constituting a unit which in close cooperation with the King determines the direction of overall policy. Some members of the Al Su'ud hold the governorships of the provinces and cities of the Kingdom, while others occupy significant positions in the executive and administrative arms of government. Even those whose positions are not in the higher echelons of government, moreover, can perform a useful role for the state, providing information to the leadership (through the channel of personal relations) on the economic, social, political and security problems facing the country. Given the size of the royal family, consisting of some 7,000 princes, the royal family's political role can be compared to that of a political party in a single-party state: its members are embedded in all parts of the military, security and administrative frameworks, holding the most sensitive positions in the state infrastructure, providing information to the leadership, and sometimes acting as channels of communication between parts of the population and the government.

Yet it would be difficult to describe the Al Su'ud as a state entity. They do not all hold positions, and many are active in the private sector rather than in the state administration (although a significant number are now active in both). Their influence on government decisions may reflect interests which are external to the state, especially if they are involved in commerce. Members of the more outlying parts of the family – those who are not descendants either of King 'Abd al-'Aziz or of his siblings – may not even benefit substantially from easy access to decision-makers.

The religious constituency

The term 'constituency' is to indicate a rather broader grouping than that constituted by the main religious leaders, the *'ulama*. By virtue of the critical source of ideological legitimacy associated with the religious constituency, the latter inevitably constitutes a vitally important circle of cooperation. The relationship again straddles the line between civil society and the state. The Wahhabi *'ulama* draw their incomes, and also most of the financial resources for the operation and expansion of their activities, from the state. They have played a key role in legitimising government policies.

Yet the *'ulama* are not simply an arm of the state. The influence which they carry with the monarch stems from his recognition that they occupy a position of strength in civil society. It is recorded that King 'Abd al-'Aziz 'shook with terror' when he encountered 'Abd al-Latif Al al-Shaikh (the leading 'alim in the early part of 'Abd al-'Aziz's reign) in the streets, and when 'Abd al-Latif died in 1924 commented that 'only now am I truly free.' The *'ulama* enjoy the respect of significant parts of the wider religious community, and they can use this basis of respect to influence broad sectors of popular opinion.

The tribal constituency

The close relations between the leaders of the major nomadic and semi-nomadic tribes and the Al Su'ud stem from the process of expansion and conquest through which the contemporary Saudi state was formed. Whether they had initially supported the spread of Saudi control or not, the tribal leaders came to play a crucial role as guarantors of the quiescence of the tribal peoples and interlocutors between them and the King. The oil economy, and the development programmes instituted by the government, were to lessen the significance of the role of tribal leaders. Tribal solidarity, however, has remained a powerful force which has been used to ensure the loyalty of the military and security institutions.

The Najdi constituency

Central Najd (see Maps) has constituted the heartland of power for the Al Su'ud. While there is an overlap here with the tribal constituency, as the core tribal support for the Al Su'ud has come from the nomadic tribes of the Najd, the wider Najdi dimension also covers the settled agricultural and urban population. The interaction between this basis of support and the ruling regime is more difficult to define than in the earlier categories, given that there is no body identifiable as a Najdi leadership. The Al Su'ud have nonetheless benefited from a special relationship with the central Najdi population, which discourages the other regions (Hijaz, 'Asir, al-Hasa and to some extent northern Najd) from asserting their particular interests against the regime.

The merchants/commercial bourgeoisie

The merchants and commercial bourgeoise have also been crucial elements in the development of the modern Saudi state. The nature and composition of this grouping, and its relationship with the state, however, has varied very substantially over time. Their evolution is given attention in Chapters 2, 3 and 4, and will therefore not be covered in detail here.

The administrative elite

A crucial role in the development of Saudi Arabia is played by those Saudis who have the professional and technical expertise and skills to serve the growing needs of the state. The senior individuals within this grouping gain access to the political leadership decision-makers in the course of their work. Their advice and practical abilities are needed, and on that basis they carry influence. The state machinery could not operate or carry through its development policies without them, and as such they are crucial to the state's eudaemonic legitimacy. While there are members of the ruling family who have become part of the administrative elite, most members of this grouping come from commoner (although perhaps prominent) families.

The external constituency

The character of this circle of cooperation is, of course, different from those covered earlier. It does not relate to any element of the Saudi state's legitimacy. Nonetheless, throughout the period since the establishment of the contemporary Saudi state, the regime has cooperated with individuals and governments which have, through this process, established a privileged basis on which to exert influence. In some cases, this has involved individuals acting independently. Under 'Abd al-'Aziz most of the key advisers to the King were foreign nationals, some from the Arab world (such as Hafiz Wahbah, an Egyptian who advised on foreign policy issues) and some from Western countries (such as the Briton, St John Philby). These advisers were there to promote 'Abd al-'Aziz's interests rather than those of their own home countries. Through the expertise, knowledge and informed opinion which they brought, and for which they were valued, they played significant roles in the formulation of policy under 'Abd al-'Aziz.

At another level, there have been the governmental relationships where external powers have provided elements of military, intelligence, strategic or economic support deemed critical to the survival of the regime or the security of the country. The close cooperation and coordination inherent in such a relationship with an external power, framed around the common interests of the Kingdom and the power concerned, has been an important basis for influence. No doubt that influence has flowed in both directions, especially at those times when the outside world has been most dependent on Saudi oil, but the concern here is specifically with Saudi decision-making.

The policy processes

The operation of the policy processes are best conveyed through the account of how the Saudi state developed, as is done in the subsequent chapters. The intention here is simply to cover the definition of some of the terms used.

'Political leadership' refers to those who take the key policy decisions. It is important to separate this from the role of the Council of Ministers. Both in the Basic Law, which now defines the role of the different organs of state, and in historical practice, the King stands at the centre of the policy-making process. It would, however, be misleading to define political leadership in terms of the monarch alone. In practice key strategies and policies are developed by the King in consultation with senior princes, and occasionally with other members of the web of contacts around him, whether they hold formal positions or not. The balance of influence between the King and senior princes, and among the latter, has varied over time. Under King Khalid (1975–81), for example, much of the effective decision-making was left in the hands of Crown Prince Fahd. Between 1995 and 2005, Crown Prince 'Abdallah acted as regent following the King's medical incapacity. His powers, however, were not equivalent to those which kings have wielded and which he now wields as King. A delicate balance of power characterised the relationship among the senior princes in the political leadership during the 1995–2005 period.

The role of the Council of Ministers has at all times been subsidiary to that of the political leadership. In Figure 1 the Council of Ministers and the administrative machinery which it controls are located at a later point in the decision-making process, reflecting their role in giving practical effect to the overall strategies and policies determined by the political leadership.

The 'domestic environment' is taken here to include all aspects of the social, cultural, political and economic make-up of the country – excluding the formal processes through which policy decisions are made and implemented. As such, the domestic environment forms the base for other elements in the system. The circles of cooperation around the political leadership, for example, are rooted in wider phenomena present in the domestic environment. The tribal and religious leaders who figure among the circles of cooperation around the political leadership draw their significance from the strength of tribal and religious groupings in the domestic environment. The influence of the merchants and commercial bourgeoisie, similarly, depends on the structure of the economy and the role played by the private sector. The administrative elite has its base in the technically and professionally skilled elements emerging out of the expanding educational system. The aspects of the domestic environment most important to the analysis, and whose development is traced through in the subsequent chapters, are the character of Saudi civil society (with particular reference to the non-state dimensions of Wahhabism), the structure of the economy (focusing on the transition from an agricultural economy to one characterised by oil rentierism) and the changing patterns of social stratification.

The 'international environment' consists of all events and developments outside of Saudi Arabia which impinge upon it. Three crucial dimensions of this environment can be identified. First, the global order: how Saudi Arabia relates to the great powers and their roles, the international institutions and the balance of international power. Second, the Islamic world where Saudi Arabia has claimed the right to a leadership role. Third, the regional environments. 'Environments' need to be plural as Saudi Arabia forms part of two different , but linked, regional sub-systems: that of the Gulf, where the issue of Gulf security and the relationships with Iran and Iraq are crucial; and that of the Arab world/Middle East, where the Arab–Israeli conflict forms an inevitable focus of attention.

The structure of the book: chapters and themes

As the objective of this book is to bring out the dynamics shaping events, stressing the interconnections between different factors, the chronologically-phased chapters (Chapters 2, 3 and 4) are not limited to domestic political developments. Issues in foreign relations and the economy need to be integrated into the analysis. Each chapter ends with a summary of the overall dynamics characteristic of the period concerned, described in terms of the analytical model already presented. The two final chapters (5 and 6) focus specifically on foreign relations and the economy. Even in these chapters, however, the linkages with domestic developments (and between economic and foreign policies) are given attention.

Chapter 2, 'State formation', covers the emergence of the contemporary Saudi Arabian state, starting with the aspects of continuity which link today's state with the emirates which the Al Su'ud ruled in Arabia in the eighteenth and nineteenth centuries. The process whereby King 'Abd al-'Aziz Al Su'ud re-claimed his family's historic heartland in 1902, and then expanded his territorial control to encompass the greater part of the peninsula, is described. The focus then moves to the impact which oil wealth had on the political and social structures of the kingdom through to 1962. Contrary to the approach of most other books on Saudi Arabia, the modern Saudi state is seen as having been instituted in 1962 rather than in 1902.

Chapter 3, 'Faisal and the new polity, 1962–79', covers political and economic developments in the kingdom between 1962 and 1979. The chapter provides backing for the contention that it was Prince (later King) Faisal's regaining of the Prime Ministership in 1962 which marked the institution of the modern Saudi Arabian state. The policies initiated and implemented by Faisal changed the dynamics of the kingdom, politically and economically, transforming the character of the state. This period when the modern state was being laid down and developed is seen as continuing through to 1979, despite Faisal himself having been assassinated in 1975. The four years following his death did not see any marked change of direction.

Chapter 4, 'Redirecting the polity: 1979 to the present', examines political and economic developments from 1979 to the present day. The framework of the state, as instituted by King Faisal, was still in being. A new set of problems and dilemmas was arising, however. Three significant events for the Saudi regime occurred in the course of 1979: the siege of the Great Mosque in Makkah, the Islamic revolution in Iran, and Shiite demonstrations in the Eastern province. The regime responded by strengthening the Wahhabi identity and infrastructure of the state, which served its short-term interests both domestically and externally. These policies, however, were to lay the basis for the crises faced by the Saudi state during the 1990s and into the new millennium. The first Gulf War, and the entry of US troops into Saudi Arabia, highlighted the contradictions inherent in Saudi domestic and foreign policies. Opposition came to be focused around an Islamist critique. Elements of the opposition moved outside of the country. Some of the most basic strategies and policies of the regime have now undergone reassessment, but the pace of actual change has been slow.

Chapter 5, 'The challenge of economic reform', looks at the key economic dilemmas facing the Saudi Arabian state today, set within the context of the country's overall political economy. While the economic development of the country has proceeded quickly, there remain key critical areas where severe problems remain: the provision of adequate and economically productive employment for the population (both male and female), the achievement of a reasonable level of equity in the distribution of rewards from the economy, the creation of economic structures appropriate for the long-term (non-oil) viability of the economy, and the creation of a social and physical infrastructure adequate for popular needs.

Saudi Arabia's application for membership of the World Trade Organisation makes urgent the resolution of these problems.

Chapter 6, 'Foreign policy: dilemmas of the alliance with the United States and the challenge of international terrorism', examines the central issues confronting Saudi foreign policy-making in recent years. Emphasis is placed on the interplay between two opposing, yet linked, realities. On the one hand, Saudi Arabia is highly dependent on the United States for its security. On the other hand, the informal alliance with the United States has created or intensified some of the country's security problems. Regional and domestic opposition to the Saudi regime has often been shaped by antagonism to the country's alliance with the United States. The interplay between these two realities has an impact on many critical realms of Saudi foreign policy: coping with international terrorism, fostering security and stability in the Gulf region, playing a leadership role in the context of the wider Arab world, and confronting pressures to cohere with international human rights conventions and uphold democratic freedoms.

The last chapter, 'Conclusion: crisis, reform and stability', draws together the themes pursued in the book, giving an overall assessment of the future of the monarchical system in Saudi Arabia.

2 State formation

Traditional dynamics and the changing domestic and international environments

The pattern of Saudi rule on the Arabian peninsula from the eighteenth century through to the initiation of oil exports in 1948, over the periods when a Saudi state existed, did not change greatly. It rested throughout on the Al Su'ud managing such territory as they controlled through alliance with religious leaders and cooperation with tribal leaders. The dynamism of religion helped to spread the territorial reach of their authority. The limited resource base ensured that there was no significant change in the size of, or roles played by, different social groupings. The domestic environment, therefore, remained relatively static. With regard to how the Saudi rulers related to the international environment, however, there was substantial change. Up to the twentieth century, the international environment was largely restrictive: it prevented the Saudi statelets from expanding. When Saudi activities became threatening to the stability of the region or challenged Ottoman interests, the Saudi state was destroyed. There were no significant sources of external support on which they could or did draw. In the twentieth century the international environment combined restrictive and support dimensions. Britain, and subsequently the United States, provided the material assistance and international diplomatic backing which enabled the Saudi state to maintain a modicum of domestic stability and international acceptability. But they also limited the scope of the Saudi state's regional ambitions.

The character of the domestic and international environments was to change radically after 1948. The massive new resource base stemming from oil revenues had an immediate and substantial effect on the balance between different groupings in society. Most aspects of life in the Kingdom were affected by the new revenues reaching the central institutions and personalities of the Saudi state. The Kingdom's interaction with its international environment also underwent change: the Saudi state now had the ability to exert more influence in the regional and global arenas, yet in some respects it was also more dependent than before. The development of the oil resources required an increased level of external involvement in the Kingdom and security support to protect these resources against external predators.

Yet the policies emerging from, and the practices of, the political leadership did not change in character in the decade following 1948. These were now better-financed than before, but the allocation of resources still depended on the *ad hoc* decisions of the King. As before, they were geared towards satisfying the interests of the circles of cooperation on which the monarch had always depended: the wider royal family, religious leaders, the tribal leaders and some leading merchants. The creation of new institutions, such as the Council of Ministers, did not substantially change the *modus operandi* of decision-making. Even the details of policy were still being shaped by the interactions between the King and the tradition-based circles of cooperation. The gains from oil production were going to a small group at the centre, rather than being used for a coordinated plan to promote development and transform the social and economic co.nditions of the population. Legitimacy, therefore, remained centred on its religious and traditional foundations, rather than shifting towards a broad-based eudaemonic support among the population.

The failure of the political leadership to adapt its policies and practices to the changing conditions wrought by the export of oil led to political crisis in the late 1950s and early 1960s. The combination of widening social and economic divisions, the evident wastage of oil revenues (such that, paradoxically, the country was forced to seek assistance from the International Monetary Fund) and the incompetent political leadership created unrest and undermined the coherence of the state. Changes in the regional and wider international environments, moreover, added to the threat. Arab nationalism was a growing force in the Arab world, invigorated in particular by Nasir's leadership, and the spirit of the movement was republican and socialist. Both strategic and anti-colonial motivations inclined Arab nationalism to look towards the Soviet Union for support. The Saudi monarchy appeared increasingly as a relic left over from a previous age, ready to be swept aside by the tide of history.

The last section of this chapter looks at the power struggle which occurred within the Saudi political leadership when confronted by this deteriorating situation. By the end of the period, a transformation in the character of the state was under way. The policies and practices of the political leadership were undergoing substantial change.

The historical background covered in this chapter is intended specifically to bring out the legacy which contemporary Saudi Arabia has inherited from the past. The aspects of the historical record presented are those which help to explain the structure and dynamics of the state as it exists today. The impact which the historical developments have had on the present will, where appropriate, be made specific.

The Saudi emirates of the eighteenth and nineteenth centuries and their legacy

The Saudi–Wahhabi alliance

Of key importance among the historical, economic, environmental and social factors which have shaped the contemporary Saudi state has been the link between the Al Su'ud and the *salafi* movement commonly known as Wahhabism. The link originated with the alliance which the religious leader, Muhammad ibn 'Abd al-Wahhab, forged with Muhammad ibn Su'ud, the ruler of the statelet of Diri'iyah in Najd, in 1744. The conception of the Saudi state being shaped by the intertwining of temporal power and religious activism has remained a constant in subsequent Saudi rule on the Arabian peninsula. This can be traced through all three historical articulations of the Saudi state: the first (1744–1818), second (1843–91) and third (1902–present). While the term 'Wahhabism' has not always been acceptable to the religious leaders of Saudi Arabia, it is difficult to find a different term to describe the particular variant of Salafism which is predominant within the Kingdom. The followers of the movement historically referred to themselves as *muwahhidun* (upholders of the one-ness of God), due to their emphasis on *tawhid* (the one-ness of God and all that pertains to his universe). The common use of the term *salafi* did not come into use until the late nineteenth century.

The bases of ibn 'Abd al-Wahhab's thought

The heart of Muhammad ibn 'Abd al-Wahhab's doctrine lay in the concept of *tawhid* and the rejection of anything which smacked of idolatry (*shirk*) or polytheism. Many of the practices which had grown up around Islam over the centuries – such as the veneration of saints' tombs, the special rites of the Sufi orders and the reliance on holy men to intercede with God on behalf of the believer – were rejected as polytheistic accretions to Islam's unitarian vision. Muslims must return to the pristine purity of early Islam, draw their inspiration primarily from the Qur'an and the *sunnah* (the reported sayings and deeds of the prophet), follow the practices of the *salaf al-salih*, direct their worship to God alone and purge the Islamic community of the laxity and corruption which had taken root within it. Innovation (*bida'ah*), defined as any action or belief which the Qur'an, the traditions of the prophet and the prophet's companions did not expressly prescribe, was forbidden.

The image of ibn 'Abd al-Wahhab which has become established in the Western world, and significant parts of the Islamic world, conveys the impression of a religious fanatic who was outside the framework of religious thinking of his day, inclined to take a literalist interpretation of religious texts, ignorant of the Islamic traditions of the great cities of the Islamic world, intolerant of those who differed from him, discriminatory in his attitudes towards women, antagonistic towards Shiites and Sufis (and more so towards Christians and Jews) and committed to the use of violence in the spreading of his idiosyncratic religious ideas (DeLong-Bas 2004: 4–5).

While traditional Wahhabi interpretations of ibn 'Abd al-Wahhab's thought have tended to emphasise the more rigid aspects, some interpretations (both by Wahhabi and non-Wahhabi writers) have given prominence to elements of flexibility in his thinking. Which interpretation is the most valid can be – and has been – debated. The existence of the different interpretative approaches, however, is in itself significant. It suggests that there is a basis on which religious and political leaders could contest some of the restrictive and apparently discriminatory aspects of the Wahhabi tradition.

It is important, therefore, to explain how the more liberal and flexible approach mentioned earlier has interpreted ibn 'Abd al-Wahhab's thinking. Emphasis will be given here to the work of Natana DeLong-Bas, both because this constitutes the most comprehensive English-language assertion of flexibility in ibn 'Abd al-Wahhab's thought, and because it reflects ideas promoted by some (but certainly not all) authorities within Saudi Arabia itself. The line of interpretation described here will be referred to as 'the flexibility approach'.

The flexibility approach stresses that the common perceptions of ibn 'Abd al-Wahhab's thinking are misleading. He came, it contends, from a family which was associated with religious learning, and his intellectual weight is reflected in the 14 large volumes of theological works which he wrote. He had studied under significant religious thinkers, both on the Arabian peninsula and in Basra, and his works show that he was aware of the major religious trends which had moved the Islamic world (DeLong-Bas 2004: 17–19).

Ibn 'Abd al-Wahhab's thought, as interpreted by those who take this approach, coheres with a line of religious thinking which was not uncommon in the eighteenth century Islamic world. There was a widespread perception that Islamic societies had become debased, and a strong tendency among Islamic revivalists to emphasise the need to return to the beliefs and practices of early Islam. These trends were to be found even at the heart of the great Islamic cities. The debasement of Islamic societies was seen as characterised both by loose personal conduct (especially that of the rulers) and by religious practices which had no foundation in the Qur'an and *sunnah*. They saw the existing religious authorities as subservient to political masters who themselves were betraying Islamic principles, oppressing the populations over which they were ruling and drawing illicit gains from their positions. They called for radical reform where Islamic belief and practice would be centred once more on the foundations of Islam, and where rulers and people would be expected to adhere to and practice proper Islamic values. They rejected practices which had no basis in the Qur'an and the *sunnah*, finding unacceptable in particular the worship of saints' tombs – where the Qur'anic emphasis on the one-ness of God was being traduced. They emphasised the continued importance of *ijtihad* (interpretation of religious texts), where every believer in every generation had the right and the duty to interpret the meaning of religious texts rather than to rely on what earlier generations and thinkers had said. They rejected *taqlid* (tradition) as a basis for religious belief and practice, except where the traditions went back to the foundational period. All of these elements are present in the thinking of ibn 'Abd al-Wahhab (DeLong-Bas 2004: 8–14). It is contended, therefore, that he was by no means unusual in the religious stance which he took. In the context of Christianity, the attitudes of these religious revivalists have some resonance both with English puritanism of the seventeenth century and the Christian fundamentalism which became prominent in Victorian England.

Despite the radicalism of ibn 'Abd al-Wahhab's religious message and his desire for state protection and promotion of his religious message, the flexibility approach points to his emphasis on dialogue and discussion. These, it is maintained, were intended to be the main instruments through which people were to be drawn to accept his message. Much of his work, advocates of the approach say, stresses education as the main channel for leading Muslims to a correct understanding of their religion, rather than the instrument of armed *jihad*. The latter is seen as the collective duty of a community, to be determined by the religious and not the temporal powers. Rather than forcing the adoption of a particular straightjacket of religious beliefs, indeed, he lays emphasis on intention, where correct motivation may be more important than correct action (DeLong-Bas 2004: 18–19).

When he did advocate the use of force, it is maintained that he defined closely the conditions which were required and which would justify it. His emphasis was on gaining adherents to true Islam rather than causing death and destruction. In the later part of his life, he abandoned his formal position as *imam* of the Saudi emirate so as to devote himself to religious thought and education. He did not issue *fatwas* (religious rulings) giving legitimacy to all of the wars fought by the early Saudi rulers, and he specifically rejected the use of force when it involved the loss of life by civilians. He did not write about issues of martyrdom nor did he project the image of a paradise to which those who died in the cause of faith would go. Christians and Jews are referred to in the traditional Islamic context as 'people of the book', deserving the status of *dhimmis* (protected people) under an Islamic state (DeLong-Bas 2004: 60–1; 201–224).

Again contrary to the conventional image, the flexibility approach contends that ibn 'Abd al-Wahhab gave considerable attention to the role of women in society, emphasising the balance between men and women and the rights which women should be given. This is not to suggest that he advocated a liberal approach to women's issues. He approved on one occasion the stoning of a woman for adultery. Yet, it is maintained, he insisted on rights which were not widely acknowledged at the time when he was writing: the need for a woman's consent before getting married, a woman's right to control of the dowry given by her husband on marriage, rights to divorce and rights not to be subject to physical maltreatment at the hands of her husband. Rather than insisting that women should cover themselves completely when in the presence of men outside of the family, he advocated that the faces, hands and feet of women could be exposed. A certain amount of mixing of unrelated men and women was possible when this occurred for business or medical purposes. Specific mention was made of the right of women to engage in commercial activities (DeLong-Bas 2004: 123–191).

While the existence of a line of interpretation emphasising flexibility is significant, particularly with regard to Wahhabism's scope for adapting to political and social reform, the historical reality is that the more rigid interpretation of ibn 'Abd al-Wahhab's thought has prevailed. Some would see this as part of the inevitable process of simplification and distortion which occurs when religious and ideological systems become vehicles for state power. The need to control the population and expand territory dictated the way in which the ideas were used. The *muwahhidun* who spread ibn 'Abd al-Wahhab's message by force across the Arabian peninsula were not likely to be attuned to fine distinctions in religious texts. The interests of the state and religious leaders were, moreover, served by utilising and indeed encouraging the intolerant militancy of the *muwahhidun*. By this means they could control the population and spread Saudi power. Even on this count, however, the framework had been set by ibn 'Abd al-Wahhab: it was he who insisted on the need for the temporal authorities to provide protection for, and promote, his religious ideas. The movement built on ibn 'Abd al-Wahhab's thinking was, at times, certainly guilty of promoting some of the repressive and discriminatory attitudes to women, Shiites, Sufis, Christians and Jews mentioned earlier (Vassiliev 1998: 75–78). While this may not have been unusual in the context of the eighteenth and nineteenth centuries, it became increasingly problematic as the twentieth century advanced.

Some of ibn 'Abd al-Wahhab's own militant actions, furthermore, were themselves easily taken as patterns of behaviour to be applied in every circumstance. The stoning of a woman for adultery, for example, probably did more to licence the use of repressive violence towards women than any preaching to the contrary. His destruction of the tomb of Zayd ibn al-Khattab (one of the Prophet's companions) in al-Uyaynah, on the grounds that it had become a site for the worship of a human being rather than God, proved similarly symbolic. It may not have been intended to lead on to the rampant destruction of all tombs, shrines and associated property, but it was an example clearly inspiring some *muwahhidun* towards acts which others would deem vandalism. Wahhabism became, through these processes, associated more with intolerance than with the dialogue which ibn 'Abd al-Wahhab (on some occasions) sought.

Yet it would also be wrong to suggest that the Wahhabi movement has been monolithic and universally restrictive. Surrounding conditions have moulded it in different ways over time often leading to significant differences of approach between prominent *'ulama*. Individual adherents to Wahhabi ideas, moreover, have wrought their own balance between the varying elements making up this framework of religious thought.

The expansion and retreat of the Saudi emirates

The expansion of Saudi power, during the first Saudi state, did not happen quickly. Relatively little was achieved, in fact, while Muhammad ibn Su'ud was alive or while Muhammad ibn 'Abd al-Wahhab was *imam*. Ibn Su'ud died in 1765 and was succeeded by his son 'Abd al-'Aziz. The latter ruled the emirate of Diri'iyah and the associated conquered territories through to 1803. Ibn 'Abd al-Wahhab lived till 1791 but abandoned the position of *imam* in 1773 so as to devote himself to a more quietist role in religious writing, counselling and propagation (DeLong-Bas 2004: 35–40). The spread of Saudi political control over the whole of southern and central Najd, the future heartland of Saudi power, was itself not completed until 1773. Some of the population in these areas had in fact accepted the principles of Wahhabism before they came under Saudi control. The expansion of the Saudi polity at this stage, therefore, tended to be the outcome of prolonged ideological and religious proselytism, indicating that a gradualist approach was being pursued. The reality was that the Saudi emirate was surrounded by emirates which were initially stronger, and the scope for forceful expansion was therefore limited. There was a practical reason for concentrating first on converting the populations to the new religious line.

In the early part of 'Abd al-'Aziz's rule, then, the expansion of Saudi-controlled territory continued at a gradual pace. It was not until the late 1780s that northern Najd was subjugated, and the largely-Shiite eastern Arabia (al-Hasa) did not fall under Saudi hegemony until 1792. From the later part of the 1790s the pace of expansion quickened, with Qatar and Bahrain coming under Saudi suzerainty in 1797. Raids were launched into Mesopotamia (and on occasions even parts of Syria) after 1801, which led up to the sacking of the Shiite holy city of Karbala in 1803. The latter event in turn brought about the assassination of 'Abd al-'Aziz. No systematic Saudi control over these parts of Mesopotamia was established, however, in part because the local Shiite population had no ground for cooperation with the Wahhabi invaders. In the sacking of Karbala some 4,000 Shiites were killed, and holy Shiite shrines including the tomb of Husain ibn 'Ali were destroyed. At the same time, and more controversially for the Islamic world, the Saudi emirate was spreading its control into the Hijaz, gaining control of Ta'if in 1802, Makkah in 1803 and Madina in 1804. These latter developments took place under the rulership of 'Abd al-'Aziz's son Su'ud, whose mother was a daughter of ibn 'Abd al-Wahhab. In the takeover of Ta'if there was considerable violence used against the inhabitants, with the massacre of some 1,500 people (De Corancez: 24). Neither Makkah nor Madina were subject to a similar scale of violence, although some of the shrines were destroyed, some leaders of the community were executed and the Turkish population of the cities was expelled.

The spread of Saudi–Wahhabi power, however, had become a threat to the coherence of the Ottoman Empire. The Ottoman Sultan gave its Viceroy in Egypt, Muhammad 'Ali, authority to send an expeditionary force to the Arabian peninsula and regain control of the holy cities. Initially the Saudi forces, under the command of Su'ud's son 'Abdallah, enjoyed military success against the Egyptian military force which had landed on the Arabian peninsula in 1811 – driving the Egyptian forces back to the sea. The arrival of more Egyptian troops under the command of Muhammad 'Ali's son Prince Tusun, however, shifted the balance against the Saudi emirate. The Egyptian forces took control of Madina in 1812, then of Makkah and Ta'if in 1813. The death in 1814 of Su'ud, who had proved the most able of the early military commanders from the Al Su'ud, further weakened the Saudi position. He was succeeded by his son 'Abdallah. The Egyptian forces then spread out across the Arabian peninsula, finally razing Diri'iyah to the ground in 1818 (Vassiliev 1998: 154). This brought the first Saudi state to an end.

The second Saudi state was created under Turki ibn 'Abdallah Al Su'ud in 1824. The Egyptian troops had not remained in Najd, concentrating their attention more on control of the cities of the Hijaz which were their main interests. The new state was based on the same Saudi–Wahhabi alliance as had been characteristic of the first, but was limited mainly to Najd. The most successful stage of the second state was between 1843 and 1865 under the rule of Faisal ibn Turki. Over these years the state was effectively pursuing a 'Wahhabism in one country' policy, rather than seeking to expand outside of central and eastern Arabia. Faisal acknowledged Ottoman overlordship through the payment of an annual tribute, and in return achieved recognition of his own position (Safran 1985: 17). The second Saudi state, however, was bedevilled by intra-Su'ud divisions, and this in due course led to the dismantlement of the state in the later part of the century. Ibn Rashid, ruler of the emirate of Ha'il in the north of the peninsula, eventually captured the Saudi capital of al-Riyadh in 1887 and annexed the area to his emirate. 'Abd al-Rahman ibn Faisal, the main claimant to the leadership of the Al-Su'ud, fled to Kuwait and remained there through to 1902 with his son 'Abd al-'Aziz (Al-Rasheed 2002: 24–25).

The form of rule over the first and second Saudi states was remarkably consistent, and indeed was to be little changed when 'Abd al-'Aziz established the third Saudi state in 1902. The linkage between the religious and temporal powers characterised all three states, with the *'ulama* playing an important role in shaping social attitudes in all three.

The legacy

The relationship between Wahhabism and the Saudi political system, in all three of the Saudi states, has been close and supportive. Without the support of the Al Su'ud, Wahhabism would not have gained a predominant position within the Islamic framework of the Arabian peninsula, and without the militant support of the Wahhabi movement it is unlikely that the Al Su'ud would have gained territorial control of the peninsula. Wahhabism provided the basis on which the Al Su'ud could claim legitimacy both for their control of existing territories and for the expansion of their control.

The relationship has, however, also had a restrictive element – defining the parameters within which each has been able to move. The state, for its part, has had to act within the circle prescribed by the Wahhabi *'ulama* so as to retain the support of this vital movement. Policies which might offend the religious sensibilities of the *'ulama* have had to be avoided. But the necessary involvement of the *'ulama* in the regulation of Saudi society has not been limited simply to influencing government policy. More significant have been the direct responsibilities devolved to the religious leaders enabling them to mould the character of Saudi society. Their control of the mosques (a powerful instrument for shaping popular opinion) is natural, but they have also played a prominent role in the educational system and in regulating social conduct through the Committees for the Promotion of Good and the Prevention of Evil. The extent of their powers in these spheres has varied over time, but a powerful influence in shaping Saudi society has been consistently maintained. At times this has run counter to the needs and objectives of the state's political leadership, imposing a straightjacket which has limited the scope of socio-economic development. The state's often-repeated desire to reduce dependence on migrant labour, for example, is complicated by some of the restrictions on the employment of women in a non-segregated environment – which tend to be vigorously upheld and monitored by the Organisation of the Committees for the Promotion of Good and the Prevention of Evil.

The exclusion of other Islamic religious trends from the central processes of the state has simplified the task of socio-religious organization within the country, creating a unifying central ethos to the state. Yet the absence of religious pluralism has underpinned the rigidity of the views promoted by the religious leadership. Rather than having to engage with the wide range of religious trends present (yet submerged) in Saudi territories – the Shiites in the east of the country and the religious leaders adhering to non-Hanbali traditions in the Hijaz – the Wahhabi *'ulama* have tended more to assertion than dialogue (Galindo 2001: 149–152). The rejection of aspects of the religious practice of heteredox Islamic trends and sects was part of ibn 'Abd al-Wahhab's message, but those who adopted his religious ideas in other parts of the Islamic world were sometimes more adventurous in their religious thinking. The Egyptian intellectual and religious thinker Rashid Rida, for example, framed his ideas around ibn 'Abd al-Wahhab's approach to Islam, yet his engagement with other religious trends enabled him to develop well-integrated conceptions of how Islam could react and respond to the challenges created by the incursions of the West into the Islamic world (DeLong-Bas 2004: 3).

The very vitality of the popular Wahhabi movement, furthermore, has posed problems for both the religious and political leaderships. Ibn 'Abd al-Wahhab's puritanical and inherently egalitarian message – where any Muslim could become a *muwahhid*, live without the trappings of luxury and devote himself to promoting the creed – exerted a powerful hold on the popular consciousness. Those swayed by these ideas could turn against the state, and the religious leaders associated with the state, if they perceived the state to have betrayed the Wahhabi ethos. This occurred at the end of the 1920s when parts of the *Ikhwan* movement rose in revolt against 'Abd al-'Aziz, and more recently in the radical Islamist opposition which developed from the late 1970s, gaining initial prominence with the seizure of the Great Mosque in Makkah in November 1979. The dilemmas inherent in this situation were in fact already apparent when ibn 'Abd al-Wahhab was alive. Seeing the wealth which was accumulating in the hands of those who had gained from the expansion of Saudi power, he criticised the conduct of those concerned. His withdrawal from the official position as *imam* may have been triggered by a desire to dissociate himself from such conduct (DeLong-Bas 2004: 38–40).

The Wahhabi dimension in the make-up of Saudi Arabia is, thus, not simply an aspect of social life and belief. It is integral to the character and dynamics of the state, underlying the legitimation of the political and social orders. In this perspective, Saudi Arabia requires no constitution, because the Islamic *shari'ah* provides the framework within which government operates and law is formulated; representative institutions are unnecessary, because the consultation (*shurah*) which the Qur'an prescribes is already practised through the open access which Saudi citizens have to those who govern; liberal democracy is, furthermore, undesirable in so far as it provides opportunities for the undermining of Wahhabi/ Islamic values. The state must act positively to counter any 'laxity or looseness' in society, and it does this by permitting religious-based organisations to promote and enforce the relevant Wahhabi/Islamic modes of conduct.

Capturing power and spreading control: establishing the third Saudi state, 1902–32

The creation of the contemporary Saudi state (or, historically, the third Saudi state) is usually dated from 1902. In that year, 'Abd al-'Aziz ibn 'Abd al-Rahman Al Su'ud and 24 companions broke from their exile in Kuwait and launched a successful assault on al-Riyadh which up to that time had been held by the Al Rashid, rulers of Ha'il in northern Arabia. The re-conquest of the Al Su'ud's traditional domains in Najd followed. By 1906, most of Najd was under 'Abd al-'Aziz's control. In 1913, the Eastern province of al-Hasa fell to his forces, and in 1920 most of the 'Asir region was brought under the Al Su'ud (with some further slivers of formerly-Yemeni territory added after the Saudi–Yemeni war of 1934). In 1926 the last vestiges of the Hashimite presence in the Hijaz were swept away. The country, first known as the Kingdom of Najd, Hijaz and its Dependencies, formally adopted the name Kingdom of Saudi Arabia in 1932 (McLoughlin 1993: 103–122).

The armed force which established 'Abd al-'Aziz's authority over the major part of the Arabian peninsula was composed largely of ex-bedouin. It would, however, be wrong to see the movement which 'Abd al-'Aziz led as incorporating or reflecting bedouin interests. Over the first four years which followed the capture of al-Riyadh, the armies which 'Abd al-'Aziz raised for battles with the Al Rashid consisted primarily of townspeople and settled agriculturalists. Those who fought returned to their everyday occupations once battle was finished. To expand his power beyond central Najd, he needed an organised force whose members would be ready for military action at any time. Tribal contingents supplied by bedouin tribal leaders could not fill this need: they were too fickle in their loyalties. 'Abd al-'Aziz turned, therefore, to the idea of settling numbers of bedouin in agricultural settlements (*hujar*), where they would renounce the nomadic life and be welded through religious instruction and military training into an instrument which could spread Wahhabi belief and Saudi power throughout Arabia. They became known as the *Ikhwan*. Despite their bedouin origin, the *Ikhwan* were shaped, financed and maintained by the political and religious leadership around 'Abd al-'Aziz (Habib 1978: 16–17).

The Kingdom's political processes prior to oil, 1932–48

The domestic bases of support

Although the circumstances which surrounded the emergence of the contemporary Saudi state hold few parallels within the Arab world, the form of the state established by 'Abd al-'Aziz fits into a pattern familiar to many traditional societies before the onset of colonialism. The exercise of the monarch's political authority required close collaboration with, and support from, other members of the royal family, the religious leaders, the tribal leaders and the major merchants. The pattern and exercise of authority, indeed, was similar to that which had existed in the first and second Saudi states.

Within the royal family, despite 'Abd al-'Aziz's pre-eminent position, other prominent members of the family could nonetheless pose a threat to the monarch if they were not conciliated. For much of 'Abd al-'Aziz's reign, for example, the King's brother, Muhammad ibn 'Abd al-Rahman, formed an opposing pole to 'Abd al-'Aziz within the royal family – continually competing for influence among family members and among the Al al-Shaikh (descendants of ibn 'Abd al-Wahhab, who retained the prime positions in the country's religious leadership). Despite the fact that the King's eldest son, Su'ud, had been nominated Crown Prince by the King in 1933, Muhammad hoped still to swing the succession to his side of the family. Members of the royal family and of families linked to the Al Su'ud by marriage, moreover, played a critical role in administering the King's realm. Prince Su'ud ibn 'Abd al-'Aziz was viceroy of Najd; Prince Faisal ibn 'Abd al-'Aziz was viceroy of the Hijaz; the Jalwi family supplied governors for al-Hasa (subsequently called the Eastern region) and the Sudairi family governors for 'Asir. While all of these held office at the King's pleasure, they nonetheless occupied entrenched positions and could not lightly be disregarded.

The tribal leaders effectively ensured the loyalty of their tribal followings to 'Abd al-'Aziz. The relationship between them and 'Abd al-'Aziz, therefore, was one of mutual dependence. In return for subsidies provided by the public treasury and the recognition given by 'Abd al-'Aziz to their administrative authority within their own areas, the tribal leaders secured and maintained the political acquiescence of a significant part of the population. The assurance of direct and frequent access to the King reinforced the tribal leaders' involvement with the Al Su'ud, as also their ability to influence the decisions which the King took. Links were further strengthened by intermarriage between the Al Su'ud and the families of tribal leaders; 'Abd al-'Aziz himself took wives from the leading families of each of the major tribal groupings.

Given the religious element built into the Saudi state, the role of the religious leaders was bound to be important. The *'ulama* helped to shape the type of state which emerged, and they in turn were used by the King in the achievement of his political objectives. They promoted the expansion of religious education using this to inculcate a common value system in the rising generation of the new state. Controlling the legal system, they spread uniform legal practices. Through the authority which they held over the 'Committees for Encouraging Virtue and Forbidding Evil', they exerted a very real influence over the behaviour of the populace. A regular weekly meeting with the King guaranteed their access to the centre of political power.

The *'ulama*'s power to issue *fatwa*s on any issue which concerned them was a useful instrument to promote governmental objectives, but so also could that power thwart governmental objectives. The importance to 'Abd al-'Aziz of maintaining the support of the *'ulama* was apparent in his strenuous attempts to persuade them to sanction the introduction of Western mechanical equipment into the country – wireless communications, telegraph and automobiles – and in his willingness to delay the introduction of such machinery until the sanction was given. Furthermore, when the *'ulama* in 1950 objected to the King's plans to celebrate a golden jubilee marking the 50th anniversary (in lunar years) of the capture of al-Riyadh from the Al Rashid, the project was duly abandoned.

The commercial establishment and the political leadership were also bound together by ties of mutual dependence. The principal sources of funds for the public treasury between 1926 and 1933 (when the first royalties for oil exploration were paid), and continuing as a substantial source of revenue up to 1947, were dues levied on the pilgrim traffic to Makkah and custom dues. Both sources depended on the vitality of the commercial sector to provide the necessary services for pilgrims and to maintain a thriving trade from which duties would be payable. Moreover, merchants were frequently called upon to 'donate' money or provisions for particular purposes – whether to finance a military campaign or to fill the store houses from which grants of provisions were made. A further aspect of the commercial establishment's importance, moreover, was its strong connections with village and town leaders; the latter, indeed, were often engaged in trade in a major way. On the occasions when 'Abd al-'Aziz took economic decisions which were inimical to the interests of the commercial establishment, he frequently found himself forced to retreat – as in 1926, when he sought to confiscate all supplies of tobacco in the Hijaz, and in 1933, when he granted a concession to the Soviet Vostgostorg trading company to import freely into Saudi Arabia and undertake its own retailing (Niblock 1981: 14–17).

It was the limited scale of resources at his disposal which impelled 'Abd al-'Aziz to take cognisance of the interests of the groups mentioned in the previous paragraph. As the state did not have the funds to create strong administrative or military structures, or to pursue an extensive programme of economic development, other means for defending the country's security, territorial integrity and coherence were needed. The links which the Al Su'ud maintained with the tribal leaders, the *'ulama* and the commercial establishment in turn made it unnecessary to develop a strong central administration. Governmental organisation remained skeletal. At the end of 1947, there were only three government ministries – those of Foreign Affairs (est. 1931), Finance (est. 1932) and Defence (est. 1944). There was no Council of Ministers and no position of Prime Minister. Such policies as were developed, and such decisions as were taken, emerged largely from the royal court. There the opinions of the King interacted with those of the groupings which had access to him. The small circle of royal advisers – mainly non-Saudi Arabs – helped to formulate relevant documents and the precise strategy (Niblock 1981: 16–18).

International bases of support: from Britain to the United States

The major external alliance which King 'Abd al-'Aziz maintained through the early part of the twentieth century was with Britain. The initial pressure to establish close relations came very much from the side of 'Abd al-'Aziz rather than the British. 'Abd al-'Aziz had opened up links with British representatives in the Gulf almost immediately following his capture of al-Riyadh in 1902, apparently with a view to establishing a relationship with Britain where his emirate would have British-protected status, similar to that of Kuwait and the Trucial States. Such a status would not only secure him against threats from other local states/emirates, but would also enable him to have access to subsidies and weapons. Further overtures were made to British personnel in the Gulf in 1903 and 1906, but with no outcome from the British government – although some of the local British officials did press their government to establish relations with 'Abd al-'Aziz. The British policy was to confine their concerns to the coasts of the Gulf rather than to become involved in developments in the interior of the peninsula. Britain was also eager that its relationship with the Ottoman Empire should not be damaged, given that the Ottomans still claimed overall suzerainty over the Arabian interior. Even when Saudi forces took control of Al-Ahsa in 1913, thereby reaching the Gulf coast, Britain gave 'Abd al-'Aziz no commitment (Al-Damer 2003: 55–66).

Britain's position changed radically with the outbreak of the First World War, especially after 30 October 1914 when Turkey declared war on Britain, France and Russia, in alliance with Germany and Austro-Hungary. Negotiations for a treaty of alliance between 'Abd al-'Aziz and Britain were opened in December of that year, leading eventually to the signing of a treaty one year later – on 26 December 1915. Although the treaty described 'Abd al-'Aziz as an independent ruler, responsibility for the emirate's foreign affairs was given to Britain which in return guaranteed the emirate's territories against external attack. Britain then began to supply 'Abd al-'Aziz with a limited amount of weaponry and similarly limited subsidies. The extent of British involvement, however, remained small: Britain did not have any permanent representation in 'Abd al-'Aziz's territories until 1926 when 'Abd al-'Aziz completed his conquest of the Hijaz; relations were handled through British representatives in the Gulf and in Iraq, and Britain failed to restrain the Saudi King's territorial expansion into northern and eastern Arabia – leading to the removal from power in Hijaz of Britain's ally Sharif Husain (Al-Rasheed 2002: 42–43). Britain did, however, play the central role in determining the course of Saudi Arabia's borders with Kuwait, Transjordan and the new Iraq state.

Soon after the 1915 treaty was signed, in fact, it had become evident that British control of 'Abd al-'Aziz's external relations was not a realistic option. 'Abd al-'Aziz was intent on expanding his territorial control, and the British had no inclination to prevent him (Al-Damer 2003: 55–77).

In February 1926 Britain recognised 'Abd al-'Aziz as 'King of Hijaz, Sultan of Najd and its Dependencies', and proceeded to negotiate a new treaty which was concluded in May 1927. Under this, the Treaty of Jeddah, Britain recognised the 'absolute independence of the dominions' of 'Abd al-'Aziz, and in return the latter agreed to respect British treaties with the Trucial shaikhs, suppress slavery and facilitate the pilgrimage of British subjects. By 1930 the two countries had exchanged ambassadors (Troeller 1976: 236–237).

While the link with Britain may have figured little in Britain's overall international strategy, it was of considerable importance in enabling 'Abd al-'Aziz to maintain himself in power, and strengthen his regional position, through the period during and after the First World War – upto the Second World War. The flow of support, in finance and weaponry, was limited, but it was nonetheless crucial to the coherence and stability of the Saudi kingdom. The relationship was, moreover, of some regional importance to Britain, ensuring that the British-protected territories in neighbouring countries were not subject to subversion from across the borders. The Saudi role even became of some significance with regard to Palestine, following the outbreak there of the Palestinian uprising in 1936. 'Abd al-'Aziz used his influence to persuade Palestinian representatives to attend a conference on the future of Palestine in 1937.

Despite the benefits which both sides drew from the relationship, the limits to which Britain was prepared to go were also apparent. When 'Abd al-'Aziz sought British security guarantees in the late 1930s to secure his position against the Italian presence which was building up in Yemen, he failed to obtain the assurances which he wanted (Al-Damer 2001: 28–30). Britain had failed, moreover, to fight for the oil concession which was on offer in Saudi Arabia, with the Anglo-Persian Oil Company putting forward a bid which fell well short of what the US Standard Oil Company of California (SOCAL) was bidding.

In the course of the 1940s, Britain was replaced as Saudi Arabia's main international partner by the United States. US interest in Saudi Arabia was very limited at the outset. Even after the Hijaz had been incorporated into Saudi territories there was no contact between the two sides. In 1928 'Abd al-'Aziz asked the United States to extend recognition, but it was not until May 1931 that this was done. Diplomatic recognition, moreover, was not followed immediately by an agreement on consular or diplomatic representation. The latter was in due course concluded in November 1933, six months after SOCAL had secured its oil concession in Saudi Arabia, and the initial representation was only at the consular level. The discovery of oil in commercial quantities in 1938 led to a US decision in June 1939 to upgrade the representation to the ambassadorial level, such that the US ambassador (then known as Minister) in Cairo was appointed non-resident Minister in Saudi Arabia (Vassiliev 1998: 324–327).

During the 1930s SOCAL had begun giving some financial assistance to the Saudi Arabian government, and from 1942 the US government began giving a small amount of aid. The latter became much more substantial from 1943, stemming largely from a realisation of the strategic importance of Saudi Arabia's oil now that the United States had joined the war against Germany, Japan and Italy. The broadening of the US combat role in Europe and the Pacific also suggested that the Kingdom would be of importance for air and supply links involving North Africa and the Far East. While the United States had previously been eager to leave the initiative in Saudi Arabia to Britain, and was wary of impinging on British interests, this was no longer the case after 1943. In February of that year, President Roosevelt issued an executive order stating that 'the defence of Saudi Arabia is vital to the defence of the United States.' On this basis, Saudi Arabia became eligible for substantial funding through the lend-lease arrangements which the United States had in place for its allies. This, then, was the crucial turning point. In the course of 1943–45, Saudi Arabia had begun receiving significant assistance from the United States, at a time when Britain was reducing its own contribution (Al-Damer 2003: 98–101). By 1945 there was no doubt that the United States was the main financial support for the Saudi government. Military links, initially in the form of the United States' establishment of an air base for its own use, also developed in 1945.

Policies and structures

The type of government which this system produced was effective in keeping the country together. When part of the *Ikhwan* turned against 'Abd al-'Aziz in 1928, claiming that he had abandoned the principles for which they had fought, the Saudi state appeared to be poised on the brink of disintegration. The *Ikhwan*, after all, had played the major role in achieving the state's territorial expansion. Yet by 1930, 'Abd al-'Aziz had overcome the threat; popular support had been mobilised to his side through the tribal, religious and commercial networks which were bound into the Saudi state (Kostiner 1993: 125–140).

The country's internal coherence was sufficient for an oil concession agreement to be concluded with SOCAL in 1933 and for the latter company to decide to develop oil production and exports when oil was discovered in 1938 (although, due to the outbreak of the Second World War, substantial exports did not start until 1948). Regional foreign policy objectives could, moreover, be pursued: initially strained (or non-existent) relations with Egypt and Iraq were followed by reconciliation and some cooperation (after 1932 in the case of Egypt, after 1933 in the case of Iraq); a Saudi government position in support of the rights of the Palestinian Arab population developed after 1936 (within the context of the Arab uprising which occurred during 1936–39); the country's integrity was maintained through the Second World War, despite the manoeuvring of the Great Powers in the area; and Saudi Arabia played a part in the formation of the Arab League in 1944 (Holden and Johns 1981: 118–122). Declaring war on the Axis powers in the last month of the Second World War, Saudi Arabia became a founder member of the United Nations.

The system did not, however, create structures which could promote the country's long-term development. Secular education was neglected, and the limited resources which were available mostly went into security-related projects (such as the establishment of wireless communications linking the different centres of population to the royal palace in al-Riyadh), subsidies to the bedouin and maintaining the royal court, rather than into schemes of agricultural, industrial or infrastructural development (Niblock 1981: 94–95). No clear distinction was drawn between the state finances and the King's personal treasury.

Oil revenues and their impact on state and economy, 1948–58

Impact on governmental administration

With the beginning of oil exports, in the course of 1948, the scale of the financial resources at the disposal of the Saudi Arabian government was transformed. Over the years between 1938 and 1946, annual government revenue had averaged $14–16 million. In 1948 it came to over $53 million. By 1950 it had passed $100 million, and in 1960 it stood at $337.7 million. The type and the size of the expenditure which the Saudi government (effectively the King) could undertake changed accordingly (Philby 1955: 328).

The new resources made possible the development of some of the administrative institutions of a modern state. A decree signed by 'Abd al-'Aziz shortly before his death brought a Council of Ministers into being in 1953, and a full range of ministries was created in the course of that decade. Among the new ministries were those for Agriculture and Water (est. 1953), Education (est. 1953), Communications (est. 1953), Commerce and Industry (est. 1954) and Health (est. 1954). Some development funding went into projects coming under the purview of these ministries, especially in education, health and communications, but such funding remained limited. Development expenditure in the mid-1950s does not appear to have exceeded 20 per cent of total public expenditure (Niblock 1981: 16–18).

Initially, the political dynamics of the Saudi state were not changed significantly by the new resources and new institutions. The institutions constituted an overlay on the established system rather than a radical change to it. Despite them, policies and the allocation of funds were still determined largely through the King's interaction with the wider Al Su'ud, tribal and religious leaders, and the commercial establishment.

Policies, structures and the social balance

The entry of substantial revenues into a political framework which had grown up under very different material conditions, however, created stresses and instabilities which led the Saudi Arabian state into severe crisis. First, the social situation was marked by ever-widening inequalities. The major beneficiaries of the new revenues were the King and the groupings who surrounded him. Up to the late 1950s, a major part of the oil-generated revenues was at the direct disposal of the King. The state budget for 1952/53, for example, allocated almost one quarter of total expenditure to an item entitled 'Riyadh affairs' (Holden and Johns 1981: 163). This was destined for the King's personal treasury; it was used by him on the royal palaces and establishments, and on providing subsidies and favours to other members of the Al Su'ud, the tribal leaders and some religious leaders. The commercial establishment drew its benefit through the reduction of import duties and the relaxation of import controls. It was significant that, when income tax was introduced into the country for the first time in 1950, members of the royal family, the 'ulama and merchants were declared exempt (Holden and Johns 1981: 163).

The wealth of the royal household, and of the groupings which surrounded it, stood in stark contrast to the continuing poverty of much of the population. Some parts of Saudi society, indeed, were actually impoverished by the economic processes which the oil wealth had set in train. The opening up of the economy to imports, which so benefited the commercial establishment, virtually destroyed the handicrafts sector of the economy and seriously damaged the agricultural and pastoral sectors. Agricultural production declined in the early 1950s. Without any strong governmental policies directed towards fostering or protecting local production, traditional producers suffered (Niblock 1981: 96).

A second source of instability was the rise of new social groupings. One of these was the workforce in the oil industry, complemented by that in associated service establishments. In 1952 ARAMCO, the oil company responsible for all Saudi oil production at that time, had a total of 24,006 personnel on its payroll, of which more than 60 per cent were Saudi Arabian nationals. The possibility of this workforce playing a concerted role in Saudi society and politics was evident in 1953 and 1956 when strikes were organised. On the second occasion, the strike was overtly political, having a slant which was antipathetic both to the United States and to the Al Su'ud (Lackner 1978: 90,95). Another expanding social grouping was that of trained, administrative and professional personnel – working in or for the new ministries which had been established or for the armed forces (Lackner 1978: 67). The total number of Saudis working in these capacities at the beginning of the 1960s decade probably came to about 15,000. Although not readily susceptible to political mobilisation, the members of this grouping were nonetheless well capable of articulating dissatisfaction.

The unequal distribution of wealth, combined with the emergence of social groupings whose interests were not well catered for by the established political system, created the conditions for an unsettled polity. Of significance also, however, was the incompetence of the political leadership and the recklessness with which it squandered the country's resources.

In the final years of 'Abd al-'Aziz's rule, the King spent lavishly on building new palaces. The long-serving Minister of Finance, 'Abdallah Sulaiman, had neither the capacity nor the inclination to limit such expenditure. Following 'Abd al-'Aziz's death in November 1953 and the succession of Su'ud ibn 'Abd al-'Aziz, the scope for resource wastage spread from personal consumption and corruption within the royal entourage to expensive, ill-conceived and mismanaged undertakings – at home and abroad. These included a deal with the shipping magnate Aristotle Onassis to create a company which would hold a quasi-monopoly over the shipment of Saudi oil (in contravention to existing agreements with ARAMCO), the purchase of sophisticated weaponry for the Saudi armed forces (but without the training which would have enabled soldiers to use it) and a financially-supportive relationship with Nasir's Egypt through the mid-1950s (ending eventually with Su'ud providing finance for an attempted assassination of Nasir in 1958). The scale of the financial crisis facing the country through profligacy and mismanagement was evident when the Saudi government had to turn to the International Monetary Fund for a loan in 1958, and was forced to accept an IMF expert to investigate the country's economic problems (Bligh 1984: 62).

Changing dynamics in the regional and international environments

The domestic economic and political difficulties were aggravated by changes in the regional political environment. The mid-1950s saw the strengthening of the pan-Arabist trend in Arab politics, with Nasir gradually establishing a pre-eminent position in the region's politics – especially after the 1956 Suez war. King Su'ud initially sought to conciliate Nasir and to share some of the nationalist aura. Between 1954 and 1957, Saudi Arabia gave financial support to Nasir's Egypt; it formally adopted the positive neutrality which Nasir advocated, terminating in 1954 the Point Four military assistance agreement which had been concluded with the United States in 1951; and during the 1956 Suez war it gave strong support to the Egyptian position, breaking off diplomatic relations with, and banning oil shipments to, Britain and France. The association with Nasir's Egypt gave a veneer of nationalist legitimacy to some of the conflicts of interest which the Saudi Arabian government had with Western governments and organisations at this time: the dispute with ARAMCO over oil shipment contracts, and the confrontation with Britain over Saudi claims to the Buraimi oasis (which were pressed most strongly over the 1954–56 period) and Saudi support for Imam Ghalib bin 'Ali in the 'imamate revolt' against the authority of the Sultan of Muscat and Oman (1954–59) (Al-Rasheed 2002: 106–114).

Yet Nasir's populism and his nationalist militancy ultimately ran counter to the Saudi monarchy's most fundamental interest: that of maintaining the established social order on the Arabian peninsula. In 1957, after a visit to the United States, Su'ud gave his support to the Eisenhower doctrine. A strong US role in the area, coupled to the provision of military and economic assistance to friendly regimes, would, he stated, constitute a means for keeping the area secure from the threat of communism (Holden and Johns 1981: 190–191). The collaborative relationship with Nasir finished abruptly.

Over the decade which followed, a bitter confrontation raged between the Egyptian and Saudi regimes. The gravity of this confrontation for the Saudi monarchy lay in the influence which the Egyptian news media held over Arab public opinion, and in Nasir's ability to mould regional developments. The regular denunciation of the 'feudal pro-Western Saudi monarchy' in the Egyptian news media and Nasir's effective hold over the movement of Arab nationalism – especially between 1958 and 1961, when Syria and Egypt were in union under his presidency – gave an added dimension to domestic discontent with the Al Su'ud. The revelation in March 1958 that Su'ud had paid a £1.9 million bribe to 'Abd al-Halim Sarraj, the Syrian chief of intelligence, to secure the assassination of Nasir emphasised the isolation and discomfiture of the Saudi regime. The overthrow of the Hashimite monarchy in Iraq in July 1958 deepened the isolation and encouraged speculation that the Al Su'ud would soon share a similar fate (Vassiliev 1998: 372–377).

The challenge to the government and to Su'ud's leadership

Opposition to the rule of the Al Su'ud began to find expression in the second half of the 1950s. A number of underground movements came into being with such names as the National Reform Front, the Free Saudis and the Free Officers (Bligh 1984: 62). Executions of army officers in May and August 1956 and March 1958 indicated that the army was touched by disaffection. The strengthening of Arab nationalist sentiment which followed the 1956 war, and the confrontation with Nasir which developed after Su'ud had expressed support for the Eisenhower doctrine in March 1957, added a further dimension to the popular discontent. Rather than trying to resolve the economic and political problems from which the unrest stemmed, Su'ud adopted repressive measures such as the temporary ban which was placed on young Saudis studying abroad in the middle of 1956 (Bligh 1984: 62).

The struggle for power: determining the future of the Saudi state, 1958–62

The crisis confronting the Saudi regime in the late 1950s, then, was many-faceted. It was clear that, if the monarchy was to survive, some fundamental changes in the conduct and operation of the state were needed. Two different approaches to restructuring now emerged within the leading councils of the Al Su'ud. The 1958–62 period witnessed a struggle for power between the two approaches' adherents, with King Su'ud having no clear or consistent programme of his own but utilising what means he could to retain his personal position and authority. The struggle was of crucial importance, for its outcome set the pattern for Saudi Arabia's development over the two decades which followed.

One tendency within the Al Su'ud saw the way ahead as lying in political reform and democratisation (accompanied, no doubt, by economic development). At the core of this grouping was Prince Talal bin 'Abd al-'Aziz, who had been Minister of Communications in the early 1950s and was appointed Minister of Finance and Economy in 1960. Also prominent were Princes Nawwaf, Bandar, Fawwaz, 'Abd al-Muhsin and Majid.

The contrary tendency placed the emphasis on greater centralised control, both of the economy and of the political system. Discontent could, in this perspective, be defused by a coherent economic and social development programme. The wastage of public resources would be terminated and funds re-directed so as to create a more widespread sense of well-being. The Crown Prince, Faisal bin 'Abd al-'Aziz, was associated with this approach (Niblock 1981: 99–100).

Although Faisal had held the title of Prime Minister since August 1954, Su'ud had in fact retained control of government. Decision-making rested in the hands of a small circle of advisers around the King. The gravity of the problems facing the Saudi monarchy early in 1958 brought about a shift of authority. Sensing that the survival of the monarchy was at stake, the King's uncle 'Abdallah bin 'Abd al-Rahman convened a meeting of senior princes, religious leaders and tribal leaders. The meeting, held in mid-March over a four-day period, reached a consensus that full responsibility for all governmental affairs should be transferred to Faisal. The King, confronted now by the most significant circles of cooperation underpinning the political leadership, had no option but to accept. Su'ud kept the title of King and the ability to interfere sporadically in the processes of government (Vassiliev 1998: 354–356).

The first two years of Faisal's governmental authority saw little progress towards the coherent planning of economic and social development. The main focus was, necessarily, on austerity and retrenchment. Revenue and expenditure were brought back into balance, in accordance with guidelines laid down by the IMF, and the external debt was reduced. Faisal's political position, moreover, was not secure enough to enable a longer-term strategy to be pursued. Su'ud was intent, over the 1958–60 period, on re-building his political following. He courted the significant circles, whose support he now badly needed, assiduously: on visits to tribal domains, he entertained the tribal leaders lavishly and furnished them with substantial subsidies (a royal prerogative which he still retained); he re-instituted regular meetings with the *'ulama* and used these to emphasise his interest in promoting religious observance; and he lent a ready ear to royal family members' complaints over Faisal's tight controls on spending (Lackner 1978: 62).

In 1960 Su'ud, having gathered substantial support within the royal family and among the tribal and religious leaders, found the means to regain control of government. The instrument was the adoption of a programme for political reform, opening the way for him to forge an alliance with the grouping of liberal princes. Early in 1960, rumours were circulated that Su'ud wished to introduce a parliament (albeit a nominated one) and to institute some other political reforms (Bligh 1984: 67). The liberal princes were given encouragement to take up the initiative. In June 1960 Talal and his colleagues put forward their programme. They submitted a demand for a partially-elected body with legislative powers, a limited monarchy and a draft constitution (Niblock 1981: 100). Faisal rejected the demand. In December of that year, Su'ud refused on procedural grounds to sign the national budget which Faisal had submitted for 1961. With his governmental authority effectively undermined, Faisal announced on December 19 that he would 'cease to exercise the powers vested' in him.

Contending that Faisal had resigned his Prime Ministerial position, Su'ud proceeded to appoint a new Council of Ministers. He named himself as Prime Minister and gave the position of Minister of Finance and National Economy to Talal. 'Abdallah ibn Hammud al-Tariqi, a commoner known for his nationalist views, was chosen to head the newly-formed Ministry of Petroleum and Mineral Resources. On 24 December it appeared that substantial political reforms were in prospect: Radio Makkah announced that the Council of Ministers had approved a draft for the establishment of a national assembly in which at least two-thirds of the members would be elected (Holden and Johns 1981: 213). Three days later, however, the story was denied. Evidently Su'ud, having regained governmental authority, was no more willing than Faisal to envisage democratisation.

The events of December 1960 proved crucial to the prospects of the liberal princes. Neither Su'ud, nor the influential figures from the traditionalist circles of cooperation who had rallied to his support, would accept the programme which had been advanced. Talal became increasingly critical of the regime and, after voicing some of his criticisms publicly at a press conference in Beirut on 14 August 1961, was dismissed from Ministerial office. Two other liberal princes, 'Abd al-Muhsin and Badr, lost office at the same time. In July 1962, Talal and his closest companions left Saudi Arabia, re-stated their political demands at a press conference in Beirut in mid-August and subsequently settled in Egypt. From there, Talal denounced the Saudi regime as being 'steeped in backwardness, underdevelopment, reactionary individuals and tyranny', and called for the establishment of a national democratic government (Holden and Johns 1981: 227).

The threats confronting the Saudi monarchy again conspired to shift governmental authority from Su'ud to Faisal. The public dissension within the Al Su'ud, made more serious by the support which Talal and the liberal princes were receiving outside of Saudi Arabia (from quarters committed to the overthrow of the Saudi monarchy), raised demands within the royal family for a stronger and more resolute leadership. External developments enhanced the alarm. Iraq's claim to Kuwait, pronounced trenchantly by President 'Abd al-Karim Qasim in July 1961 (within two weeks of the termination of the British protectorate over Kuwait), heightened security fears along Saudi Arabia's eastern border (Holden and Johns 1981: 217). The secession of Syria from the United Arab Republic in September 1961 led Nasir to intensify his campaign against 'reactionary forces' in the Arab world, with Saudi Arabia picked out as the 'centre of feudalism and pro-Western intrigue'. And the overthrow of the Hamid al-Din dynasty in Yemen in September 1962 brought a pro-Nasirist regime, under 'Abdallah Sallal, to Saudi Arabia's south-western borders. Su'ud, suffering from ill-health and blamed by senior princes in the Al Su'ud for the dissension which was destroying the regime's coherence, was compelled to concede Faisal a role in government (Vassiliev 1998: 362–364).

In October 1961, Faisal resumed some government functions (while Su'ud underwent medical treatment abroad). In March 1962 the two brothers agreed on what was effectively a coalition government: Su'ud remained as Prime Minister and Faisal assumed the posts of deputy Prime Minister and Foreign Minister. In October 1962 Faisal took over the Prime Ministership, regaining full control over the conduct of government (Niblock 1981: 100). Although Su'ud attempted to regain governmental authority once more, in 1964, Faisal had now established a strong enough basis of support – among the senior princes in particular, with additional backing from religious and tribal leaders – to defeat such a challenge. Following contacts between senior princes, the *'ulama* and tribal leaders at the end of October 1964, Su'ud was deposed on 2 November and Faisal became King.

Conclusion

The third Saudi state, instituted in 1902, can be referred to as 'the contemporary state', in so far as there has been an unbroken line of succession within the political leadership. In the years before 1962, however, the 'modern state' of Saudi Arabia had not – in a significant sense – come into existence. The monarch governed in a similar fashion to his predecessors in the first and second Saudi states. Legitimacy rested firmly on personal, ideological and traditional bases. There was no attempt to create a eudaemonic legitimacy for the system, employing a strong state apparatus to distribute benefits directly to the population. Support, rather, was gained through pay-offs to individuals. The significant circles of cooperation, whose support was needed by the King and who were the main beneficiaries of his new-found wealth, were the traditionalist circles of ruling family, tribal leaders, major merchants and *'ulama*.

The substantial influx of oil revenues after 1948 substantially increased the resources at the disposal of the political leadership, but the political processes remained static. The increasing interaction of Saudi Arabia with the outside world, economically and politically, required a government which could respond to change and handle the opportunities offered and problems created. Under the incompetent leadership of King Su'ud, the state was unable to transform itself and therefore incapable of devising an appropriate response to change.

The problems confronting the state came both from the domestic and the international environments. Domestically, new social forces were taking shape, with new types of social, economic and political demands – often influenced by wider regional trends dismissive of the legitimacy claims of traditionalist monarchies. A mood of political discontent spread among significant parts of the population. Fortunately for the Saudi regime, the discontent did not develop into a popular movement capable of taking power, whether through military or civilian means. This was probably due to the rather narrow social basis of the new groupings and the continuing strength of religious and tribal affiliations. The development was, in any case, pre-empted by the realisation among senior princes that the Al Su'ud's hold on power was threatened. Faisal relied on the traditionalist circles of cooperation in giving him uncontested authority, but the policies which he was to institute effectively reduced the influence of these circles in the Saudi state.

3 Faisal and the new polity, 1962–79

Faisal, Khalid and the centralised state, 1962–79

Centralising authority

Over the period between 1962 and 1979 the Saudi Arabian state underwent an important transformation. The threat to the political survival of the Al Su'ud, and the steadily rising oil revenues, had created conditions in which the state's political leadership could set the agenda for the country's development. It was no longer inhibited by influences from the tribal and religious leaders or the commercial establishment. Substantial programmes of planned economic and social development were initiated, accompanied by legal and administrative reforms, and by institutional expansion. These programmes and reforms both reflected and reinforced the power of the state's leadership.

The religious and tribal leaders and the commercial establishment retained prestige within the Saudi state, but they had lost much of their importance as intermediaries between the population and the state. The role which the governing institutions now came to play in fostering economic and social development, and in guiding every aspect of social and communal life, meant that there was little room left for intermediaries. Bedouin tribal acquiescence to the Saudi regime remained important, but this could best be assured by direct government subsidies and welfare policies. Commerce was still important, but the commercial establishment was no longer regarded as an important ally in rallying urban opinion. Again, state policies could achieve that objective. Even in the religious sector there was a change in the balance. Religion retained its crucial importance to the self-identity of the Saudi state, but the state now played a more central role in religious affairs. This found expression both externally and domestically. The state was more active in projecting the Islamic dimension in foreign policy and in guiding the religious sector domestically.

Over most of the period covered by this chapter, Faisal was in charge of government policy. In the early years (up to November 1964) he was Crown Prince and Prime Minister, and thereafter (through to his death in July 1975) he was King. In practice he exercised an equivalent authority throughout. There was a marked consistency and continuity of policy over these years. The composition of the Council of Ministers formed by Faisal in November 1962 was largely unchanged when he died. The gradual transformation of the Saudi Arabian state was, thus, closely associated with Faisal. This stage in the transformation of the Saudi Arabian state, however, effectively continued beyond his death through to 1979. Over the four years which followed Faisal's death, the dynamics of the Saudi state remained much as before. Decision-making became more collegial (among the senior members of the Al Su'ud) when Khalid bin 'Abd al-'Aziz acceded to the throne in July 1975, but the problems facing the country and the manner in which the government dealt with them initially underwent little change. The Second Five Year Development Plan (1975–80), which shaped the country's economic strategy in the late 1980s, had been drawn up under Faisal's direction. The economy continued to benefit from substantial oil revenues, reflecting both rising prices and rising production. An important concern of the government, with both domestic and external dimensions, was to control and weaken socialist/communist forces and influences in the region, just as it had been under Faisal.

Saudi statistics covering the 1962–79 period, especially those related to social rather than economic developments, are generally unsatisfactory. The Central Department of Statistics was not operational until the mid-1960s, and even then the statistics produced in the early years were patchy. Most of the available statistical time-sequences on population and employment in Saudi Arabia do not go back before 1970. To provide an accurate picture of developments between 1962 and 1979, it is therefore necessary to focus mainly on the years since 1970. Estimates for the earlier years can at times be extrapolated by examining the subsequent rate of change.

Reforming the administration

Administrative reforms and developments reinforced and enhanced the power of the state. The central government administration grew, both in the number of personnel and in the institutional divisions. In 1962, the government employed a total of 36,776 administrative and clerical personnel; by 1971 this had grown to 85,184 (Awaji 1971: 134). In 1979 the total number exceeded 250,000. The Ministry of Information (formerly the General Directorate of Broadcasting, Printing and Publishing) was established in 1963; the Ministry of Justice in 1970 and Ministries of Higher Education, Municipal and Rural Affairs, Planning (formerly the Central Planning Office), Public Works and Housing, Commerce (formerly part of the Ministry of Commerce and Industry), Industry and Electricity, and Posts, Telegraphs and Telecommunications in 1975 (Al-Rawaf 1980: 420). The Royal Commission for Jubail and Yanbu was established in 1975 to oversee the development of these two heavy industry centres, and the Saudi Arabian Basic Industries Corporation in 1976 to take responsibility for a wide range of industrial undertakings. Local administration was reorganised by royal decree in 1963, giving more authority at local levels to government officials and reducing the scope of responsibility of tribal shaikhs (Khashoggi 1979: 93). The key element in the 1963 decree, however, was not put into practice until some three decades later: the creation of provincial councils carrying significant responsibilities over their local affairs (Al-Rawaf 1980: 426–468) Also important was the establishment of a social security system, making the state directly responsible for the care of the poor, rather than leaving this to the munificence of the royal family, tribal leaders or religious charities. A Social Security Law was introduced at the end of 1962 ensuring that those over the age of 60, the incapacitated, orphans and women without means of support could obtain a minimum annual payment of 360 riyals. Under the law, homes for the old and disabled, orphanages, reformatories, and schools for the blind, deaf and dumb were established (Holden and Johns 1981: 258).

Legal reform phased out some outmoded aspects of social practice and established a more unified system of law. In November 1962 slavery was abolished (there had, up to this point, been some 30,000 slaves in the kingdom). In 1969 labour legislation was introduced, revising and improving working regulations and establishing a system of arbitration committees (Holden and Johns 1981: 258). The establishment of the Ministry of Justice in 1970 brought all courts in the country under a single administrative system, and the Supreme Judicial Council (created in 1975) was made responsible for reconciling modern legislative requirements with the *shari'ah* law. Authority again shifted away from tribal and religious leaders, who had in certain fields wielded judicial power in the past, leaving the state in direct control (Vogel 2000: 107–109).

Re-shaping the economy

Planning the transformation of the economy

The government's development planning, although not always an accurate indication of how money was actually spent, reveals the main components of the strategy pursued in transforming the social and economic life of Saudi Arabia. A Supreme Planning Board had been brought into existence in January 1961. This, however, did little more than oversee the spending plans of the different ministries. Soon after Faisal had resumed the Prime Ministership in October 1962, he issued a 'Ten Point Programme'. The Programme made clear his commitment to a planned and structured approach to development, proclaiming 'the government's solicitude for social matters and education' and pledging a 'sustained endeavour to develop the country's resources and economy, in particular roads, water resources, heavy and light industry, and self-sufficient agriculture' (De Gaury 1966: 147–151). Although the Ten Point Programme set the scene for the massive schemes of infrastructural, industrial and agricultural development which were to transform Saudi Arabia in the 1970s, the institutional framework for planning and implementing Faisal's developmental vision was not quick to emerge. The establishment of the Central Planning Organisation (CPO) in January 1965 – becoming the Ministry of Planning in 1975 – marked the beginning of a concerted government-led development effort. The CPO assigned priorities for development expenditure in the late 1960s and then drafted the two development plans which set the framework for the country's transformation in the 1970s: the First Five-Year Development Plan (1970/71–1974/75) and the Second Five-Year Development Plan (1975–80).

The 1970/71–1974/75 plan defined the development objectives as being to raise the rate of growth of Gross Domestic Product (GDP), to diversify the economy and reduce the country's dependence on oil, to lay the foundation for sustained economic growth and to develop human resources so as to enable the different elements of society to participate more fully in the process of development.

The 1975–80 plan was framed around similar objectives, but on this occasion wider political and social objectives also achieved expression: to maintain 'the religious and moral values of Islam', to assure 'the defence and internal security of the Kingdom,' and to increase 'the well-being of all groups within society... and foster social stability under conditions of rapid social change' (KSA-MP 1975: 4).

The outlays envisaged under the two plans differed both in size and in make-up. The first plan projected public expenditure reaching SR 41.3 billion over the 1970/71–1974/75 period. SR 18.4 billion of this would be for projects, and the remaining SR 22.9 billion for current expenditure. The overall sum was very substantial in comparison with the level of public expenditure in the 1960s – greater, in fact, than total public expenditure over the whole decade of the 1960s. GDP was to increase from about SR 16 billion to SR 26 billion during the plan period, at an average

Table 1 Sectoral expenditure under the first and second plans

Sector	1970–75 plan % of total	1975–80 plan % of total
Economic resource development	10.7	18.5
Human resource development	18.1	16.1
Social development	4.4	6.7
Physical infrastructure development	25.1	22.7
Development subtotal	58.3	63.9
Administration	18.6	7.7
Defence	23.1	15.7
External assistance	—	12.7
Other subtotal	41.7	36.1

Source: KSA-CPO 1970; KSA-MP 1975.

annual growth rate of about 9.8 per cent. Nonetheless, expenditure under the first plan was small in comparison with that projected for the 1975–80 period. Under the second plan, total public expenditure was set at a massive SR 498.2 billion. Of this, SR 318.4 was for projects and SR 179.8 was for current expenditure. GDP was expected to grow at 10 per cent per annum. Over both the 1970/71–74/75 period and the 1975–80 period, actual expenditure in fact exceeded planned expenditure, reaching SR 86.5 billion in the earlier period (more than twice the projected total) and about SR 632 billion in the later period (El Mallakh 1982: 156 and 201).

As can be seen from Table 1, there were some important differences in the relative share of public expenditure which the two plans devoted to different sectors. Whereas the first plan allocated 41.7 per cent of total expenditure to creating and maintaining the security and administrative trappings deemed appropriate to a modern state, and a further 25.1 per cent on physical infrastructure, the equivalent percentages under the second plan fell to 23.4 per cent and 15.7 per cent respectively. Conversely, the development of the country's economic resources attracted only 10.7 per cent of projected total expenditure under the first plan, but 18.5 per cent in the second plan. Taking into account the vastly higher level of public expenditure in the second plan period, this meant that more than 12 times as much money was allocated for the development of Saudi Arabia's economic resources between 1975 and 1980 as it had been between 1970/71 and 1974/75. While the early 1970s saw rapid administrative expansion, the construction of an extensive educational infrastructure, the development of communications and the expansion and modernisation of the security forces, then, it was not until the 1975–80 period that major investment began to go into Saudi Arabia's industrial and agricultural sectors (KSA-CPO 1970; KSA-MP 1975).

Economic outcomes

The development programmes of the 1970s, despite attracting more funding than the plans had envisaged, did not always attain the targets set for them. GDP grew at an average rate of 13.2 per cent per annum over the 1970/71–1974/75 period (as against the projected 9.8 per cent), but much of this growth stemmed directly from rising oil prices and production. Agricultural production grew at 3 per cent per annum (as against a projected 4.6 per cent), and industrial production at 11 per cent (as against a projected 14 per cent). Over the 1975–80 period, GDP grew less than envisaged (at an annual rate of 8 per cent as against the projected 10 per cent), but the non-oil economic sector exceeded its projected growth rate (15.1 per cent annually as against a projected 13.3 per cent). Such success as was achieved, moreover, was perhaps dependent less on the existence of a coherent development strategy than on the vast sums of money which were at the government's disposal. Annual revenue from oil ranged between $400 million and $600 million in the early 1960s, rising to $1–2 billion at the beginning of the 1970s, and to $22–36 billion in the mid-1970s. In 1979 it reached $48 billion (El Mallakh 1982: 62). The country's foreign holdings, which had been negligible in 1962, gave Saudi interests a substantial role in the international financial order by 1980. Public foreign assets probably totalled some $100 billion in that year, although accurate figures are difficult to obtain. Saudi citizens and commercial banks owned a further $30 billion.

Nonetheless, the scale of Saudi Arabia's economic and social transformation between 1962 and 1979 was very substantial. Per capita income rose by a factor of 40 between 1962 to 1979, from about $550 per annum in 1962 to about $22,000 per annum in 1979. Crude oil production rose from an average of 1.64 barrels a day (b/d) in 1962 to 9.53 b/d in 1979 (El Mallakh 1982: 55). The largest gas-gathering scheme in the world had been created. At Jubail and Yanbu, the two centres developed specifically for heavy industry using gas as a fuel or feedstock, a web of oil refineries, steel rolling mills, and plants for petrochemicals, methanol, metal smelting, fertilisers and aluminium extrusion had come (or was coming) into being. Elsewhere, there were vehicle assembly plants, integrated grain-silos, flour and feed mills, and factories for food processing, construction materials and consumer products. In the field of petrochemicals, Saudi Arabia was preparing to claim a major stake in the international market.

While the agricultural sector grew less quickly than any other sector over the 1962–79 period (on average between 3 per cent and 4 per cent per annum), the basis was laid for a substantial increase in agricultural production. The instrument for this was the Public Land Distribution Ordinance of 1968. The ordinance reflected the realisation that substantial tracts of land, hitherto deemed barren, were in fact cultivable now that sufficient resources were available to draw water from underground aquifers. The First Development Plan stated that 'even in agriculture more resources exist than many believed possible before studies were made.' Plots of up to 10 hectares were allotted to individuals, and up to 400 hectares for companies, conditional on the land being brought into agricultural use (Hajrah 1982: 71). Large capital-intensive schemes were initiated which were to make Saudi Arabia self-sufficient in some agricultural products – especially barley and wheat – early in the 1980s. The social and environmental costs of this development, however, were high. It rested on massive state subsidisation of the water supply and was accompanied by a sudden drop in the underlying water table and an increase in its salinity (Nahedh 1989: 202–209).

Spending in the social and educational fields was substantial. Whereas in 1960 only 22 per cent of boys and 2 per cent of girls had been enrolled at school, by 1981 these figures stood at 81 per cent and 43 per cent respectively (Metz 1993: 97). At the University level, enrolments rose from less than 3,000 in 1964 to more than 36,000 in 1979. The overall numbers of those in education at all levels stood at less than 150,000 in 1962, rising to 547,000 and to 1,462,000 in 1979 (making up almost 20 per cent of the total population) (Al-Rawaf 1980: 243; KSA-MP 2005). There was also a substantial increase in the number of hospitals and health centres. Medical services had been very rudimentary in the early 1960s, but by 1979 there were 67 hospitals and 824 health centres in existence. The social security budget rose from SR 2.6 million in 1963/64 to 22.8 million in 1973/74 and to 146.5 million in 1977/78 (Al-Rawaf 1980: 220). The numbers benefiting from this rose from about 127,000 in 1963/64 to almost 750,000 in 1978/79.

The physical infrastructure appropriate to a semi-industrialised state was put in place: all the major population centres were linked in a paved road network (some 13,066 km being constructed in the second plan period alone), large sums were spent on municipal development (making them 'healthier, more comfortable, more enjoyable, but less costly places in which to live, work and travel', to use the second plan's terminology), the rate of house-building rose from 17,500 units per year in the first plan period to 40,000 in the second (whether through direct government involvement or through the activities of the private sector aided by government-supplied credit), the generation and provision of electricity was increased such that the capacity of the electricity network in 1979 was approximately 20 times what it had been in 1962 and the supply of water (whether through groundwater supplies or through desalination) rose by a similar factor (KSA-MP 2000). Airport and port facilities were developed beyond recognition to what had existed in 1962.

The 1962–79 period, therefore, was one where massive state spending transformed Saudi Arabia's economy, and its social and physical infrastructure. The state became central to the population's welfare, in a manner which it had not been previously. State resources directly fashioned the population's living conditions and every individual's opportunities for employment and self-improvement.

Social dynamics of the new polity: the stabilising social milieu

The social and economic developments outlined in the previous section had substantial effects on the Kingdom's social and political dynamics. The oil rentier characteristics of the economy were shaping a new social and political reality, forming social groupings which were unable or disinclined to organise politically or to articulate opposition. The skill with which the government pursued its policies also contributed to the country's political quiescence. In the long term, new forces would arise which changed the balance, but for most of the 1960s and 1970s the government was able to cope with such opposition as expressed itself – largely from Nasirist and socialist elements.

Migrant labour

Of central importance in enforcing political quiescence was the substantial part played by migrant labour in the economy. The element in the Saudi workforce comprised of manual workers, which in other developing countries might have formed the social basis for radical political movements, was in the case of Saudi Arabia largely migrant. The latter were neither able nor inclined to political activism.

The numbers of migrant labourers in Saudi Arabia grew slowly through the 1960s, but very quickly after 1970. In 1963 there were some 115,000 non-nationals employed in Saudi Arabia, making up about 14 per cent of the labour force. In 1970 the total had risen to 320,000 (27 per cent of the labour force), rising further to 668,500 in 1975 (40 per cent of the labour force) and 1,347,000 in 1979 (53 per cent of the labour force) (Sirageldin *et al.* 1984: 32). It was significant that the proportion of migrant labourers constituted by non-Saudi Arabs declined steadily over the years, while that constituted by labourers from the Indian sub-continent and the Far East rose. In 1975, only some 5 per cent of foreign labour came from the Indian sub-continent or South-East Asia. In 1979 the percentage stood at 15 per cent (Birks and Sinclair 1980: 114–115).

While there are no reliable figures covering the proportion of the non-agricultural manual workforce constituted by migrants, it seems likely that by 1975 the Saudi component of this workforce came to no more than 20 per cent of the total. The proportion would have continued to fall subsequently. The two sectors which employed most non-agricultural manual labour were manufacturing and construction. In the former, migrant labour made up about 90 per cent of those employed in 1975, and in the latter about 85 per cent (Birks and Sinclair 1980: 108).

Most of the non-Saudi labour force was employed on short-term contracts, lasting two years or less. When contracts expired, or were terminated by employers, employees were obliged to leave the country. Most migrant labourers came to Saudi Arabia without their families. Inevitably the major concern of this group of labourers was to support their families at home, and a substantial part of their earnings was remitted overseas. Many of the country's larger development projects were sited on 'enclave developments': industrial areas, such as Jubail and Yanbu, which were distant from the main towns and established centres of population. In these enclaves contacts between migrants and the local population was limited, and the return of the migrants to their home countries once a project was finished assured. Some contracting companies (especially those from the Far East) imported the labour they needed from the company's home country, accommodating the workers in project-based camps (Birks and Sinclair 1980). In such camps, the contact which migrant labourers had with Saudi society was usually minimal, and the cultural environment in which they lived and worked was frequently that of their home country.

A labour force of this kind was not likely to be drawn into Saudi politics. Far from constituting fertile ground for the development of radical political movements (whether secular or religious), the industrial and service workers in Saudi Arabia scarcely figured as a social grouping impinging on the country's political processes. Such Saudis as there were in the manual labour force benefited from higher wages and better conditions than migrant workers. The socio-economic and ethnic/cultural composition of Saudi Arabia's labour force, therefore, meant that there was no grouping which could cohere together, acting as a politicised Saudi working class.

The new middle class

The emergence of a new middle class also reinforced the mood of political quiescence. This social grouping was based largely on public sector employment in administrative and other non-manual occupations, which the enlarged and expanding public sector had spawned. In 1979, some 26 per cent of the country's total labour force was working in the public sector. Rather more than one-third of the Saudi workforce was employed in occupations which were administrative, professional/technical, clerical, commercial or skilled (KSA-MP 1980).

Some analysts (e.g. Rugh 1973, and Heller and Safran 1985) saw this new middle class as constituting the social basis for political change: an educated and technically-proficient grouping which, it was contended, would demand the right to participate in political decision-making and would become increasingly restive at the restrictions which traditionalist authority imposed. Yet the practical experience suggests the opposite. Dependence on the state for employment discouraged political activity. When state employees sought to raise political or social demands, and to pursue them outside of the framework of their public sector employment, they could be (and were) dismissed from their positions. Public sector employment, then, constituted an instrument through which potential opposition could be countered.

Public sector employment also defused potential opposition in a more general sense. It provided employment for the large number of educated Saudis emerging from the schools and universities. Whereas there were only some 200 Saudis graduating with university degrees (whether from Saudi or foreign universities) in 1964, the number rose to 808 in 1970 and 5,124 in 1980. The total number of Saudis in education at any level rose from about 30,000 in 1962 to 48,865 in 1970, and to 159,738 in 1980 (KSA-MP 2005). If jobs had not been available for the graduates of these schools and universities, an articulate yet discontented social grouping could have developed – posing a threat of instability to the regime.

Merchants and the commercial sector

The large commercial sector, and the leading role played by the established merchant families in this part of the economy, added further to the forces favouring the political status quo.

In 1975 about 27 per cent of the total workforce was employed in commercially-oriented activities (defined here as covering the categories of trade and finance, transport and communications, and construction). The proportion had risen to 36 per cent by 1980 (El Mallakh 1982: 26). This stemmed from the characteristics of the oil rentier economy and the policies pursued by the state. The flow of oil revenues provided the wherewithal for large-scale consumer imports; the government's liberal economic philosophy determined that the resulting trade should be handled primarily by the private commercial sector, and the scale of consumer imports limited the expansion of (or diminished the size of) other parts of the private sector. The private sector, therefore, was effectively dominated by commerce rather than manufacture, and the heart of the commercial activity was in the import–export trade. Local craft manufacture and industrial manufacture experienced difficulties in competing with imports. For private investors, there was little incentive to invest in these fields.

The interests of the merchant families which dominated the commercial sector clearly favoured political accommodation with the government. Much of their wealth stemmed from trading on the basis of the agencies they held for Western companies and corporations (Field 1984). The liberal economic framework which the government had created, the openness to international trade and the substantial state expenditure on development, all underpinned their prosperity. The maintenance of political stability, and of close and cooperative relations with Western countries, was important to them.

Such manufacture as there was tended to be linked to the commercial sector, undertaken by merchants whose main activity was in the import–export trade. The production of light bulbs, for example, was undertaken by the al-Rajhi company, which was the country's main importer of light bulbs, and the largest cigarette producer was the National Cigarette Company, which also undertook the distribution of Marlboro cigarettes. Much of the 'manufacturing', moreover, involved the assembly of goods whose components were imported, or else the finishing and packaging of imported materials. Even the agriculture sector was increasingly linked to the commercial sector. Under the kingdom's Public Land Distribution Ordinance (1968), commercial companies could (in any one distributive programme) be allocated holdings up to 400 hectares, whereas the limit for individuals was 10 hectares. Substantial grants of land were made to companies under this ordinance. Commercial interests also obtained land through the *iqta'* system. The latter involved royal grants of land to tribal leaders, but merchants linked by family relationship to the tribal leaders often obtained the land (Hajrah 1982: 63–68).

Settled farmers and pastoralists

Over the 1960s and 1970s, the rural communities of Saudi Arabia declined in number and also became more dependent on the state.

Whereas there had been some 2 million Saudis living off animal husbandry in the mid-1960s (Nyrop 1985: 83), the total number of those employed in the agricultural sector (both settled and nomadic) in 1980 came to no more that 426,000 (El Mallakh 1982: 418). State support was now critical for all parts of the rural community. While individuals may have been disaffected, therefore, the interests of the communities overall again lay in political accommodation. State support took the form either of direct grants (per animal owned etc.) or else of family members being employed in the National Guard or other state bodies. The rural population no longer depended for their livelihoods primarily on the sale of produce.

The conduct of foreign policy

Links between the domestic and international environments

The regional and international roles which the Saudi government played over the 1962–79 period developed in close interaction with domestic needs and conditions. The period was one in which the regime was confronting, and ultimately helping to contain, the forces of secular radicalism within the region. The challenge posed by the growth of radical political movements in the Arab world, as shown in Chapter 2, had itself formed the crucible transforming the Saudi Arabian state.

The Nasirist challenge, 1962–67

The major challenge came from Jamal 'Abd al-Nasir's Egypt. Between 1962 and 1967 the confrontation was at its height, with Egypt and Saudi Arabia engaged in an ideological struggle linked to wider regional developments. Nasir, enjoying paramount influence in the Arab world and intent on preventing the rising trends of Ba'thism and Marxism from outflanking his brand of Arab nationalism, waged rhetorical war against Saudi Arabia. Broadcasts from the Cairo-based Voice of the Arabs denounced Saudi Arabia as a 'feudal monarchy', a 'focal point of Arab reaction and Western intrigue'.

In response to the Nasirist challenge, Faisal sought to build-up international networks of support. From 1965 onwards he actively pursued an initiative to convene an Islamic summit meeting, which would enable Saudi Arabia to demonstrate its importance to the wider Islamic world (Madani 1977: 88–91). This was intended both to strengthen the perceived international legitimacy of the Saudi state and to lay the basis for practical support from some of the powerful Islamic countries outside of the Arab world.

Diplomatic and military relations with Western countries were also strengthened. The relationship with the United States held some elements of tension. The United States was seeking in the early 1960s to retain a relationship with Egypt, with the objective of discouraging any further strengthening of the Egyptian–Soviet relationship (Holden and Johns 1981: 229–231). This imposed some limits on the support which could be extended to Saudi Arabia. The centrality of the Palestine issue to Faisal's thinking also caused problems to US administrations. Nonetheless, there was a gradual build-up of US military assistance to Saudi Arabia.

The pivot of Saudi–Egyptian confrontation was the Yemen. There, Egyptian forces supported the republican regime (which had come to power after the coup of September 1962), while Saudi Arabia gave financial and logistic support to the insurgent royalist forces under Imam Muhammad Badr. The number of Egyptian troops in the Yemen rose at its height to 60,000 (Holden and Johns 1981: 243). As Egypt became steadily more entangled in the morass of the Yemeni civil war, unable to quell the insurgency yet unwilling to abandon its republican allies, the vituperation which Nasir directed at the Saudi regime increased. This reached a peak at the end of 1966 when ex-king Su'ud was welcomed on a visit to Cairo and was permitted to use the facility of the Voice of the Arabs to re-assert his right to the Saudi throne (Holden and Johns 1981: 250–251).

The 1967 war and the changing regional balance

The Egyptian defeat in the June 1967 Arab–Israeli war had an immediate impact on the dynamics of the Yemen conflict in specific and on Egyptian–Saudi relations in general. Egypt could no longer afford, either militarily or financially, to maintain a strong military presence in Yemen. Some troops had already been withdrawn from Yemen shortly before the outbreak of war, so as to reinforce the Egyptian forces facing Israel in Sinai. Following the war, the pace of withdrawal increased. Decisions taken at the August 1967 Arab summit held in Khartoum effectively limited the Egyptian government's scope for manoeuvre in Arab politics. The Egyptian economy stood in danger of collapse, faced with the loss of Suez Canal revenues while required to bear the costs of military reconstruction. The heads of state of Saudi Arabia, Kuwait and Libya committed their governments during the conference to make an annual subvention to Egypt of $266 million, with an additional $122 million going to Jordan. The Saudi contribution to the subventions came to $140 million (LAS 1985: 144).

At a meeting with Faisal in Khartoum on 30 August, Nasir agreed to abandon the Egyptian military role in Yemen. All contingents of the Egyptian expeditionary force left Yemen by the end of November.

Although the Yemeni civil war continued through to 1970, it no longer constituted a focus for Saudi–Egyptian confrontation. A phase of inter-Arab politics which had seen Saudi Arabia pitted against the most populous and influential Arab state had come to an end.

In seeking to contain and weaken the forces of secular radicalism within the region, the Saudi government was in a stronger position than it had been before the 1967 war. The absence of Egypt from the radical forces confronting Saudi Arabia was important. Over the 1967–73 period, the Saudi–Egyptian relationship moved gradually from resentful accommodation to close collaboration. In 1972 the Saudi government played a prominent role in persuading President Sadat to expel Soviet military advisers from Egypt. In the run-up to the October 1973 war, Faisal and Sadat agreed on the overall strategy to be pursued. The latter had particular relevance for Saudi Arabia's orchestration of an oil boycott on states deemed hostile (Heikal 1975).

The Saudi government also achieved some success in affecting the political balance within the Palestinian national movement. From the spring of 1969, Saudi financial and logistic support began to flow, for the first time, to the Palestinian resistance. Some of that support went directly to Yasir Arafat's *Al-Fatah* movement, while some went to the Palestine Liberation Organisation (PLO). As the PLO had, following the fifth meeting of the Palestine National Council in February 1969, fallen under the predominant influence of *Al-Fatah* (marked by Arafat's election as PLO chairman), both destinations strengthened the position of *Al-Fatah*. Early in 1969, the PLO had effectively been bankrupt; Saudi support enabled the organisation, under *Al-Fatah*'s guidance, to build up the infrastructure on which Palestinian national leadership could realistically be claimed and maintained (Al-Angari 2002: 303–314). Those Palestinian movements which advocated revolutionary change within the Arab world as a whole, such as the Popular Front for the Liberation of Palestine (PFLP) and the Popular Democratic Front for the Liberation of Palestine (PDFLP), gradually lost influence – forced to operate on (or beyond) the fringes of the PLO. By 1973, *Al-Fatah*'s strategy of seeking to unite the different elements of Palestinian society in a common national struggle, while cooperating with such Arab governments as were prepared to help, faced only a weak challenge from other factions.

A pillar of Gulf security and the containment of regional radicalism

Between 1967 and 1973, the contest between Saudi Arabia and the forces of secular radicalism within the region remained intense. Despite the change in the Egyptian government's position, radical movements retained a strong influence on popular opinion. Indeed, in the aftermath of the 1967 war, the radical trend gained new positions of strength. Military coups brought regimes to power in Iraq (July 1968), Sudan (May 1969) and Libya (September 1969) which were perceived as being more radical than their predecessors. The withdrawal of Britain from Aden in November 1967 left power in the hands of the Marxist National Liberation Front, which then fashioned the institutions and policies of the People's Democratic Republic of Yemen (PDRY). The Dhofar Liberation Front in Oman was transformed during 1968 into the Popular Front for the Liberation of the Occupied Arab Gulf, now bearing a Marxist ideology and a wider regional concern. A spectrum of Palestinian organisations came into being, some of which (such as the PFLP and the PDFLP) called for popular insurrections against the traditionalist regimes of the area – as a necessary precondition for the liberation of Palestine. Moreover, although Egyptian troops had been withdrawn from North Yemen, a republican regime remained in power there and was, with Soviet, Syrian and Algerian support, resisting attempted advances by the royalist forces.

The British decision to withdraw from the Gulf area, announced in January 1968 and completed in November 1971, created a new arena for competition between Saudi Arabia and regional radicalism. The United States now became more closely engaged in the Gulf, promoting a 'twin-pillar' policy in the Gulf which involved the provision of increased military assistance to Saudi Arabia and Iran, and reliance on these two countries to maintain the security of the Gulf region. The Saudi role in the twin-pillar policy was minor beside that of Iran, yet the additional military assistance was significant for the Saudi regime's own sense of security.

The combination of the increased US military support, the recognition of Saudi Arabia's role in Gulf security, growing financial resources, political stability at home and the developing relationship with Egypt gave the Saudi government the confidence and the ability to extend its attempts at containing regional radicalism. Such attempts were not always success-ful. Military help was given in mid-1968 to anti-government insurgents in South Yemen. The insurgents were, however, soon defeated and the overall effect of the Saudi aid was to strengthen the position of leftist elements in the South Yemen government. In March 1970, the need to intensify pressures on South Yemen led Faisal to reach agreement with the repub-lican regime in North Yemen. A unified government of North Yemen was formed comprising moderate royalists and republicans. The new government received economic assistance from Saudi Arabia, and border conflicts between North and South Yemen ensued. South Yemen, however, withstood the pressures and moved further towards the left, changing its name to the PDRY in 1971 (Holden and Johns 1981: 272–273).

Some of the Saudi government's 'containment' policies, however, were more successful. Working together with Iran, Saudi Arabia helped to create political conditions in the formerly British-protected Gulf statelets which proved durable. The rulers of the Trucial States were coaxed into the federal structure of the United Arab Emirates, despite Saudi Arabia disputing the territorial delimitation of the new political entity (an outcome of the overlapping claims of Abu Dhabi, Oman and Saudi Arabia to the Buraimi oasis which had caused conflict between Britain and Saudi Arabia between 1953 and 1955). The issue of Iran's claim to Bahrain was defused (Halliday 1980: 218). Radical nationalist groupings in the area, sometimes supported by Iraq or Syria, were given no opportunity to benefit from Britain's withdrawal.

The 1973 war and the oil embargo

Over the period between the October 1973 war and the overthrow of the Shah of Iran in February 1979, the Saudi regime occupied an even stronger position *vis-à-vis* the forces of secular radicalism in the region. The regime, buttressed now by the huge revenues brought in by rising oil prices and production (in the wake of the October war), could now pursue more ambitious objectives than before. Placing itself as a (or perhaps the) central arbiter of Arab politics, it sought to promote the establishment of a stable Arab order. So as to achieve such an order the Saudi government would orchestrate relations among Arab states, ensuring that common objectives were pursued and instability avoided. Destabilising forces would be collectively controlled (Gros 1976: 143–152). Saudi Arabia also began from the mid-1970s to extend to the wider international stage its attempts to contain the forces of secular radicalism.

The relationship with Egypt remained central to Saudi regional policy over most of this period. A key element in this relationship was the common perception that the United States had the power to resolve some of the region's most critical problems. The two countries pursued a coordinated strategy of seeking to draw the United States into brokering a settlement of the Arab–Israeli conflict, through the influence which it could exert on Israel. The October war, combined with the associated oil boycott, was conceived as a means to bring this about. The Egyptian–Israeli disengagement agreements of 1974 and 1975, negotiated by US secretary-of-state Henry Kissinger, were the product of this strategy. The Saudi government was closely involved in the discussions which surrounded them (Al-Angari 2002: 350–351). The Egyptian government's renunciation of its treaty of friendship with the Soviet Union in 1976, indicating further the trust now placed in the United States, brought Saudi and Egyptian policies into yet closer alignment. Saudi Arabia and Egypt also sought to cooperate in the production of military goods.

When Sadat announced to the Egyptian National Assembly on 9 November 1977 that he would be prepared to visit Jerusalem, the Saudi government was taken by surprise. While senior Saudi officials (in particular Kamal Adham, head of Saudi intelligence) had sought to move the Egyptian government towards greater flexibility in its negotiating stance towards Israel, the announcement was strongly criticised in Saudi government statements. Sadat's initiative was described as having departed from the 'unified Arab stand' and being at variance with Arab League resolutions (Al-Angari 2002: 389–390). There was good reason for the Saudi government's displeasure, as the announcement and the subsequent visit rendered incompatible some of the strands of policy which the Saudi government had been pursuing. The deep resentment which Sadat's action engendered in many parts of the Arab world threatened to unravel the stable and collaborative Arab order which the Saudi government was seeking to promote. The direction of events immediately prior to the announcement, moreover, increased the complexity of the dilemma faced by the Saudi government. The latter shared with the Egyptian government a concern that the re-convening of the Geneva conference, which had been planned for December 1977, would re-introduce a Soviet role into Arab–Israeli peacemaking. Both preferred to restrict superpower involvement to the United States. There was, therefore, rather more understanding of the concerns which had moved Sadat than existed in most Arab countries. In an attempt to keep the notion of a collaborative Arab order in being, the Saudi government sought to mediate between Sadat and the more hard-line Arab states. In November 1978, after the signature of the Camp David agreements, it promoted a scheme whereby Egypt was offered substantial economic assistance (some $5 billion, most of which would come from Saudi Arabia) if it reneged on the agreements (Holden and Johns 1981: 491–495). The offer was not accepted.

Saudi Arabia's relationship with Syria was also of central importance. The Saudi government played a crucial role in persuading Syria to accept the 1974 disengagement agreement with Israel. Perhaps more important for the long term, however, was the Saudi role in containing the regional impact of the Lebanese civil war, which broke out in 1975. The need, from the perspective of the regional order which the Saudi government was seeking to create, was to prevent the Lebanese crisis intensifying inter-state rivalries and destabilising the whole area. The Saudi government's strategy was to create a framework within which the Arab League states could collectively exert some influence on Syria's military involvement in Lebanon, but where individual Arab states gained little opportunity to weaken Syria's position in the country (Cobban 1985: 143–145). The Lebanese civil war was not brought to an end, but its potential as a catalyst for regional instability was reduced.

In the Gulf area, the Saudi government's attempts to work towards a more stable regional order were facilitated by the more accommodating approach which Iraq adopted towards its Gulf neighbours in the second half of the 1970s. Shortly after the March 1975 Algiers agreement, which resolved (for the time being) Iraq's differences with Iran over the Shatt al-Arab, the Saudi government indicated to the Iraqi government its wish for a closer relationship (Holden and Johns 1981: 424). Over the years between 1975 and 1979, Iraq was drawn into the network of cooperative relations among the Arab states of the Gulf which the Saudi government was promoting – becoming a participant member of some of the new regional corporations and institutions which were being set up (such as the United Arab Shipping Company and the Gulf International Bank), attending regional Ministerial meetings and benefiting from some Saudi and Kuwaiti investment. Although differences remained over how Gulf security should be managed, with Iraq intent on a security arrangement for the Gulf area independent of any Western involvement or dependence, a broadly collaborative relationship was maintained (Niblock 1982: 146–147).

The Saudi government's attempts to draw the Yemens into a new and stable regional order were less successful. The PDRY retained its radical policies and its strong relations with the Soviet Union, both of which were deemed threatening by the Saudi government. Governmental instability in North Yemen meant that gains (as perceived by the Saudi government) achieved in one period were liable to be lost at a later stage.

Domestic political outcomes

Political power in Saudi Arabia over the 1962–79 period became progressively more established and less contested. Although Su'ud lacked sufficient support within the ruling family to challenge Faisal's effective control of government, his deposition in November 1964 removed a symbol around which potential dissent in the country could cohere. Between December 1966 and June 1967, Su'ud made one last attempt to regain his crown – but now from exile in Cairo. With the support and encouragement of President Nasir, Su'ud protested that the *'ulama* had acted illegally in securing his deposition, claimed that the CIA had been instrumental in removing him and denounced the presence of forcign troops in Saudi Arabia. He sought, and gained, support from 'Abdallah Sallal's republican regime in Yemen and attempted to pass subsidies to tribal leaders in Saudi Arabia who he believed might favour his cause. No significant response, however, came from within Saudi Arabia. After the June 1967 Arab–Israeli war, Nasir abandoned his support for Su'ud who was left politically isolated and suffering from declining health. He died in February 1969. Some of Su'ud's sons remained disgruntled, but they carried little influence either within or outside of the royal family.

All of the liberal princes had returned to Saudi Arabia by the middle of the 1960s. Talal, effectively the leader of the group, returned in February 1964, bearing with him an admission of guilt. Most of the former liberal princes, but not Talal, were given governmental and munic-ipal positions and were integrated into the ruling group around Faisal. In 1965 'Abd al-Muhsin was appointed governor of Madina, in 1968 Nawwaf became Faisal's special adviser on Gulf affairs and Badr became deputy commander of the National Guard, and in 1971 Fawwaz was made governor of Makkah. After Faisal's death, Talal too was given some official (but non-governmental) roles.

Radical opposition to the regime, outside of the confines of the Al Su'ud, remained significant through the 1960s. Although Faisal's policies were directed towards dissipating the social tensions which had provided fertile ground for the growth of opposition in the late 1950s, the country's social and economic problems were not easily or quickly resolved. The Union of Peoples of the Arabian Peninsula (UPAP), led by Nasir Sa'id, was perhaps the most substantial of the opposition movements active at this time. Pursuing an Arab nationalist line and benefiting in the mid-1960s from the backing of the Egyptian government, the UPAP's support seems to have been strongest among the Shi'a of the eastern region. With the Arab defeat in June 1967, Egypt stopped providing finance and broadcasting facilities for the UPAP. Nevertheless, the UPAP and some smaller Ba'thist and communist organisa-tions drew some advantage from the government's economic difficulties between 1968 and 1970. The stagnation of oil and petroleum revenues, the payment of $140 million annually in subventions to Egypt and Jordan, and the increased defence spending made necessary by regional instability forced the government to cut back both on its programmes of economic develop-ment and its provision of social welfare. In June 1969 some 150 people were arrested on suspicion of plotting to overthrow the government. Most of those arrested were members of the air force, army or police. Such conspiracy as there was probably went no further than the establishment of a secret society, mainly comprising members of the Royal Saudi Air Force. The incident showed, however, that disaffection did exist – even among elements on whom the regime relied for its security and protection.

Radical secularist opposition appears to have declined through the 1970s. The huge resources now at the disposal of the government, and the adoption of reasonably coherent development plans enabled potential discontent to be defused. The increased effectiveness of the government's security organisation (now better-resourced than before), moreover, rendered organised opposition more difficult. The General Security Service, established in the mid-1960s, kept a check on domestic disaffection; the National Guard, recruited from tribal elements traditionally loyal to the Al Su'ud, was expanded and strengthened as a counterpoise to the army; and the loyalty of the security forces was further assured by placing members of the royal family in key positions in each branch. Equally important was the decline in external support for such opposition as did exist within Saudi Arabia: Nasirism lost its expansionist dimension after the June 1967 war and seemed no longer to constitute even a viable model from the early 1970s; Syrian Ba'thism adopted a more accommodating attitude towards the monarchies of the Gulf after Hafiz al-'Asad's 'corrective' movement of 1970; and after the March 1975 agreement between Iraq and Iran, the Iraqi Ba'thists abandoned (temporarily) their attempts to subvert the Saudi monarchy and began to seek a collaborative relationship. Following the 1973 Arab–Israeli war and Saudi Arabia's orchestration of the oil boycott, moreover, Faisal had gained some Arab nationalist credentials. The boycott, crafted by the Minister of Petroleum Ahmad Zaki Yamani, proved an adept and effective weapon. The pursuit of pan-Arab objectives, and the preparedness to make sacrifices for wider Arab causes, were no longer so closely identified with anti-Saudi political movements.

Conclusion

By the end of the 1970s, then, the Saudi state had been transformed. A powerful centralised state had been created, based on a capable administrative machinery. The political leadership was now creating a eudaemonic basis to the state's legitimacy, with benefits flowing direct to the population from the state – rather than though intermediaries. The claim to eudaemonic legitimacy, although never expressed in such terms, constituted a significant element in securing popular acceptance of the Saudi state. The circles of cooperation remained as allies of the political leadership, but were no longer of great significance as bases of support. The state–population relationship no longer required intermediaries.

Both the domestic environment, and Saudi Arabia's relationship with the international environment, had been transformed. Substantial overall economic and social development had occurred: massive industrial and agricultural projects had been undertaken, per capita income had risen by a factor of 40 (since 1962) and the population was benefiting from a level of social welfare (through health and education services, and subsidies) far in excess of what had previously been the case. The internal political scene had been stabilised, with the secular radical opposition defused and weakened. Externally, the regime had defended itself successfully against the radical forces in the region previously antipathetic to it, and the country had come to enjoy a significant measure of international and regional influence.

4   Redirecting the polity

1979 to the present

New problems and new areas of confrontation

The economic and social foundations of the state which were laid between 1962 and 1979 continued to underpin developments in Saudi Arabia in the subsequent period. Social and economic developments proceeded along similar lines to before. Developmental expenditure, previous and ongoing, began to exert a deepening impact on people's lives.

A new set of problems was, however, now emerging. Some aspects of Saudi Arabia's emerging society and economy were viewed critically by parts of Saudi society. A cultural and religious alienation was beginning to take hold, soon finding expression in political opposition. The dynamics of the domestic environment, in short, were beginning to shift, requiring a re-thinking of government policies. At the same time significant changes were taking place in the regional and wider international environments, similarly putting pressure on the government to re-think its strategies. The policies which the Saudi state now adopted, in response to these changes in its domestic and international environments, followed naturally from the state's historical origins and its bases of legitimacy. They were, however, problematic and can in historical perspective be seen as fuelling the crises which Saudi Arabia was to face from the 1990s. It can be suggested, indeed, that the threats which confronted Saudi Arabia in the late 1990s, and especially after 9/11 2001, have their origins in policy-decisions taken in the early 1980s.

The change in the domestic environment was reflected in the character of the oppositional critique now finding expression. This became dramatically apparent in November 1979, with the seizure of the Great Mosque in Makkah by Juhayman al-Otaibi and his associated group of radical Islamists. Through all the subsequent period, the main threat to the Saudi regime has come from radical Islamism rather than from the Arab socialist and nationalist trends which had been predominant in the past. Political, economic and social factors were intertwined in the Islamist challenge to the regime. It was significant that some of those who regarded the changing scene in the country most negatively came from sectors of society whose militant support had created the Saudi state. The state was threatened, in short, by Wahhabi militants whose social base was in the Najdi heartland and whose fathers and grandfathers had formed the backbone of the *Ikhwan* who had fought for 'Abd al-'Aziz in the creation of the third Saudi state. The situation bore comparison with developments in the late 1920s, when a section of the *Ikhwan* had rebelled against 'Abd al-'Aziz's attempts to confine Wahhabi expansionism to the territorial confines of the Saudi state.

The focus of the Islamist critique was on social conduct and political legitimacy, seen from a radical Wahhabi viewpoint. Juhayman's formulation of this found expression as a raw outburst of rage, but the critique was to develop in the 1990s into a more sophisticated (yet still fundamentalist) discourse. A sense of loss underpinned the militancy, drawing on the character of the social change under way and expressing itself in a religiously-inspired attack on the political legitimacy of the regime. Those at the top of the system were deemed to have betrayed the principles of Wahhabism, with Saudi society now shaped by alien values. The massive foreign presence encouraged the spread of these values. Saudi Arabia's cultural coherence was seen as being undermined by the largely-Western technical and professional elements entering the country, the increasingly-Asian migrant labour force and the corruption of the ruling elite.

Changes in the regional environment also challenged the Islamic legitimacy of the Saudi state. In February 1979, the Shah of Iran was overthrown and the Islamic Republic of Iran came into existence. The impact on Saudi Arabia was immediate and substantial. A strategic regional ally, which had emphasised secular values and strategic cooperation with Saudi Arabia under US patronage, was replaced by an Islamist regime challenging the Saudi claim to Islamic leadership. The Islamic revolution's attitude to the Saudi regime, expressed softly in governmental statements but harshly through the media and mosque sermons, was uncompromising and stark. The Kingdom was portrayed as outdated, corrupt, compromised by its relationship with the United States and (for all these reasons) unfit for a leadership role in global Islam. Iran was now promoting change within the Islamic world, seeking the establishment of regimes based on radical Islamist principles. There was no doubting the appeal which this approach held for many Muslims around the world.

There were also economic problems. The rising price of oil initially promised huge increases in revenues, encouraging vast increases in development and defence spending. The Iranian revolution led to the price of crude oil rising abruptly from an average $14.3 per barrel in 1978 to $37.9 in 1980. The price remained high in 1981, mainly as a result of the outbreak of the Iran–Iraq war. Thereafter, however, prices began to fall back. The initial falls in prices were gradual, such that the price still averaged between $25 and $30 between 1982 and 1985. In 1986, however, there was a sudden collapse. The price fell back to where it had been pre-1979, averaging $14.4 for that year. Over the ten years which followed, the average price generally remained below $20, falling to a low point of $12.7 in 1998. Only in 2000 was there a sustained recovery of prices, with the average price moving between $25 and $30 through to 2003 (KSA-MP 2005). In the second half of 2004 the price rose sharply, reaching $55 per barrel in September of that year. In June 2005 it touched $60.

The impact of these price changes on Saudi oil revenues was proportionately even more substantial, as Saudi Arabia was acting as the international oil market's swing producer. This meant that it was producing close to its capacity when the oil price was high (in an attempt to keep the price down) and limiting its production sharply when prices were low (in an attempt to keep prices up). The value of oil revenues rose from $38 billion in 1978 to $116 billion in 1980. After a further rise to $118 billion in 1981, revenues declined rapidly over the subsequent five years, reaching a low point of $14.5 billion in 1986 – the lowest annual oil revenues which the Kingdom had received since 1972. Over the 14 years which followed, the oil income fluctuated between $16 billion and $55 billion, varying substantially from year to year. A high and stable plateau was not reached until 2000: revenues remained thereafter above the $55 billion level (KSA-MP 2005). Even in 2004, however, they had not regained the peak reached in 1981.

Given that oil revenues made up the major part of government revenues over this period, ranging between 60 per cent and 90 per cent of total revenues, the impact of the changing levels on Saudi Arabia's economic development and stability was substantial. Plans made at the beginning of the 1980s decade were being implemented, in the later part of the decade, with revenues only a fraction of that available at the time of planning. Every year between 1984 and 1999 saw a deficit in the Saudi budget. The dilemma was resolved in a variety of ways: borrowing on the international financial market, selling foreign assets (thereby inevitably reducing the reserves which Saudi Arabia needed to maintain in preparation for its post-oil future), and cutting expenditure in such fields where this was feasible. In practice, the government safeguarded those elements of expenditure which were crucial for regime stability and national security, or where there were contractual agreements which could not be broken, and reduced other elements of spending. This did not make for a coherent pattern of economic and social development.

Three main areas of a re-shaped governmental strategy, in response to these various challenges, can be identified. First, the Islamic and Wahhabi identity of the state was given new stress. This was done by widening the role of the religious leaders, strengthening the religious strands in the educational system, associating the state more closely with Islamic symbols, curbing public behaviour deemed to be un-Islamic and promoting Saudi Arabia's Islamic role more actively in the international arena. Second, the strategic partnership with the United States was strengthened. The intention here was to buttress both the stability of the regime (in the face of domestic threats) and the security of the country (against external threats). The policy involved substantial arms purchases and close strategic coordination, with some joint action, at the regional and international levels. Third, social expenditure was increased in areas critical to regime stability: subsidies paid to the more marginalized elements of the population were increased, salaries were raised in the public sector and educational provision was expanded (especially in the religious schools and universities) to absorb more students.

This three-pronged strategy embodied a top-down approach to the population. Such an approach had, in practice, been characteristic of Saudi rule since oil had begun to be exported. The population would be managed through enhancing the powers of the religious authorities; domestic and international threats would be met by more extensive security arrangements (backed by the United States) and welfare policies would give most social groupings an incentive to remain quiescent. No new avenues were provided for governmental engagement with the population or for people to participate in institutions which shaped their material and social environments. People could enjoy the benefits of governmental munificence, but they could not play any part in determining how their communities ordered themselves.

The three strands of policy carried some in-built contradictions. The additional protection given to Wahhabi Islam, in a setting where wider religious and political pluralism was forbidden, gave strength to the less compromising and more fundamentalist tendencies in Wahhabism. This was the milieu which had fostered Juhaymam's extremism. The expansion of the religious universities, moreover, created a link between religious-based criticism and socio-economic grievance. A significant part of the curricula in the religious universities was taken up with study of the Islamic sciences. While there were jobs for some such graduates, many encountered difficulty in finding appropriate employment. For most jobs in the central government ministries and the private sector, they were less qualified than the graduates of the mainstream universities.

The values of simplicity and equality inherent in Wahhabi Islam, moreover, sat uneasily with the social dimensions of the emerging economic order. Inequalities were growing, sometimes stoked by corruption. '*Asabiyah* capitalism was becoming predominant in the private sector, with members of the Al Su'ud adding control of large parts of the business economy to their established social pre-eminence. The inequalities in the system, the suspicion that corruption was the critical factor creating the wealth of the super-rich and the involvement of members of the royal family in the commanding heights of the private sector, all created a belief that the inequalities were unjustified and damaging to society. Meanwhile society was changing through the impact of the massive migrant labour force. Much of this labour force espoused very different social values to those of the Saudi population. The call for a return to more simple and authentic Islamic values, therefore, carried weight in the developing socio-economic environment. The grounds of the political discontent which was to achieve expression in the 1990s were, unwittingly, being cultivated.

The close security relationship with the United States posed further problems. The value of this relationship was perhaps understandable to Islamists for as long as the Soviet Union was in existence. Saudi Arabia and the United States could be portrayed as engaged in a joint struggle against the forces of communist atheism. US–Saudi support for the Islamic resistance to the Soviet-backed regime in Afghanistan constituted the high-point, and most alluring symbol, of this joint struggle. But with the retreat of Soviet power in the late 1980s, and the subsequent collapse of the Soviet Union, the relationship with the United States could no longer be perceived in the same light. The focus of US concern was now directed towards the Islamic world, and the military actions and economic retaliation undertaken by the United States after 1990 were largely against Muslim countries. The failure of the United States to use its power to curb Israeli settlement in the occupied territories deepened the perception of US antagonism towards the Islamic world. To the more radical trends in Wahhabism, then, the collaborative US–Saudi relationship was becoming a symbol of Saudi subservience to an anti-Islamic agenda. International developments combined with domestic policies to broaden the support for radical Islamism within the country.

Western commentators and governments after 9/11 2001 were to be highly critical of the policies pursued by the Saudi political leadership over the two previous decades. They criticised in particular the failure to control religious extremism (linking this to allegations that regressive ideas were promoted through the educational system), the lack of democracy and the failure of the regime to create the employment opportunities needed by the growing population. At the time when these policies were being pursued, however, there was little such criticism. On the contrary, Saudi political and economic strategies through the 1980s and 1990s were made possible, and effectively encouraged, by the United States. The security relationship, with the massive arms purchases which underpinned it, was critical to US international strategy. It was pivotal in US attempts to confront and weaken the Soviet Union through the 1980s. The perception that the Gulf was being encircled by Soviet military power led the United States (and to some extent its Western allies) to favour solutions which avoided short-term instability. A concern with human rights and democratisation in Saudi Arabia was seen as potentially destabilising. US advisers played key consultative roles in Saudi development planning, and the US economy benefited massively from the privileged relationship which the US enjoyed with the country. The United States economy gained both through lucrative contracts and from the huge investments which Saudi investors made in the United States. The lack of democracy was seen as a perhaps-regrettable necessity in ensuring the stability of the Kingdom and through that the security of the Gulf and Indian Ocean regions. Criticism of the social values enforced within the Kingdom was muted with the contention that these values were inherent in Saudi society and useful in restraining secular radicalism (Simons 1998: 220–221). The key element in Saudi Arabia's external circle of cooperation, therefore, was not a factor encouraging liberalisation. Rather, it supported the political environment promoted by the government.

Economic development and the problems of *'asabiyah* capitalism

The economic outcomes of development over the past 25 years, and the problems which have arisen, are covered in Chapter 5. This section is intended simply to highlight three dimensions important to an understanding of Saudi Arabia's ongoing political processes.

Development with fluctuating resources

As indicated earlier, the oil revenues earned by Saudi Arabia from the mid-1980s through to the end of the 1990s were substantially less than had been expected in the late 1970s and early 1980s. Whereas government expenditure doubled between 1978 and 1981, remaining high for the three years which followed, therefore, it fell back to the 1978 level in 1985. It remained low for the rest of the 1980s and most of the 1990s – with the notable exception of 1990–92 when it was forced up by the Iraq war. Defence and security expenditure generally made up between 25 per cent and 40 per cent of the total annual budget. Through to 2005, total expenditure had still not regained the peak achieved in 1981 (KSA-MP 2005). Gross Domestic Product, despite the growing contribution of the non-oil sector, reflected the same trends. In the light of the growing population, the effect on per capita income was even more dramatic. Whereas Saudi Arabia in 1981 had a per capita GDP of $28,600 (roughly equivalent to that of the United States), in 2000 per capita GDP came to less than $7000 (US-E 2004). In the United States, per capita income in 2000 had reached $35,027.

Despite this, the impact of development expenditure was nonetheless making itself felt. Non-oil GDP rose steadily between 1987 and 2005. The rise in agricultural production was of particular significance within this, largely as a result of the re-distribution of public lands, which was accelerated after 1979. The number of factories in operation more than doubled between 1979 and 1989, and doubled again between 1989 and 2001. The increase in support for the less well-off parts of the population was apparent from the sums being paid out to Saudi citizens for social security, which tripled between 1979 and 2001. Hospital beds in the country also increased three-fold between 1979 and 2001. The growth in higher education was exceptional, with a ten-fold increase in the number of graduates emerging from the University system: from about 5,000 in 1979 to almost 50,000 in 2001. In the latter year there were in total some 400,000 students in higher and technical education. The schools also underwent substantial growth. The number of students emerging from the school system increased by about three-fold over this period, such that in 2001 almost 500,000 students finished school. (KSA-MP 2005). The education figures provide some indication of the employment needs which were now arising (covered further in Chapter 5).

Some writers have suggested that, given the reduction in Saudi oil revenues in the late-1980s and 1990s, Saudi Arabia had ceased to be an oil rentier state by the mid-1990s (e.g. Champion 2003). Despite the substantial nature of the change, however, Saudi Arabia continued to rely on oil rent for more than 90–95 per cent of its export earnings, 75 per cent of its budget and 35–40 per cent of its GDP (KSA-MP 2005). As such it still had the characteristics of an oil rentier state. Most crucially, the government retained a substantial ability to use resources so as to buy political support. The writing-off of the oil rentier dimension was, in any case, premature. The rapid rise of the oil price from the summer of 2004, reaching an unprecedented $60 a barrel in June 2005, brought massive new revenues into the hands of the Saudi state. There was every indication that the price of oil would remain high, although perhaps not at the same level.

Migrant labour

Despite the consistently-expressed intention in all of the development plans from 1985 onwards to reduce reliance on foreign labour, the number of non-Saudi workers in the country rose steadily through the 1980s, reached a plateau in the 1990s and began to rise again at the end of that decade. The Seventh Development Plan estimated the numbers of non-Saudis in the labour force in 1999 at rather more than 4 million. This figure is some 1 million higher than that provided by the Central Department of Statistics, but the difference may be accounted for by the latter covering only those employed legally. The overall pattern of increase is reflected in the total numbers of non-Saudis present in the country (whether working or not). According to the World Migration Organisation (WMO) the number grew from 1,804,000 in 1980 to 4,220,000 in 1990 and then to 5,255,000 in 2000 (WMO 2005: table 23.10). In November 2004 the Saudi General Statistics Authority estimated the number of non-Saudis at 6,144,236 (SA-IR 2005a). It seems clear that the non-Saudi component in the workforce remains higher than the Saudi component, despite the steady growth of the latter. The Central Department of Statistics' figures for Saudi labour, based on 2002 data, put the Saudi labour force at about 3,114,000 (KSA-CDS 2005). The vast expenditure on education within the Kingdom has not so far succeeded, then, in reducing the need for foreign labour.

The national composition of the foreign labour force over the 1990s underwent change. With the Saudisation of professional and technical jobs, the numbers of Westerners working in the economy and for the civil authorities declined gradually (although the absolute numbers of Westerners increased, with the enhanced US military presence between 1990 and 2003). The proportion of the non-skilled labour force coming from Arab countries also declined, especially after 1991 when the government expelled some 750,000 Yemenis from the country due to their government's stand in opposing military action against Iraq. Asian labour was now taking up a larger proportion than before, and within that category the proportion from the non-Islamic parts of Asia was growing. This was to be of some significance for those Saudis who felt that their culture and religion were under threat.

The phenomenon of 'asabiyah *capitalism*

The period after 1979 saw a change in the character of the economic elite in Saudi Arabia. Whereas previously the private sector had been dominated by the big merchant families, based predominantly in Jiddah, now the role of members of the Al Su'ud was becoming increasingly prominent. The focus of the sector began to shift away from Jiddah and towards al-Riyadh. The change can be traced through the contents of two books, one published at the beginning of this period and the other a recent publication. Michael Field's *The Merchants: the Big Business Families of Arabia* (Field 1984) covered the families which were seen in the early 1980s as forming the core of Saudi Arabia's private sector: the Alirezas, bin Ladins, bin Mahfouz's, Juffalis, Olayans and others. A significant number of these families were Yemeni in origin (from Hadhramout), and had been established in Jiddah over a prolonged period. Sharaf Sabri's *The House of Saud in Commerce* (Sabri 2001), covered what the writer described as 'a dynamic critical mass' of the private sector – that coming from the royal family. His book shows the substantial role played, at the very centre of the private sector, by members of the Al Su'ud, mainly the descendants of King 'Abd al-'Aziz but including some from cadet branches of the royal family. The merchant families had not been displaced from the economy, but rather were now playing a less prominent role, and in many cases were in partnership with members of the Al Su'ud.

The economic position which members of the Al Su'ud were able to build-up was based initially on land grants from which they had benefited during the 1960s. King Faisal had made these grants, mostly in and around the major cities, with a view to separating members of the family from the public purse: to ensure that they had an independent economic base and would not be dependent on state finances. At the time, the value of the land was often insignificant. With economic development, and the expansion of the cities, the land acquired value rapidly. From the late 1970s, members of the Al Su'ud found themselves in possession of very substantial resources which could be used for investment.

Some of the investment which followed was pursued within the proper bounds of economic enterprise, and reflected the business acumen of the individual concerned. The most successful investor, indeed, accumulated his huge wealth through business conducted outside of the Kingdom. Prince Alwaleed bin Talal, listed by Forbes Magazine in 2001 as the sixth richest man in the world, built his financial position on investments in the US banking sector – buying into banking operations which were in difficulty and promoting their transformation into profitable and valuable assets. Four years after his acquisition of a major share in Citibank in

1988, his share-holding was worth 20 times what it had been and he was the major shareholder in the largest banking operation in the United States. Nor was Prince Alwaleed alone. The value of Saudi private investments in the outside world had reached some $650 billion by 2004. A significant part of this was simply investment in Western bonds and shares, invested for safe-keeping away from the perceived risks of investment in Saudi Arabia or the wider region. There was, however, a significant number of Saudi investors (among them members of the royal family) who were active in managing business operations in many parts of the world. Some of the investors were benefiting the Saudi economy through bringing both the gains from their investment, and some of the associated technical and business skills, back to Saudi Arabia.

Some of the gains from royal family investment within the Kingdom, however, can not be attributed to skill or acumen. It was clearly possible for some Al Su'ud investors to use their family connections to promote their interests – whether through privileged access to bank loans, preference in the award of contracts or (in the worst cases) political manipulation to exclude competitors. There was, in any case, a widespread perception in the longer-established parts of the business community that the private sector was no longer operating on a basis of fair competition. Without contacts within the royal family, many believed, successful business operation was difficult or impossible.

Responding to the new Islamist challenge: the 1980s

Juhayman al-Otaibi and the seizure of the Great Mosque, 1979

The material threat to the Saudi state posed by the small band of extremists who seized control of the Great Mosque in Makkah on 20 November 1979 was insignificant. The 200–300 Islamist insurgents who took control of the mosque were soon surrounded by Saudi troops and their actions won little support from the population. Symbolically, however, the event was important: the Al Su'ud were being challenged on their own ground, accused of having betrayed the Wahhabi basis on which the Kingdom had been founded. Their inability to ensure the security of the most holy site in Islam, moreover, appeared to demonstrate a weakness at the centre of power. The impact of the seizure was enhanced by its timing. November 20 was the Muslim New Year. There were, therefore, large numbers of pilgrims from all over the Islamic world present in Makkah to say prayers on the first day of the Islamic century's fifteenth century, 1400 AH. The seizure took place immediately after the imam of the mosque had recited the dawn prayers, with some 100,000 people present.

The message conveyed by Juhayman and his supporters was raw, carrying little theological sophistication. Juhayman's origins, and the context in which his beliefs had developed, however, gave a dimension of significance to his actions. He was born in the settlement of Sajir in Qasim, whose population was descended from those who had – inspired by Wahhabi ideas and zeal – fought for 'Abd al-'Aziz in the early part of the twentieth century. Both by virtue of belonging to one of the main tribes of Najd, which had been a mainstay of support for the Al Su'ud, and coming from the religious tradition which was the ideological backbone of the Kingdom, he was by no means a peripheral figure (Buchan 1981: 120–123).

The activities and beliefs of Juhayman and his companions, moreover, were bolstered by the formal structures of Islamic teaching which had been put in place by the Saudi state and the Wahhabi *'ulama*. Some of the group, including Juhayman himself, had attended lectures in the faculty of law at the University of Madinah. Many of these lectures were given by religious leaders who enjoyed national prominence. The rector of the University was Shaikh 'Abd al-'Aziz bin Baz, later to be the grand mufti of Saudi Arabia, and for a time Juhayman seems to have been inspired by bin Baz's teachings (Buchan 1981: 122). Some of the other teachers who influenced the group at that time were members of the Egyptian Muslim Brotherhood who had been encouraged to take refuge in Saudi Arabia in the 1960s, as part of Faisal's attempt to strengthen resistance to Nasirist influence in the Kingdom and the wider region (Kepel 2004: 173–174). Among the latter was the prominent writer Muhammad Qutb, brother of the radical Islamist leader Sayyid Qutb. Sayyid Qutb had been hanged under Nasir's regime in Egypt in 1966. The University of Madinah was a key institution of Wahhabi religious learning within the country, financed and supported by the state.

In 1974 Juhayman turned against bin Baz, believing that he had compromised his beliefs by practical cooperation with the corrupt leadership of the country. After a period spent in Qasim, Juhayman and his associates established themselves in al-Riyadh in 1976. Their activities were now aided by financial support from some wealthy well-wishers – a phenomenon which was to be present in the longer-term growth of Islamic radicalism in the country. The content of their preaching drew them to the attention of the Ministry of the Interior, and in 1978 Juhayman and 98 of his companions were arrested and held in prison for six weeks for questioning. Bin Baz was brought from Madinah to pass judgement on their preaching, but did not find grounds on which to declare it contrary to Islam. The group was then released from prison (Holden and Johns 1981: 511–526).

Once his supporters had taken over the mosque, Juhayman proclaimed that one of his companions, Muhammad ibn 'Abdallah al-Qahtani, was the *mahdi* (sent by God to guide the Muslim community). Taking over the microphone al-Qahtani declared: 'The *mahdi* and his men will seek shelter and protection in the Holy Mosque because they are persecuted everywhere until they have no recourse but the Holy Mosque' (Buchan 1981: 122). The claim that al-Qahtani was the expected *mahdi* was easy for the *'ulama* to counter, given that the concept itself is theologically controversial within Islam – often seen as an accretion coming into Islam from non-Islamic sources.

The strength of the message which Juhayman was conveying, however, came more from the denunciation of the Al Su'ud and of the religious establishment which he unleashed. His political views had been circulating prior to the confrontation in the mosque, through pamphlets which he had produced. In these he described the royal family as corrupt, worshipping money and spending it on palaces rather than on mosques, and rewarding those who agreed with them and persecuting those who disagreed. The religious establishment was divided between those who had warned the royal family about its corruption and those who (like bin Baz) were in the pay of the Al Su'ud. His bitterness towards bin Baz was given an edge through a belief that the religious leader had shared similar ideas to those of Juhayman and his companions, but had allowed the connection with the royal family to influence his position – and in fact that he had used his position to persuade other *'ulama* to stop accusing the Al Su'ud of corruption. Juhayman maintained that people were not obliged to obey rulers who failed to follow the Qur'an and the *sunnah*, even though they might claim to be ruling in the name of Islam. The message, then, conveyed a rather unsophisticated but nonetheless powerful reiteration of the egalitarian and puritanical creed which 'ibn 'Abd al-Wahhab had first elaborated – albeit with the addition of the message that one of the grouping was the *mahdi* (Holden and Johns 1981: 513–522).

The government's attempt to dislodge the insurgents was not completed until some two weeks after the occupation had started – due in part to the determination of the insurgents and in part to the problems which the Saudi armed forces had in removing them without damaging unduly the structure of the mosque. The action taken by Juhayman and his companions appears to have enjoyed very little support among Saudis, especially as it involved the desecration of the holiest religious site in the country. It did, however, exert a powerful influence on the development of government policy through the two decades which followed.

Impact of the Iranian revolution

Unconnected to the events in Makkah, but buttressing the regime's need to respond to Islamist radicalism, was the Islamic revolution in Iran. This constituted a threat to the Saudi regime at two levels: that of external security, and that which linked ideological legitimacy with domestic stability. The concern here is primarily with the latter. Monarchical Iran's secular values had contrasted neatly but not antagonistically with the proclaimed religious values of the Al Su'ud; the contrast enhanced the religious image of the Saudi regime. But there was now a strong and militant Islamic rival to the Saudi regime, posing a direct challenge to the monarchy's ideological legitimacy. The challenge was not just to the policies pursued by the Saudi regime but to the institution of monarchy itself, which was portrayed as alien to Islamic values. The threat was intensified by the revolution's ability to reach inside the Saudi domestic environment and affect the attitudes of Saudi citizens. The substantial Shiite community in the Eastern Province of Saudi Arabia, long perceived as suppressed by Saudi Wahhabism, was acquiring a new confidence through the rise of a resurgent Shiism across the Gulf. Whether or not Saudi Shiites were prepared to be used for Iranian ends, the Iranian revolution was transforming the dynamics of their identity and cohesion. Saudi governmental antagonism to the Iranian revolutionary regime, in any case, was not shared by all Saudi Shiites. A further dimension of the Iranian reach into Saudi Arabia was through the substantial numbers of Iranian pilgrims coming to the holy places in the Hijaz, carrying with them their regime's revolutionary message and spreading this among Saudis and non-Saudis alike.

The initial Saudi reaction to the Islamic revolution was cautious but not unfriendly. Prince (subsequently Crown Prince) 'Abdallah, on 23 April 1979, claimed that the new regime in Tehran had 'removed all obstacles and restrictions in the way of cooperation', and that 'our cooperation will have an Islamic dynamism against which no obstacles facing the Muslims can stand'. He described the Saudi position as one of relief that the Islamic republic had chosen to make Islam, rather than heavy armaments, the 'organiser of cooperation and the basis for dialogue' (*Arab News*: 29.4.79).

The honeymoon phase, however, did not last long. It soon became apparent that the Iranian revolutionary leadership was dismissive of the Al Su'ud's claims to Islamic legitimacy, hostile to the close military links between Saudi Arabia and the United States, eager to promote Islamic radicalism in the wider Islamic world and intent on fostering links with opposition elements from Saudi Arabia's Shiite minority. An ideological struggle with Iran now developed, with national and international ramifications.

At one level the Saudi regime was fighting to prevent its domestic Islamic legitimacy being eroded or undermined, at another it was contesting with Iran the religio-political leadership of the Islamic world. The Iranian regime used the opportunities at its disposal to promote its radical Islamist vision, taking a militant stance in Islamic conferences and organisations, promoting links with Shiite communities in different parts of the world, using the pilgrimage season to spread its revolutionary message among pilgrims, providing logistical support for Islamist movements favourable to the Iranian vision, funding religious propagation and projecting its agenda through broadcasts and other media. Saudi Arabia constituted a key target of Iranian revolutionary criticism. Broadcasts from Tehran denounced the corruption of the Al Su'ud, the un-Islamic features of Saudi monarchical power, the oppression of Shiites in the eastern province, the compromising alliance which the Kingdom maintained with the United States and the Saudi role in keeping oil prices low in the interests of Western powers. The Saudi political leadership responded by using similar methods of ideological propagation to promote its own, very different, Islamic vision.

The ideological conflict took a material form within the Kingdom during the annual *'id al-adha* pilgrimages. Some 150,000 Iranian pilgrims attended the annual pilgrimages in the early 1980s – the largest national contingent in the 1.5 million-strong influx of pilgrims. Significant numbers of these Iranian pilgrims took the opportunity to spread the views of their revolutionary regime. Confrontations between the Saudi authorities and the Iranian pilgrims became, through the 1980s, a regular characteristic of the *hajj*. Already in the 1979 *hajj* the Iranian religious leadership had encouraged Iranian pilgrims to demonstrate in the streets of Makkah and Madina, distributing pamphlets and waving portraits of Ayatollah Khomeini. The Saudi authorities arrested some of the demonstrators, leading to allegations from Iran that its pilgrims were being harassed. This continued over the years which followed, often with the use of violence in the confrontation between pilgrims and police. The most violent conflict occurred on 31 July 1987, when Iranian pilgrims organised a major demonstration attacking US and Israeli policies in the region. The forceful breaking up of the demonstration cost the lives of some 400 pilgrims, two-thirds of whom were Iranians (*Guardian*: 2.8.87). The ferocity of the Saudi police response was denounced by the Iranian government, which permitted a public demonstration to protest against the action. Demonstrators sacked the Saudi embassy, with the death of one Saudi diplomat. The Saudi government then broke off diplomatic relations with Tehran – a measure which it had carefully avoided over the previous years (*Guardian*: 22.8.87).

As noted earlier, the Iranian revolutionary government gave particular attention to the Shiite community in Saudi Arabia, providing logistical support and ideological backing to Shiite opposition elements. The Shiite-based Organisation of the Islamic Revolution (formed secretly in Saudi Arabia after the events recounted in the next section) was permitted to open an information office in Tehran, make broadcasts aimed at the Shiite population of Saudi Arabia and coordinate its global activities from there (Al-Rasheed 2002: 147). The impact of this logistical backing, however, is difficult to assess. The most critical factor for Saudi Shiites was probably the symbolic significance of the events in Iran: a Shiite-based Islamic revolution. A new spirit had begun to spread, and while it was no doubt fanned by broadcasts coming from Tehran the assertion of Shiite identity would probably still have occurred without them.

Unrest in the Eastern Province

The seizure of the Great Mosque was rapidly followed by a further element of religio-political unrest: demonstrations, leading to riots, among the Shiites of the Eastern Province. Over a prolonged period Saudi Shiites had been quiescent, perhaps cowed by the Wahhabi religious leaders' historical antagonism towards their religious practices. Public celebration of the major Shiite ceremonies, such as the *'ashurah* mourning rituals in memory of the martyrs of Shiism, Hasan and Husain, and the building of new Shiite mosques, had been banned by the temporal author-ities in the eastern region ever since the al-Hasa region had come under Saudi rule in 1913 (Al-Rasheed 1998: 122–123). The ibn Jiluwi governors of the eastern province had provided the Shiites with a measure of protec-tion against enforced conversion by Wahhabi clerics, but this came at the cost of the community maintaining a low profile. Professionally, many Shiites had on an individual basis made progress under the rule of King Faisal, attaining positions of some significance in the public sector. Shiites also constituted a major part of the labour force for ARAMCO's oil operations in the eastern region. As a community, however, the Shiites still suffered from a lack of public recognition or acceptance.

In the summer of 1979 Shiite leaders in the eastern region announced that they intended to stage *'ashurah* ceremonies in public that year, with processions marking the event. The processions were scheduled for 28 November. By that time, feelings had of course been further inflamed by the seizure of the Great Mosque on 20 November. The processions reflected a wider politicisation: some of the demonstrators carried plac-ards calling on the Saudi government to bring about a fairer distribution of wealth in the country, end discrimination against Shiites, support the

Islamic revolution in Iran and stop supplying the United States with oil (Butterworth 1982: 106). In Qatif the demonstrations were met by a strong reaction from the security forces, and soon degenerated into general urban riots over a 24-hour period. A pent-up anger, which had deep roots within the community, was finding expression. Seventeen Shi'a lost their lives. Further violence was to occur in Qatif on 1 February 1980, when some Saudi Arabian Shiites celebrated the first anniversary of Ayatollah Khomeini's return to Iran from exile. Among the demands of those who demonstrated on this occasion was the release from prison of Shiites who had been arrested following the November 1979 events. Four demonstrators were killed in the February confrontation (Holden and Johns 1981: 524–525).

The social background of those who took a lead in demonstrations, and who formed the nucleus of the Organisation of the Islamic Revolution which was established secretly following the November events, was significant. Most were ARAMCO workers and students at the University of Minerals and Technology in Dhahran (Al-Rasheed 1998: 122–125). A technically-skilled and professionally-oriented sector of the population was mobilising a more widely-based popular movement on the basis of Shiite identity. After 1992, the Organisation of the Islamic Revolution became known as the Reform Movement. The Organisation/Movement published the magazine *Al-Jazirah al-Arabiyyah* from London during the 1980s and early 1990s.

Re-asserting the regime's Islamic credentials

The initial inclination of the political leadership after the events of 1979–80 was to promise a liberalisation of the regime. The establishment of a Consultative Assembly was mooted, with Crown Prince Fahd announcing in February 1980 that the regulations for such an Assembly would be announced within two months. The regulations, he said, would be framed in accordance with 200 provisions drawn from the *shari'ah* (Holden and Johns 1981: 536). However, no such regulations were drawn up, and the Assembly did not come into being. It was not for another 12 years, after the First Gulf War, that a Basic Law underpinning the creation of an Assembly was adopted. A major opportunity to liberalise the system, broadening support among the middle classes – who had been shocked by the extremism of Juhayman and his supporters, and were distrustful of the revolutionary rhetoric coming from Tehran – was lost.

The strategy ultimately adopted was very different. Central to this strategy was the re-assertion of the regime's Islamic credentials. The allocation of state funding for the support of religious activities increased rapidly. In the

Second Development Plan (1975–80) this stood at SR 1.26 billion, while in the Third Development Plan (1980–85) SR 9.04 billion was allocated. An intensive programme for the construction of new mosques was put in place. Additional funding was put into the country's structures of Islamic education, with a substantial increase in the numbers of students who were admitted into the Islamic universities and the provision of more generous grants than before to encourage this participation. A member of the Al al-Shaikh was appointed Minister of Justice, reinforcing the traditional alliance between the religious and temporal leaderships, and restoring control of the judiciary to a member of the Al al-Shaikh. Bin Baz was made Grand Mufti, giving him a clear leadership position in the country's religious infrastructure. The religious leadership was given a wider role than before in directing the country's social life: the Committees for the Promotion of Good and the Forbidding of Evil were re-vitalised and encouraged to play more active roles, education was put under tighter religious control, and the views of the religious leaders on restricting the role of women in the work-place and in the educational sector given more attention. Women were no longer able to benefit from government scholarships in being sent abroad for studies. In October 1986 King Fahd let it be known that in future he wanted to be known as the 'Custodian of the Two Holy Mosques', and no longer to be addressed as 'Your Majesty' or by any secular title. The social context of Saudi life during the 1980s and 1990s became more narrow than before.

The strategy also had international dimensions. This was to be expected, given the combination of regional and domestic challenges facing the regime. During the 1980s, the Saudi government was active in confronting secular radical movements on the regional and international scenes, in alliance with the United States. The most notable case of this was the support given by the government to the Islamist movements which were fighting the Soviet-backed regime in Afghanistan. By supporting a cause which had the flavour of an Islamic struggle against communist oppression, the regime was able both to underpin its domestic Islamic legitimacy and to strengthen its claim to global Islamic leadership.

There was, in addition, a socio-economic dimension. Despite the cutting back of expenditure in many fields during the 1980s, the level of subsidies and support for the more marginalised parts of the population increased. As noted earlier, there was a sharp increase in the funding going into social security, as also in the subsidies paid to those in the rural sector. More funding than before was put into the development of the areas where Shiites were predominant.

While the strengthening of the regime's Islamic credentials was consistent with the regime's historical legacy, and responded to the growing strength of Islamist consciousness nationally and regionally, the policies adopted were problematic. Strengthening the position of religious leaders who were intent on applying a rigid interpretation of Wahhabi orthodoxy encouraged a narrowness of vision within Saudi society, ultimately breeding discontents which were to threaten the regime during the 1990s and after. The position which some prominent non-Saudi (largely Egyptian) Islamists held in the Saudi Islamic universities gave an added dimension to the religious dynamic. The latter grouping had brought with them radical perceptions associated with exclusion or oppression in their own countries. Such perceptions now shaped new forms of religious discourse through the interaction with Wahhabi salafism. Radical Islamists, many drawing their inspiration from these interacting ideologies, were to pose the major threat to the regime from the early 1990s. The new Islamist trends were more sophisticated theologically than Juhayman's raw fundamentalism. This enabled them to gain a more substantial following in the population. One aspect of Juhayman's movement was to be characteristic of the period which followed: the international Islamic character of its following. Among the 65 insurgents who survived the siege, and were later executed, there were 41 Saudi citizens, 10 Egyptians, 7 Yemenis (all but one citizens of the PDRY), 1 Sudanese and 1 Iraqi (Holden and Johns 1981: 527).

An alternative strategy, also based on mobilising religious values, would have been feasible. The government could have opened up the religious arena to a wider range of Islamic expression, promoting greater intra-Islamic tolerance and pluralism. Encouragement could have been given to non-Wahhabi religious trends, from Sufis to Shi'is, to participate in the government-supported religious and educational arenas. Such an experience of Islamic pluralism would have laid the basis for more general pluralistic values to spread in Saudi society. The events at the Great Mosque had provided the popular base for such a move: there was widespread revulsion at so holy a site being defiled by violence bred of religious extremism. An initiative aimed at undercutting the well-springs of extremism through cultivating Islamic pluralism might well have gathered support. Rather than taking this option, however, the regime took the easier and opposite option: giving the established religious leadership around 'Abd al-'Aziz bin Baz greater authority to combat deviance from Wahhabi norms. The framework which underlay the rejection of pluralism was buttressed.

Responding to the changing global and regional orders: Arab disunity, Gulf insecurity, the US alliance and the Gulf wars

The dilemmas in Saudi Arabia's foreign relations are covered in detail in Chapter 6. The objective here is to give an overview of how the key events unfolded. This is necessary to an understanding of domestic developments in Saudi Arabia at that time. As will become apparent, events in the regional environment (especially the Gulf) were of central importance in shaping the problems faced by the political leadership in the domestic environment.

The Palestine issue and the Arab–Israeli conflict, which had been of central importance in shaping Saudi Arabia's foreign relations in the previous period, were now overshadowed by more direct and immediate concerns. Nonetheless, it is worth bearing in mind that Saudi foreign policy was still conducted against a backdrop of continuing concern over Palestinian and Arab–Israeli issues. The early 1980s saw some new Arab peace initiatives, most notably the Arab League's 1982 Fez Plan which was based on proposals which Crown Prince Fahd had put forward in 1981. Contacts with Egypt were gradually opened up following the assassination of President Sadat and the assumption of the presidency by Husni Mubarak in 1981. The outbreak of the Palestinian *intifadah* in 1987 (continuing through to 1990) had a powerful impact on Saudi popular opinion, just as it did in the rest of the Arab world. The reality of the continuing dispossession of the Palestinian population, and the failure of the international community to act effectively to protect Palestinian political, social and human rights, was brought to (and stayed at) the forefront of Saudi popular consciousness. The development of Saudi popular attitudes towards the Western world during the 1990s and after was heavily influenced by perceptions of the injustices inflicted on Palestinians.

Saudi Arabia was now the only remaining pillar in the US twin-pillar policy. While the United States sought to fill the gap by increasing its direct (though 'over the horizon' as far as Saudi Arabia was concerned) military involvement in the region, the Kingdom became increasingly crucial to US policy in the region. The early- and mid-1980s saw growing US concern with perceived Soviet expansionism in the wider Gulf and Indian Ocean regions, now seen as constituting an Arc of Crisis. The fear was that the strengthening Soviet and Cuban military involvement in Ethiopia after 1978, the entry of Soviet armed forces into Afghanistan in December 1979, the increase in Soviet troops in South Yemen, and the growing Soviet naval presence in the Indian Ocean, would enable the Soviet Union to encircle the Gulf and close the straits of Hormuz to Western shipping (Halliday 1982). The supply of oil to the Western world could, it was claimed, be disrupted. Close security cooperation between Saudi Arabia and the United States was seen, on both sides, as a necessity. The Saudi role in Afghanistan, to be covered in detail in Chapter 6, was of particular importance in the coordinated regional policy – a vital element in weakening the Soviet threat in the Arc of Crisis. Saudi Arabia's security relationship with the United States, therefore, deepened substantially during the 1980s. This was the period when US and Western European sales of military equipment to Saudi Arabia reached their peak. Such purchases had come to $1.798 billion between 1973 and 1977, rising to $8.085 billion between 1978 and 1981, $14.190 billion between 1982 and 1986, and $25.125 billion between 1987 and 1991 (Cordesman 2003a: 98). Saudi Arabia also became involved more widely in promoting US global strategies against leftist regimes in different parts of the world.

The outbreak of the Iran–Iraq war in September 1980 added a new layer to the insecurity in the Gulf. The Kingdom gave substantial support to Iraq during the Iraq war (1980–87), based on the premise that although Iran and Iraq both posed threats to the security of the Kingdom, Iran was by far the largest threat. Close Saudi–Iraqi cooperation was therefore necessary to buttress Saudi Arabia's own security and stability, and the Kingdom provided some $25 billion worth of assistance to support Iraq during the war (Al-Rasheed 2002: 157).

The First Gulf War

Iraqi troops entered and occupied Kuwait on 2 August 1990. At the outset, the Saudi Arabian government reacted with a stunned silence: no mention of it was made in Saudi Arabian media until 4 August, and there was no immediate governmental comment. On 3 August King Fahd met with 'Izzat Ibrahim, the Vice-President of Iraq's Revolutionary Command Council, who had been sent by President Saddam Husain to al-Riyadh to assure the Saudi government that Iraqi forces would not pose a threat to Saudi Arabia. No assurance on Iraqi withdrawal from Kuwait was given. On 4 August, the Saudi Arabian government did eventually condemn the invasion and gave its full support to the Kuwaiti government-in-exile which had already become established within Saudi Arabian territories in Ta'if. The leading circles of the Al Su'ud, however, appear to have been split on the action which now needed to be taken. While some (reportedly Princes Nayif and Salman) were convinced from the outset that US troops would be needed to defend the Kingdom, others (reportedly including Crown Prince 'Abdallah, Prince Talal and Prince Sultan) advocated an initial attempt to reach a negotiated settlement through the auspices of the Arab League. The latter approach drew support from those who were concerned at the impact which the presence on Saudi Arabian soil of non-Muslim foreign troops would have on popular opinion and on wider perceptions of Saudi Arabia in the Islamic world. The matter was resolved, however, when the US secretary of defence, Richard Cheney, held a meeting with King Fahd on 6 August, convincing the King that the security of the Kingdom was at stake. On 7 August, the Saudi Arabian government formally requested assistance from the US government, and air and naval units were duly despatched (Aburish 1994: 175–178).

There is little doubt that the Iraqi forces, if they had chosen to move on into Saudi Arabia, would have had little problem in so doing. Despite the vast amounts which Saudi Arabia had spent on its defence during the 1980s (some $200 billion), the defence forces in the north of the country were minimal. Prince Khalid bin Sultan, appointed on 10 August as the Saudi military commander, has described the 'terrible shock' he received when he went to inspect the Saudi troops on the border. He notes that 'we had discounted the possibility of being exposed to a land threat from our northern Arab neighbours', and that the Iraqi troops would have been able to reach the country's major oil fields within days (Sultan 1995: 8 and 11). The weakness and inadequacy of the country's ability to defend itself, in the light of the huge expenditure which had been incurred, was to form the basis of some of the criticism directed at the government through the 1990s.

The Iraqi government, however, did not carry out a major attack on Saudi Arabia, although there were to be some incursions into Saudi territory. Over the weeks which followed the Iraqi occupation of Kuwait, the numbers of foreign troops present in Saudi Arabia gradually built up. The major part of the military forces came, of course, from the United States, but some 20 of the coalition partners had troops present in the country. At the height of the war against Iraq there were some 750,000 foreign troops massed in Saudi Arabia, with all the weapons, vehicles and equipment which they needed for the operation. The logistical success of the Saudi Arabian government in coping with this massive force was considerable, and was perhaps underrated in the accounts given of the war from Western perspectives. The burden on Saudi Arabia during the war included its subjection to Scud missile attacks and the Iraqi attack on the Saudi town of al-Khafji, close to the Kuwaiti border, on 29 January 1991. The land war to drive the Iraqi forces from Kuwait was initiated on 24 February. On 28 February operations were halted and the war was over (Sultan 1995: 361–420).

The First Gulf War had two main effects on Saudi Arabia's domestic environment. The first was economic: Saudi Arabia bore the major financial burden of the war. The costs to Saudi Arabia were of several kinds: direct subventions to the countries which had sent troops, grants and loans to countries whose diplomatic support was needed, support for the approximately 330,000 Kuwaitis who at one time or another took refuge in Saudi Arabia, logistical support for the forces which were stationed on Saudi Arabian territory, repair and reconstruction of the country's infrastructure which was damaged in the war (whether inadvertently through the heavy demands of military movements or through the Iraqi missile attacks and incursion into al-Khafji) and the military costs of its own forces' operations. It is difficult to be sure of the overall cost, but it is likely to have been in the region of $60 billion – a sum which was only slightly less than the total reserves held by the country at the start of 1990. Of all the states which took up arms against Iraq, Saudi Arabia made by far the biggest financial contribution. The costs of the war to the United States and Britain were mostly offset by the financial contributions which Saudi Arabia, Kuwait and to a lesser extent the United Arab Emirates made to their war efforts.

Saudi Arabia went into the decade of the 1990s, therefore, in a substantially weaker financial position than it had been at the start of the 1980s. For as long as Kuwaiti and Iraqi oil was not being exported, Saudi Arabia gained through the higher oil prices which its own oil could command. By the mid-1990s, however, the oil price had sunk to a lower level than had been seen since the early 1970s. The country's financial resources were depleted by involvement in Iraq over two decades: during the 1980s through the subventions made to support Iraq against Iran, and during the 1990s through the costs of the Gulf War against Iraq.

The second domestic impact of the First Gulf War arose from the permission granted to non-Muslim troops to enter and operate from Saudi Arabian territory, in a military action against a fellow-Muslim state. As will be shown in subsequent sections, the decision opened up new divisions in Saudi society. The political leadership had clearly envisaged that the invitation would be controversial, which no doubt was one reason why it agonised over what to do. To defuse possible criticism from religious quarters, the King acted quickly in the first few days after the Iraqi occupation of Kuwait to ensure that the *'ulama* were publicly supportive. The Board of Senior *'Ulama* was asked to provide religious backing for the invitation, and on 13 August it duly issued a *fatwa* affirming that the invitation to foreign troops was 'dictated by necessity...and made inevitable by the painful reality'. Islamic law, the *fatwa* stated, provided that 'the man in charge of the affairs of the Muslims should seek the assistance of one who has the ability to attain the intended aim'. The legal basis was located in the Qur'an and the *sunnah* 'which indicated the need to be ready and take precautions before it is too late' (Galindo 2001: 197). The *mufti* ibn Baz issued a *fatwa* of his own, stressing the illegality of Iraq's attack on Kuwait and the need for the King to defend both Islam and the Kingdom. Some of the *fatwas* issued at this time emphasised that foreign troops would remain in the eastern province, well away from the sacred area around the two mosques. Some 350 leading religious figures from different parts of the world were invited to a conference organised by the Muslim World League in Jiddah on 12 September 1990 to discuss the theological basis on which non-Muslim troops were being called to defend the Kingdom (*Guardian*: 14.9.90).

Despite the support of the *'ulama*, however, the government's invitation to the United States to bring its troops onto Saudi Arabian territory engendered militant opposition within a sector of Saudi Arabian society. This is covered in the section on *The Opposition and Reform Movements, 1990 to the present*.

Re-fashioning the relationship with the United States

The First Gulf War had established the precedent of US troops being stationed in Saudi Arabia, and in the decade which followed the military relationship between Saudi Arabia and the United States now incorporated that element within it. The US military involvement was no longer restricted to the provision of military supplies and training, but covered also the stationing of some 5,000 US troops within the country. The US Combat Air Operations Centre for the Gulf region was based at a military camp close to al-Riyadh. The US presence was seen as necessary in view of the threats facing Saudi Arabia, domestically as well as externally. The military relationship between the two countries was complemented by close political and economic cooperation. As has been widely noted, the Saudi ambassador in Washington, Prince Bandar bin Sultan, enjoyed close relationships with US presidents over this period, in particular when George Bush and George W. Bush held the presidency.

The events of 9/11 and the Second Gulf War were to lead to a fundamental re-structuring of the Saudi–US relationship. This will be covered in Chapter 6.

The opposition and reform movements, 1990 to the present

The relationship between civil society and the state in Saudi Arabia, as was noted in Chapter 1, is complex. This complexity complicates the process of trying to analyse the opposition and reform movements within the country. The dividing lines between the state and civil society are not always clear. Calls for political reform have come from elements within the governing system, individuals associated with the governing system but not part of it, individuals and groupings within society which have no formal link with those in power (but who may nonetheless retain contacts with some in positions of authority) and those inside and outside of the country who are implacably opposed to all parts of the governing system and shun all contact with anyone associated with the system. These, moreover, are not discrete groups: individuals can shift from one category to another according to the political dynamics of the time. A number of groupings, indeed, have moved from rejection of contacts with the regime to an acceptance that contacts may prove worthwhile, and some have moved in the opposite direction. In some groupings, moreover, the contacts maintained with governmental authorities may be conducted simply on behalf of individuals not of the grouping as a whole.

The opposition and reform movements in Saudi Arabia over the period since 1990 can be conceived as two sets of *continua* stretching between outright opposition and intra-regime reform pressure. The two sets will be characterised here as 'Islamists' and 'modernisers'. On the Islamist side, the possible link within the system is with the religious establishment – in particular the *'ulama*. Some of the Islamist reformers/opposition are within the religious hierarchy itself, while at the outer extreme are some who denounce the religious hierarchy as collaborators with a corrupt and un-Islamic regime, against which violence is justified. On the side of the modernisers, the possible link is with the political leadership and the institutions of government. Some modernisers themselves hold government positions, while at the outer extreme are those who reject any contact with government personnel and institutions and see no solution to the country's problems short of the overthrow of the existing regime.

For both the Islamists and the modernisers there are structural problems in their relationships with the regime/religious establishment. Most Saudi Islamists are seeking a state where the Islamic hierarchy plays a more substantial role in determining the directions and limits of state policy. They are, therefore, both critics and supporters of the *'ulama*: denouncing them for their failure to promote Islamic principles effectively, but stressing that they carry the Islamic legitimacy which must underlie all state policy. For the modernisers, the state has failed (over a prolonged period) to rise to the challenge of political reform. Many would attribute the failure to the structural character of the state. Yet, for all but those seeking the overthrow of the regime, the state needs to be the channel through which reform is brought about, at least in the early stages of reform. In a system where civil associations seeking political reform are not permitted, the only available alternatives are subversion or collaboration.

The terms 'Islamists' and 'modernisers' are employed here because the protagonists tend to classify themselves in this manner. It should be borne in mind, however, that the dichotomy is not between traditional values and secularism. The Saudi Islamists see themselves as reformists, who reject *taqlid* (tradition), have developed a *fiqh al-waqi'a* (understanding of how Islamic law can be implanted in the actual situation today), carry on a sophisticated discourse which covers issues of legitimacy and rights, and operate through the most up-to-date channels of information available today – with internet sites which reach out to and interact with the modern world. The modernisers mostly stress that they are acting within the parameters of Islamic principle, taking account of the traditions and customs of the Saudi population.

Petitioning for change

Opposition critiques of the Saudi regime remained muted through the 1980s. The most active external opposition tended to come from Shiite elements outside of the Kingdom, sometimes operating with Iranian support. Even that, however, did not attract much attention or pose a significant problem to the regime.

With the arrival of foreign non-Muslim troops on Saudi Arabian territory in 1990, however, a new dynamic entered the relationship between the population and the state. This initially took the form of attempts by liberal middle class elements to press for a widening of civil and human rights. They were taking advantage of an apparent weakness in the government's previously hard-line stand on Western-inspired notions of civil rights. With so many Western journalists in the country, to monitor a confrontation portrayed as setting the forces of civilised values against those of totalitarianism and dictatorship, and with Western troops following the customs of their own societies, there was an evident discrepancy at the root of government policy. In the later part of 1990, the Saudi Arabian press became rather more open than it had been before. King Fahd announced his intention to reform the system of provincial administration, establish a National Consultative Assembly and broaden the roles which women could play in employment. In the context of the preparations which were being made for military conflict, women were encouraged to participate as volunteers providing nursing and medical assistance (Galindo 2001: 199). Some of the Chambers of Commerce informally began putting forward ideas about opening up the labour markets to more female employment and creating new structures of representation (Abir 1993: 179).

The most powerful expression of liberal middle class pressure for change was the demonstration organised by 45 Saudi women to press for the right of Saudi women to drive to be recognised. The women clearly thought they would be in a strong position: not only were the females in the US military driving military vehicles around the country, but many of the cars which had brought Kuwaiti families fleeing from Kuwait had been driven by women. The women demonstrators took care to base their stand on Islamic grounds. In their petition to the governor of al-Riyadh, they stated: 'Our demand is corroborated by religion. The traditions of our Prophet Mohammed, may God's blessings be upon him... are evidence confirming the greatness and comprehensive nature of Islam in acknowledging the rights of everyone' (Doumato 1995: 139). The demonstration took place on 6 November 1990, with 45 women driving into the centre of al-Riyadh. The women were arrested and later released under guarantees given by their male guardians. Their passports, and those of their husbands, were confiscated. They were suspended from their jobs, and some did not subsequently secure re-employment. Prince Nayif, the Minister of the Interior, issued an edict re-stating the ban, which had first been imposed by King Su'ud in 1957. He described the women demonstrators as women who had been educated abroad and had received a non-Islamic education (Galindo 2001: 201).

The demonstration constituted a turning-point both for governmental and middle class liberalism. As had been characteristic of much of the conservative political discourse since the early 1980s, the issue of women was shaping the official polemic. The political leadership and the *'ulama* now coalesced around a common cause: to ensure that the foreign military presence did not become an instrument of social or political change – at least not of a type which they could themselves not control and shape. A *fatwa* issued by bin Baz defined the social dangers which would come from women driving:

> Women driving leads to many evils and negative consequences. Included among these mixing with men without being on her guard. It also leads to the evil sins due to which such an action is forbidden... The purifying law forbids all of the causes that lead to depravity.

In sermons delivered by the *'ulama*, the female demonstrators were described as 'the worst of women' (Galindo 2001: 201). Prince Nayif, in an address to the al-Riyadh literary club, stressed the dangers of adopting Western ideas and the need to protect the youth in particular from 'destructive ideologies and suspicious imported culture' (Galindo 2001: 201).

Despite the setback to liberal discourse, a group of 43 reform-minded personalities did nonetheless go ahead with a petition to the King on political reform, which was presented to him in January 1991. The group was made up mainly of intellectuals and businessmen, among them the former Minister of Information Ahmad Abdu Yamani. The petition emphasised the adherence of the petitioners to Islamic law, indicating that they were not seeking to destroy the established system. Their reform requests were modestly phrased and in fact covered items which had already been on the state's political agenda. They asked for Consultative Assemblies to be formed at the national and provincial levels, the media to be opened up, greater scope to be given to the role of women and a complete reform of the educational system (Galindo 2001: 208). There was no immediate response from the state and given that the political leadership had already accepted that new political structures, with associated legal changes, were to be introduced, the petition acted as little more than a prompt to keep the path to political reform open. The regime was in due course to introduce the reforms which had been suggested, in 1992 (see later).

From this point forwards, the lead in petitioning the state for political change was taken by Islamists, although sometimes bringing in other elements. The rising strength of the Islamist reformists needs to be placed in context. One reason why the *'ulama* had chosen to take a strong stand on this issue was to ensure that they were not outflanked by younger and more militant religious teachers and preachers. The latter had already criticised them for having sanctioned the entry of US troops into Saudi territory – a view which held some resonance for parts of the population. At the core of the militant group which was making the critique were three religious persona with positions at religious universities in Saudi Arabia: Safar al-Hawali, Salman al-'Auda and Nasir al-'Umar. Their criticisms had been initiated within a week of the Board of Senior *'Ulama's fatwa* in support of the government's position. On 19 August, Safar al-Hawali, head of the *'aqidah* department at Umm al-Qura University, described the reliance on the United States to deal with the Iraqi invasion of Kuwait as a violation of Islamic law, asking 'how can the *ummah* of the faith and *tawhid* accept reliance on America to solve the problem instead of Almighty Allah?' (Alshamsi 2003: 130). On 28 August, Salman al-'Auda, a member of staff at the Imam Muhammad ibn Sa'ud University, broadened the criticism to suggest that neither Iraq nor Kuwait were operating on Islamic principles, with the conclusion that no Islamic obligation could arise in the conflict between them. Nasir al-'Umar, a professor at the same university, focused on the practical dimension confronting the Islamic world, contending that the United States was motivated by the desire to gain hegemonic control in the Gulf (Alshamsi 2003: 136).

The differences which the Islamist reformists had with the government over the presence of US troops in the country broadened out after the Gulf War into a general call for political reform. Their demands were put forward in petitions submitted to the government, the first of which was presented in May 1991. The latter petition, known as the Letter of Demands, encompassed many demands with which liberal critics of the regime could identify, and indeed many of the 400 signatories to the letter were liberals rather than Islamists. The broad range of support which the petition attracted, moreover, was reflected in the support which some senior *'ulama* gave to it. Even bin Baz initially issued a statement endorsing the text, although he was to distance himself from it once the text had become public and controversial (Alshamsi 2003: 164–165). Despite the broad range of support, it is worth stressing that the drafting of the text, and its presentation in its final form, had been carried out by the reformist Islamist grouping.

The content of the Letter explains the breadth of support which it was able to receive, binding together notions of civil and human rights which cohered within both liberal and Islamic traditions, and calling for improvements of conduct and practice which resonated with Saudi Arabian public opinion in general. The Letter called for the establishment of a *Majlis al-Shurah* (Consultative Assembly) to handle the state's domestic and foreign policies, according to Islamic law; the revision of all state regulations and laws in the political, economic and administrative sectors, to make them consistent with Islamic law; the choosing of 'qualified and ethical' people for state office; the establishment of justice and equality, where people have clearly defined rights and duties; the acceptance of the principle of accountability for all state officials, especially those in influential positions; the establishment of just policies for the distribution of public funds and the adoption of measures to prevent the waste and exploitation of resources, with the adoption of an Islamic economic system; the implementation of reforms in the military; ensuring that the media reflects the Islamic identity of the state; building a foreign policy reflective of the interests of the nation and avoiding alliances which contradict Islam; developing and supporting the religious and *da'wah* institutions; integrating all judicial institutions and ensuring the independent status of the judiciary and ensuring the rights of the individual and society in accordance with the *shari'ah* (Alshamsi 2003: 163).

The government's reaction to the Letter of Demands was to seek to persuade the official *'ulama* to dissociate themselves with the document, and on this they achieved some success. One of the effects of this, however, was that the next memorandum which was put forward, the Memorandum of Advice, was based more exclusively on the views of the Islamist reformists and was distinctly oppositionist in tone. It was directly critical of the monarchical regime, and did not seek to straddle different trends and incorporate a wide range of opinion. The Memorandum of Advice was presented to the government in July 1992. The demands now were more narrowly Islamist: the role of the *'ulama* and *du'ah* (preachers, literally 'callers') in society should be enhanced; the *shari'ah* should be comprehensively applied; the Islamic judicial authority should be strengthened; the violation of human rights and human dignity by the regime should be stopped; administrative reforms should be carried out so as to prevent corruption and ensure justice; an Islamic financial and banking system should be established so as to prevent existing non-Islamic financial and economic practices; the state welfare system should be reformed; the weaknesses in the country's military infrastructure, shown up by the Gulf War, should be addressed and the army should be enlarged and improved; the media should be made to maintain and protect Islamic identity, defend Islam and promote Islamic causes and values; and the country's foreign policy should encompass the propagation of Islam to all parts of the world, unifying Muslims and supporting Islamic causes. The regime was criticised for becoming involved in alliances which served colonial objectives (Alshamsi 2003: 168–169).

The petitions, then, laid out the objectives which different parts of the opposition were seeking to achieve in the early part of the decade. The relationship between the Islamist leadership and the official *'ulama* is evident from what followed the publication of the Memorandum. The Board of Senior *'Ulama* denounced the text in strong terms, saying that the way its signatories had behaved

> inspires the causes of disunity, hatred and fabrication ... and completely discredits the good features of the state. It either proves the ill-intent of the writers or their ignorance of reality ... The Board confirms that such acts violate the Islamic *shari'ah*.
>
> (Alshamsi 2003: 49–50 of vol. 2)

Yet it may be significant that 7 of the 17 members of the Board were 'absent for health reasons' when this statement was issued.

The internal Islamist critique

The main lines of the critique of the regime and its policy, coming from the Islamist side, will already have become clear in the last section. Over this period, and in the years up to 1994, the Islamist grouping continued to put across the same ideas – explained in greater detail and with more religious explanation – in the campaign they waged to bring about political change in the country. The vehicles for this campaign were lectures and sermons delivered in mosques and elsewhere, which were then reproduced on cassette tapes and circulated widely. The year 1994 is given as a cut-off point, as it was in September–October of that year that the leaders of the Islamist grouping were arrested and imprisoned. As will be shown later, the direction taken by different parts of the Islamist grouping diverged after that.

Some of the views purveyed by the Islamist leaders can be seen as simplistic and perhaps obscurantist. There was no systematic attempt to grapple with some of the most complex problems facing Saudi society, such as the need to bring more women into the workforce, or how to safeguard the rights of the Shiite part of the population (there was, in fact, a strongly anti-Shiite tenor to some of their comments about Shiites). One of the few places where women achieve a mention in the Memorandum of Advice is where the media is criticised for not providing constructive programmes which benefit 'women and the family' – locating concern with women solely in the family and not the employment context. The same section calls for programmes which 'promote decency and virtue among women' (but apparently not among men).

Yet the Islamist leaders did produce a discourse which emphasised concepts of civil and human rights, while emphasising that Islamic law was the determining criterion and sole source of human rights. Much of their critique was phrased exclusively in terms of the manner in which the rights of those who are seeking to promote Islamic causes and understanding are undermined or forbidden by the state, but there was also an attempt to make the proposed reforms of wider significance. The complete banning of torture was recommended, as also was the 'violation of the right to dignity' when police are seeking to obtain information. Individuals were to be assured of the ability to have lawyers to defend them, and should be presumed innocent unless a court of law has proved otherwise. It was recommended that departments be established in every government institution to receive claims and grievances from citizens about the negligence of their employees (Al-Auda 2003).

The tenor of the opposition tended to become more antagonistic to the regime as time passed. Shortly before his arrest in September 1994, Salman al-Auda gave an address in which he accused the regime of introducing 'oppressive and illegal measures' to prevent Muslims from spreading their ideas, saying that corruption had engulfed all aspects of life in Saudi Arabian society, with deteriorating standards of morals in all walks of life. Radical reform was needed. Yet, he said, there were people in power who were 'set against any kind of reform' (Alshamsi 2003: 207). It should be noted, however, that there was never any direct refusal to acknowledge the legitimacy of the Saudi state.

These central figures in the internal Islamist leadership spent the years 1994–2000 in prison. When they were released from prison, they were not initially permitted to give sermons or public lectures. They did, however, find many channels through which their views could be conveyed. The most effective channel was the internet sites which they established, through which they could convey their opinions on developments within the Kingdom and outside. These became major fora for political discourse on the Kingdom, from an Islamist perspective. The line which came from their pronouncements tended to be more muted in terms of criticism of the ruling family and the political leadership. Much of their criticism was now directed outwards, denouncing the global order and the injustices which Muslims were suffering under it. Over many issues in foreign policy, indeed, the Islamists now found themselves favourable to the governmental line – as in the case of Iraq. There was a sense that the whole country was under attack from outside, and that the priority was to stand together in resisting this attack rather than criticising the regime. The Islamist leadership took part in some of the meetings which were convened by Crown Prince 'Abdallah to consider the way in which the system of government could be reformed (*Guardian*: 20.6.03). Most of the leading elements in this Islamist grouping who had been prominent in the 1990s, moreover, took an active part in denouncing the terrorism which was striking at targets within Saudi Arabia in the early part of the new millennium. In one case, they helped bring some of the elements involved to the authorities. They had thus become strategic allies of the regime in confronting both domestic and international threats.

The Islamist civil critique in exile

The events in the mid-1990s led to those who were most geared to Western forms of organisation creating an organisation to press for reform. This was done through the formation of the Committee for the Defence of Legitimate Rights (CDLR) in May 1993, whose title was chosen to stress that the rights sought were ones which were rooted in the *shari'ah*. The six signatories of the initial declaration of the Committee were senior academics and legal personalities. The high status of the signatories, and their religious learning, indicated to the population that the Committee was not moving outside the religious and ideological basis of the existing system of government. One of the signatories was 'Abdallah al-Jibrin, a member of the highly important *'Ifta* Committee which was responsible for issuing *fatwa*s on behalf of the senior *'ulama*. Another was a retired judge and former head of the *diwan* of ombudsmen, 'Abdallah al-Mas'ari. The latter's son, Muhammad al-Mas'ari, acted as spokesman of the group. He was a professor of physics at King Saud University, and due to his skill in dealing with the Western media he soon became regarded as the leader of the CDLR. The Committee's aims were to make the government accountable, to regain the independence of the judiciary and to make people aware of their rights according to Islamic law. In its opening statement, the Committee called for people to provide it with information about injustices which had been occurring (Al-Rasheed 2002: 176–177).

Despite the high status of the signatories, they were nonetheless arrested and imprisoned following the Committee's creation. The Committee was banned, and the *'ulama* issued a *fatwa* condemning the Committee. A number of the activists who had been promoting the Committee then left the country, most prominently Muhammad al-'Mas'ari and Sa'ad al-Faqih, a surgeon. They then re-established the Committee in London, creating considerable publicity for the Committee, especially through the vehicle of faxes sent out to a wide range of fax numbers in Saudi Arabia, and subsequently by a web-site (Al-Rasheed 2002: 178). Through both means they spread information on the situation within Saudi Arabia and called for political reform. While not all of the information was accurate, it did open up internal as well as external discourse on developments in the Kingdom. An attempt by the British government to seek the deportation of Muhammad al-Mas'ari from Britain, on the grounds that his statements were intended to encourage the use of violence, was rejected by the British courts.

In 1996, however, a split occurred which effectively destroyed the CDLR in the form in which it had existed before. The two leaders who had shaped the activities of the external CDLR fell into dispute, with Sa'ad al-Faqih leaving the organisation in order to found a new grouping, the Movement for Islamic Reform in Saudi Arabia (MIRA). The two sides have given different accounts of the reasons behind the split, covering both personal and ideological issues, but the significant point here is how the two organisations differed subsequently in terms of the effectiveness of their organisation and the political lines which were pursued. The activities of the CDLR quickly fell away, partly due to the heavy debts which the organisation had incurred. The activities which it did retain tended to be focused on global Islamist affairs, showing an alignment with radical Islamic groups in Britain such as the al-Muhajirun. MIRA kept the focus on Saudi Arabia, running an effective web-site (which would mysteriously disappear from the web from time to time) which gave continued publicity to developments within Saudi Arabia and the campaign to bring about political change in the country. A publication which it initiated, *Arabia Unveiled*, focused on such issues as the independence of the judiciary, the accountability of the government and royal family, the oil and defence policies pursued by the regime and the socio-economic problems facing the population. Both of the organisations tended to direct their criticism more against the King, Prince Nayif (Minister of the Interior), Prince Sultan (Minister of Defence) and Prince Salman (Governor of al-Riyadh), than against Crown Prince 'Abdallah. MIRA tended to be more critical than was the CDLR of bin Baz, who was described by the former as lacking legitimacy (Galindo 2001: 227).

In December 2004 MIRA opened a radio station called *Sawt al-Islah*, broadcasting from an undisclosed European country to Saudi Arabia. Arrangements were made for Saudis to participate in the programmes interactively, through channels which could not be monitored within the Kingdom.

Turning to violence: the al-Qa'ida dimension

A separate strand of Islamist opposition was constituted by 'Usama bin Ladin and his associates, who ultimately became known under the epithet 'al-Qa'ida'. For a time in the early 1990s the organisation seemed poised to take a similar form to the exile civil movements covered in the previous section. An office was opened in London in 1994, calling itself the Committee for Advice and Reform in Saudi Arabia. 'Usama's objectives, however, were not limited to Saudi Arabia, and the means he chose to pursue them were not peaceful. 'Usama and the al-Qa'ida grouping will be covered in Chapter 6.

The liberal critique

Despite the prominence of different strands of Islamist opposition to the regime and/or its policies, it is important to stress that a liberal critique has continued. As noted earlier, the liberal critique has straddled the divide between civil society and the state. Some parts of it are clearly outside of the umbrella of the state and are antagonistic towards the regime. Other elements are linked into the circles of cooperation around the political leadership. Members of the Al Su'ud family themselves (see following section) differ in the attitudes which they take towards the process of reform – ranging from advocates of liberal democracy to those who are antipathetic to reform of any kind. Some commoner members of the government, such as the Minister of Planning Dr Ghazi Algosaibi, are often seen as being associated with the liberal reform movement, although perhaps more in seeking to implement social reforms and opposing narrow-minded interpretations of Islam, than in the public promotion of political reform (Algosaibi 2002). Some members of the *Majlis al-Shurah* have also been active in seeking the expansion of the assembly's role and its transformation into a representative body through the holding of elections.

Those parts of the liberal critique which are clearly not associated in any way with the state are both internal and external. Internally, calls for political reform – seeking the establishment of elected representative bodies with defined and significant legislative powers, at both provincial and national levels; clearer legislative protection of human rights and greater rights for women – have all been made by intellectuals and journalists. Although this has usually been done individually, it has also taken the form of collective petitions. This precedent was established in 1990/91, and was repeated in 2003. The latter petition was considerably stronger in tone than the former and led to the arrest of the key individuals concerned.

Another domestic part of the liberal critique is that which is now pursued by the members of the country's Shiite community. Developments in Saudi Arabia in the early 1990s created a new political dynamic for the Shiite community. They were now confronted by a resurgence of a militant brand of Wahhabism, seen as being hostile to Shiism. The Shiite community now had common cause with those within and outside the state structures who were calling for reforms guaranteeing human rights and representation. They could hope to achieve some protection of their rights through these means.

For an understanding of this new trend, an account of the development of the Shiite movement in the 1980s is necessary. During the latter period exiled Saudi Arabian Shiites had campaigned internationally against the Saudi regime, alleging continued harassment of the Shiite community following the unrest in the Eastern Province in 1979 and the early 1980s. The Islamic revolution in Iran, and the Iran–Iraq war, added to the intensity of the stands adopted. The group which articulated this position most actively was the Organisation of the Islamic Revolution, later known as the Reform Movement, which had an office in Tehran. From London, the organisation published a monthly periodical, *Al-Jazirah al-Arabiyyah*, which pursued a well-informed critique of Saudi government policies (Al-Rasheed 1998: 125–130). The main target of criticism from the Shiite opposition, then, was the Saudi state and its repression of the Shiite community.

The mood of the late 1980s and early 1990s, however, had changed. Shiism and Iran had both been under attack by some of the Islamist radicals who were gaining prominence at that time. One such radical, who had signed the Memorandum of Advice and was one of the founding members of the CDLR, was Shaikh 'Abdallah al-Jibrin. Shaikh Al-Jibrin issued a *fatwa* stating that Shiites were infidels and as such could be killed without a sin being committed (Fandy 1999: 206). The significance of the shaikh's statement was enhanced by his status as a member of the *'ulama's 'Ifta* committee. Safar al-Hawali, in some lectures on Shiism, maintained that Shiism was not compatible with Sunni Islam, containing substantive elements which had been brought in from pre-Islamic religions in Persia as well as from Christianity and Judaism. Salman al-'Auda was also critical of the religious bases of Shiism. The government had, moreover, been putting substantial resources into social and economic development in the Eastern Province, in an attempt to remove some of the material sources of discontent. The Shiite community in Saudi Arabia, therefore, had rather more reason and inclination to seek governmental protection than they had before. Conversely, faced now with militant Sunni Islamist opposition, the government was in need of finding new support. In August 1996 the Reform Movement reached an agreement with the government. Shiite prisoners in Saudi prisons would be released, there would be a review of the ban on travel for 2,000 Shiites, passports would be issued to those Shiite exiles who wanted to return to Saudi Arabia, and the Shiite community would be allowed cultural and religious expression (with permission to import books on Shiism, an agreement that negative references about the Shiite community in official documents would be removed and acceptance that the Shi'a constituted one of the sects of Islam) (Galindo 2001: 228).

The trend of the Shiites to seek protection through demanding the protection of their human rights was made all the more important by the religious discourse being conveyed by the most prominent Saudi Arabian Shiite religious personality, Shaikh Hasan al-Saffar. The message which Shaikh al-Saffar had been putting across from the late 1980s was linked into a wider discourse within Islam, emphasising the compatibility of Islam and democracy. The title of his seminal work, which was published in 1990, was *Al-Ta'adudiyah wa al-Hurriyah fi al-Islam* (Pluralism and Freedom in Islam). While al-Saffar was not espousing a Western form of liberalism, he was advocating that pluralism should be recognised, that the relations between different social groups should be based on tolerance and openness, and that pluralism and freedom of belief should be the bases on which the Islamic community was built. He denounced xenophobia at both the religious and intellectual levels. There was an emphasis on the need for freedom of expression, space for the population to engage in political participation, recognition of equal citizenship, and the creation of an Islamically-based boundary between private religious practice and the requirements of the state. He described civil society, with its autonomous associations, as constituting the basis on which a good relationship between the population and the state could be constructed (Fandy 1999: 210–211).

It was Shaikh al-Saffar who laid the basis for the agreement which was eventually reached between the Reform Movement and the Saudi government in 1996. He had issued a statement in June 1992 saying that any initiative for a dialogue between the government and the Shiite community would receive a positive response. Negotiations took place over the years which followed, much of it handled by Ghazi Algosaibi, who at that time was the Saudi ambassador in London, until agreement was reached in November 1996 (Al-Rasheed 1998: 136). The relationship between Shiite religious and political leaders and the government since then have not always been harmonious, as Shiites were at times under pressure from the Ministry of the Interior when terrorist acts occurred within the Kingdom, and the security authorities were slow to recognise that the main sources of instability facing the Kingdom no longer resided in the Shiite community with its links to Iran. There were arrests of a number of Shiites in 1998, with the individuals not being released until some months later. Nonetheless, there remained in being a Shiite movement which carried liberal political perspectives with it, enjoying a measure of protection by the Saudi state. In 1997 Shaikh al-Saffar published a new book, *Al-Watan wa al-Muwatanah* (The Homeland and Citizenship) which was welcomed and appreciated by those who reviewed it in the Saudi media (Fandy 1999: 209).

In 2003 and 2004 there was a renewed petition movement by modernisers within the Kingdom, calling for political reform and the expansion of human rights. Those who organised this movement were imprisoned, charged with calling for a constitutional monarchy, 'using Western terminology' in demanding political reforms and questioning the judicial system. The three central figures were all academics, Matruq Falih, 'Ali Dimaini and 'Abdallah al-Hamid. It was, however, significant that on this occasion the development was given some publicity in the Saudi media. When the accused came to court in September 2004, moreover, the court witnessed the unusual spectacle of relatives and supporters of the accused staging a peaceful protest outside the court room, followed by a vocal protest within. The session then had to be adjourned (SCCSRA 2005). There was some similarity between the ideas which were put forward in the petitions and the positions taken by Shaikh al-Saffar.

One other element in the liberal critique which requires a mention is the organisations run by Saudi exiles which campaign on human rights issues from abroad. Some of these appear and disappear within short periods, with their presence established mainly through web-sites which circulate information about human rights abuses and current developments in the Kingdom. Their strength in terms of popular support among Saudi citizens is, therefore, difficult to assess.

Re-fashioning the political and governmental system

As has been noted earlier, King Fahd made a promise of substantive political reforms in November 1990, at a time when Saudi Arabia was convulsed by the effects of the Iraqi occupation of Kuwait. The promise of political reforms, when the Kingdom was faced with threats to its stability, was by no means new. On this occasion there was perhaps more reason to believe that measures of reform would indeed be taken, given the impact which the unprecedented presence of large numbers of US troops would have on the country. Nor did the content of the reform package come as any great surprise. Over a prolonged period, promises of reform from within the political leadership, and calls for reform from those modernisers with links to government, had focused on a basic law defining the processes whereby the country was governed, the establishment of a Consultative Assembly which would comment on proposed legislation, and the creation of more coherent structures for the administration of the provinces. The reforms which were in due course made public in March 1992 duly took the form of a Basic Law of Government setting out the responsibilities and processes of the governing institutions, a Law of the Consultative Council and a Law of the Provinces.

The Basic Law, the Consultative Assembly and the reform of provincial administration

When the Basic Law was made public, government spokesmen themselves played down its novelty. It was projected, rather, as defining and regularising processes which were already in place. This was certainly true, and as such it is difficult to describe the law as constituting political reform. Indeed, in some respects it was re-stating and re-affirming the unchanged and conservative bases on which the Kingdom had always operated. Nor can the Basic Law be described as a constitution. The boundaries within which power can be exercised are not sufficiently limited and specific. The law, in any case, describes the Qur'an as

Saudi Arabia's constitution. The document is nonetheless worthy of attention as it does provide a useful image of how the political leadership sees (or saw, in 1992) the key elements of Saudi rule.

The Basic Law (under Royal Decree A/90) identifies Saudi Arabia as an Arab Muslim state whose religion is Islam. The system of government is described as a monarchy, with the rulers being drawn from among the sons and descendants of King 'Abd al-'Aziz Al Su'ud. The King chooses the heir apparent by royal decree and can also relieve him of this position. On the death of the king, the heir apparent takes over, and citizens 'shall give the pledge of allegiance (*bay'ah*)' to him, 'professing loyalty in times of hardship as well as ease'. The government 'derives its authority from the Holy Qur'an and the Sunnah of the Prophet (Peace be upon Him), which are the ultimate source of reference for this law and the other laws of the State'.

There is a continuing stress throughout the document on the Islamic values underpinning social and economic organisation: the family is described as the nucleus of Saudi society, and families shall be raised in the Islamic creed; the state shall promote family bonds and Arab/Islamic values; the aim of education is to instil the Islamic creed and ownership; capital and labour are seen as basic components of the 'economic and social entities of the Kingdom', constituting personal rights which 'perform a social function in accordance with the Islamic *shari'ah*'. The state was required to protect the Islamic creed, apply the *shari'ah*, encourage good and discourage evil, and 'undertake its duty regarding the Propagation of Islam'. These elements clearly re-state the mission which the Saudi regime had always set for itself and pronounced.

With regard to rights and duties, *inter alia* the state was obliged to protect human rights in accordance with the *shari'ah* and to provide material and social well-being through employment and other measures of social and cultural provision. The mass media were required 'to employ civil and polite language', contributing to the education of the nation and strengthening its unity. Acts leading to disorder and division were prohibited, as also were acts affecting the security of the state or undermining human dignity and rights. Foreign residents were obliged to observe the values of the Saudi community and to respect its traditions.

The central processes of government were described, but the precise operation and composition of key bodies was often obscured by the phrase 'the law shall specify'. The authority of the state was said to consist of the judicial authority, the executive authority and the organisational authority. The King was to be the ultimate arbiter of all of these authorities. The judiciary was nonetheless described as being an independent authority, whose members were appointed and relieved of their duties by royal decree – based on a proposal by the supreme judiciary council, whose composition and activities would be 'specified by the law'. The role of Prime Minister would be filled by the king, assisted in the performance of his duties by the Council of Ministers, again according to the rulings of the law. The deputy Prime Minister and the Ministers, together with Deputy Ministers and senior officials, would be appointed and relieved of their duties by royal decree. All Ministers and heads of independent authorities were to be responsible to the Prime Minister (i.e. the king, in normal circumstances) for their activities. An extensive list of duties for the King was specified, ranging from the right to declare a state of emergency to appointing and dismissing military officers. There were also provisions governing the handling of the Kingdom's financial affairs.

One link of continuity with the past, intended clearly to emphasise the royal family's long-standing claim to being open to the people, was an article asserting that councils held by the King and the heir apparent 'shall be open to all citizens and to anyone else who may have a complaint or a grievance'. No processes were specified, however, whereby this popular right could be exercised.

The *Majlis al-Shurah* Law (Royal Decree A/91), with the organisational provisions which came with it, was slightly longer than the Basic Law and very specific in defining the role which the assembly could and could not play. The justification for the law was located in a Qur'anic text ('and consult with them upon the conduct of affairs') and the establishment of the assembly was described as being 'in adherence to God's bonds and commitment to the sources of Islamic jurisprudence'. The membership was to consist of 60 'scholars and men of knowledge and expertise', to be chosen by the King. The chairman, deputy-chairman and secretary-general of the assembly were similarly to be chosen by the king. The assembly's role was defined as being to express its opinions on the general policies of the state which were referred to it by the Prime Minister. The specific areas where comment was expected were the following: the general economic and social development plans; laws, regulations, treaties and international agreements; and annual reports submitted by ministries and other government bodies. Resolutions made by the assembly were to be forwarded to the Prime Minister for consideration by the Council of Ministers.

Despite the overall reactive role which was laid down, the possibility of some pro-active element was also envisaged. The *Majlis* could submit a request to the Prime Minister for any government official to attend a meeting, and a group of ten or more members could seek the enactment of a new regulation (or the amendment of one in force) and have it forwarded to the King. The chairman of the *Majlis* could submit a request to the King for relevant government documents. Specialised committees were to cover particular fields of the *Majlis*'s interests, and these committees would have the right to invite non-members to join them.

The procedures for the operation of the assembly were laid down in great detail. Among these were instructions that the chairman's decision on asking members to speak should take into account 'the sequence of their requests and their relevance to a fruitful debate', and the ban on members speaking for more than ten minutes on any subject (unless given permission by the chairman to do so). If a member betrayed any of his duties he could be subject to censure in writing, the deduction of one month's salary or forfeiture of membership. The flavour of the precepts suggested a nervousness on the part of the authorities and a concern lest the opening of the door to criticism should unleash an uncontrollable torrent. As the members were appointed by the King, with no power base outside of the assembly, however, the possibility of such a development was limited.

The Law of the Provinces (Royal Decree A/92) combined a definition of what were in practice the existing duties of province governors with procedures for the introduction of provincial councils – with ten members of the local community who were 'eligible in terms of their knowledge, expertise and specialisation' participating in each council. The members of the local community were to be appointed by the Prime Minister, on the recommendation of the provincial governor and with the approval of the Ministry of the Interior. The parameters within which the provincial councils could operate were phrased in a rather more pro-active way than were those of the *Majlis al-Shurah*. The councils could determine the needs of the province, rank these in terms of priorities and then propose these items be included in the state's development plans. They were to analyse the province's urban and rural layout, and implement any changes once these had been adopted. The membership of the councils, however, comprised official representatives (including the governor of the province) as well as the ten from the local community, such that the latter were effectively always a minority.

The law contained the same tension between rights and duties as was present in the *Majlis* law. The initial article of the law referred to the need to guarantee the rights and liberties of citizens, within the framework of the Islamic *shari'ah*. The cautiousness over how debates in the councils might develop, however, was evident in an article which gave the ministry of the interior the power to declare null and void any resolution which was deemed to fall outside a council's powers.

The operation and development of the **Majlis** and the provincial councils

The introduction of the *Majlis* and the provincial councils was projected by some commentators at the time as the first step towards representative local and central government. Except in the sense that institutions were being created which could at some time be transformed into representative bodies, it is not valuable to see the institutions in this light. Neither at the provincial nor the national levels was there the suggestion that members of the assembly/councils were supposed to represent their communities. Indeed, the provisions that members should be 'completely impartial' and should not raise any matter which 'may serve a private interest' emphasised the separation of members from the notion of representation.

The new laws, in fact, constituted a missed opportunity to change the basis of the political system. What was needed was progress towards a political system where the radically different political trends in the country could be openly debated, where those holding particular political views could both mobilise support for them and be forced to defend them in the public arena and where provincial and national bodies would reflect the balance of opinion resulting from such a contest. No doubt such a development would have been divisive, and the dominant trend in the short term would almost certainly have been Islamist, but it would have nurtured a more sophisticated civil society. The language of political rights, used in different ways by both Islamists and modernisers, could have become the vehicle for dialogue. The strength and centrality of the Al Su'ud in the Kingdom, backed by the resources of the oil rentier state, should have been sufficient to contain the problems inherent in political competition. Far from the development undermining the religious basis of the state, so crucial for the Al Su'ud's legitimacy, the move to political competition seemed likely – at least in the short term – to reinforce that basis.

The assembly and the provincial councils did, however, have value in other respects. They widened the input into national and provincial policies, enabled these policies to become the focus of public debate (through the broadcasting of *Majlis* sessions and the reporting of debates in the media) and brought some highly qualified Saudis into close involvement with a policy-making process from which they had previously been marginalised or excluded. Saudi government spokesmen have sometimes pointed out that the *Majlis* members are more highly qualified, with a wider range of technical and specialist knowledge and skills, than could be found in representative institutions elsewhere in the world. This is certainly true: a substantial number of the members hold doctoral degrees. Yet this is a reflection of its unrepresentative character, as well as its utility in enabling government legislation and policy to benefit from specialist advice and scrutiny. The value of the assembly in terms of providing the government with greater access to specialist advice was enhanced when, in July 1997, the number of members was increased from 60 to 90 and again in May 2001 when it was further increased to 120.

The possibility that the new institutions could be converted into representative bodies did not arise until the Kingdom was confronted with a new threat to its stability: the impact of 9/11, with the associated progression towards war over Iraq and the intensification of terrorism within the Kingdom. The possibility which did arise, moreover, was for the moment limited to the provincial councils; it did not cover the assembly. Crown Prince 'Abdallah in 2002 announced that the local community members of provincial councils would in future be elected, with the elected members comprising 50 per cent of the councils' membership. The putting into effect of this decision was slow, with the proposed date of elections continually being put back, but elections were in due course held in February 2005. There had been indications that women as well as men would be able to compete in the elections, as well as vote in them, but in the event this was 'not possible due to difficulty in making practical arrangements'. The ban on autonomous political organisation was not lifted, so candidates were competing on an individual basis. Many commentators were of the view, however, that candidates favourable to Islamist viewpoints had performed well. The move towards representation was no doubt of some significance, but the system still fell far short of permitting meaningful political competition based on mobilised opinions and interests.

The debate on reform and the struggle for power within the Al Su'ud

Different attitudes towards political reform within the royal family have, of course, been present for a long time. As was seen in Chapter 2, the divisions in the late 1950s and early 1960s were so deep that they led to one part of the family taking refuge abroad. After reconciliation had been achieved in the mid-1960s, differences remained muted through to the later part of the 1990s. The debate covered in this section, therefore, covers the later part of the 1990s decade and the early part of the decade which followed. The roots of the differences, however, need to be understood within the context of what had gone before.

It is impossible to separate the debate on reform from wider struggles for power and influence within the royal family. The issue of reform was to become one of the elements around which the different poles competed. At times, however, it has been unclear whether reform positions adopted by members of the royal family do in fact represent genuine desires to implement change or are simply counters in an intra-family power struggle.

Western observers have tended to conflate pro-Western tendencies with an inclination to political reform, assuming that those members of the royal family who behave in a Western manner, advocate Western norms of social behaviour and favour close relations with the United States are likely to be proponents of political democratisation. This assumption, however, may be mistaken. In the current divisions within the Al Su'ud, for example, King 'Abdallah has often been described as representing the more conservative side of the family, closer to the traditional Islamic and tribal hierarchies, more attuned to Islamic values, more at one with Arab nationalism, less supportive of the relationship with the United States (Kechichian 2001). For all these reasons, therefore, he is assumed to be less inclined to opening up the political system and making it more representative. On the other side, the 'Sudairi seven' – the princes who share the same mother as King Fahd, most notably the Minister of Defence Prince Sultan, the Minister of the Interior Prince Nayif and the Governor of al-Riyadh Prince Salman – are seen in the opposite light. They are described as being socially at ease with Western customs, supportive of a close relationship between Saudi Arabia and the United States, less influenced by traditional Islamic and tribal dimensions, and eager to see Saudi Arabia integrate itself more closely into the global economy. For all these reasons they are seen as being favourable to the system moving towards a constitutional democracy.

Yet the reality would appear to be the opposite. In recent years, the pressure within the Al Su'ud for a more representative form of political system appears to have come primarily from Crown Prince (now King) 'Abdallah and those princes who are closest to him. It is significant that some of the princes who are most aligned with the Crown Prince in the ongoing power struggle were formerly part of the 'Free Princes Movement' of the early 1960s. Prince Talal bin 'Abd al-'Aziz, holding no official post but nonetheless wielding some influence, and Prince Nawwaf, the head of intelligence (2002–05), both fall into this category. It is significant that Prince Talal is the only one of the senior princes who has consistently spoken and written in favour of Saudi Arabia becoming a constitutional monarchy, with a government emerging out of competitive elections.

A further element in support of liberal political reform within the Al Su'ud comes from the sons of King Faisal, who include the Foreign

Minister Prince Su'ud, the former head of intelligence and current ambassador in Washington Prince Turki and the governor of 'Asir Prince Khalid. They were reported to have submitted a joint petition calling for political reform in 1991 and appear to have continued to support this line in the years which have followed.

Key members of the Sudairi seven have tended to see the needs of the system in terms of security rather than greater representation. Prince Nayif, in particular, has downplayed political reform, insisting that the central necessity is to defeat the terrorist threat facing the Kingdom. There are reports that the introduction of elections for the provincial councils was opposed by Prince Nayif and some of the other Sudairi princes, on the grounds that such a move could undermine the stability of the Saudi state. 'Abdallah, while Crown Prince, was certainly frustrated by the slow pace at which progress towards elections was made, reportedly believing that there were personalities in the system who were deliberately blocking change.

The ability of 'Abdallah to carry through the political reforms which he appears to favour was, of course, limited by his position while Crown Prince. His powers increased after 1995, when he began deputising for Kind Fahd under an article in the Basic Law which permits the King to 'delegate part of his authority to the Heir Apparent by royal decree'. Fahd became increasingly incapable of exerting influence on the course of events in the Kingdom. It was reported that for extended periods he was unable to focus on the affairs of government. 'Abdallah's powers, nonetheless, remained substantially less than those he now has as King. All significant royal decrees, and all of the main policy decisions, still had to bear the King's signature. For those who wanted to frustrate policies pursued by the Crown Prince, therefore, the way was open for intrigues which used Fahd's position to block the adoption of new measures. Fahd's wishes, moreover, usually had to be conveyed through princes who were close to him, increasingly his son 'Abd al-'Aziz. The gatekeeper to the King could, of course, have an agenda of his own.

The limitations on 'Abdallah's position, moreover, were reinforced by the key positions in the government held by the Sudairi seven and other princes allied to them. The Sudairi seven's control of the Ministry of the Interior, through Prince Nayif, and the Ministry of Defence, through Prince Sultan, meant that 'Abdallah had limited influence over the two key ministries responsible for the internal and external security of the state. He did have control of a parallel security apparatus, being head of the National Guard and having allies in charge of intelligence, but this created a balance of power rather than giving him the power to determine the shape of security policy.

'Abdallah's position as King is, of course, substantially different. Indeed, in one respect he enjoys greater power relative to the Al Su'ud's senior princes than earlier Kings did. The 1992 Basic Law gave the King the right not only to appoint the Heir Apparent but also to change the line of succession if he so chooses. While Prince Sultan was appointed Crown Prince by 'Abdallah immediately after he became King, therefore, he holds that position at 'Abdallah's pleasure. The law did not apply to 'Abdallah when he was Crown Prince, as his appointment pre-dated the law. 'Abdallah's position as King, moreover, is strengthened by his personal reputation. He is regarded as having integrity, working for the country without seeking to advance the economic interests of his immediate family or to ensure that his children are given positions in government. Sharaf Sabri's book on the financial linkages of members of the royal family indicates that the financial holdings of his sons, relative to those of other members of the royal family, are marginal (Sabri 2001: 95–97). He is also respected for his piety. In contrast, some of the Sudairi princes have been deemed too eager to promote their own interests, using their political influence to enhance the value of their financial investments.

Some writers see current changes in the political leadership as of little significance, contending that a re-shuffling of positions among an aging generation ('Abd al-'Aziz's sons) will bring no real reform. The major issue, they claim, is how the kingship will pass to a new generation within the royal family and whether it might even skip a generation to bring fresh thinking to the leadership of the state. No doubt the generational shift will be significant, but the age and characteristics of the monarch may not be the most critical factors for the future. As will be suggested in the conclusion to this book, the more crucial concern may be how the exercise of political power can be made accountable. Rather than focusing on the changing balances of power within the royal family, therefore, the focus should be on processes which move effective governmental power into new channels.

Conclusion

The period covered in this chapter has encompassed two crises for the Saudi state, one at the beginning of the period and one at the end. Both involved challenges to the state coming out of the domestic and international environments, rather than stemming from conflict or division within the state apparatus. To some extent, the challenges were in each case created by policies pursued by the government. In responding to the 1979–80 crisis, the government undertook a limited re-ordering of its policies and practices, putting more authority in the hands of the religious leaders and strengthening the alliance with the United States. Events in the 1980s appeared to show the soundness of this strategy. The deepening of the ideological/religious claim to legitimacy cohered well with an international policy which confronted secular radicalism abroad, in alliance with the United States. The First Gulf War and the end of the Cold War, however, created the ground for increasing disharmony between aspects of domestic and international policy. This finally came to a head following 9/11 and the Second Gulf War. Political reforms were introduced, albeit not to a degree which substantially altered the relationship between the population and the state, or made state institutions accountable to the population. The implications of these developments for the future of the Saudi state will be considered in the overall Conclusion.

5 The challenge of economic reform

Introduction

The focus of this chapter is on the reform of the Saudi economy: the progress which has been made and the challenges which lie ahead. The analysis will have a prescriptive element to it. The objective is to indicate the kinds of reform which will be needed if the economy is to satisfy the needs of the population.

Before examining the record, some consideration needs to be given to the concept of reform and how this applies to the Saudi economy. Most observers have approached this from the perspective of the 'Washington Consensus' – a concept which embraces the Washington-based international financial institutions, in relation to the package of reforms they normally promote (IMF 1999). The focus of the Washington Consensus is on fiscal discipline, tax reform, trade liberalisation, privatisation, deregulation, competitive exchange rates, measures which encourage investment (especially foreign investment) and the redirection of public expenditure to fields which offer high economic returns. The approach usually carries an overall prescription for the state to retreat from direct participation in economic production. Indeed there is a tendency to regard the state as part of the problem, rather than part of the solution, of the economic dilemmas facing developing economies.

A significant part of this chapter will be concerned with progress (or lack of progress) made on reforms within the scope of the Washington Consensus. However, the argument pursued is that such reforms offer only a partial solution to the problems facing the Saudi economy and that the major changes required to ensure effective economic growth are not compatible with a retreat of the state. On the contrary, the state needs to be more intensively engaged in shaping the economic life of the Kingdom.

The analysis must start by identifying the areas where the Saudi economy is currently failing to provide satisfactory outcomes for the country's population. This will form a basis for assessing the character of the reforms which are needed and therefore the role which the state will need to play in bringing about these reforms. It is contended that there are four major areas where the Saudi economy and its management are currently failing to provide satisfactory economic outcomes for the population. The problem areas are covered in the section which follows.

The listing of problems should not obscure some of the strengths which Saudi Arabia has in facing the challenges of economic development. The Kingdom has some 260 billion barrels of oil in proven reserves, 230 trillion cu. ft. of recoverable gas, significant mineral reserves (aluminium, gold etc.), at least $650 billion in foreign assets held by private individuals and companies (some estimates have put the figure as high as $1 trillion [*Arab News*: 11.11.04]), a high savings rate and a reasonably developed infrastructure (Zahid 2004). Saudi Arabia has the largest GDP in the Middle East, with the exception of Turkey and Iran.

Areas of existing economic inadequacy

Provision of employment

The level of unemployment of Saudi citizens, in an economy where there is a very large migrant labour population, constitutes a major economic failing. Until the early 1990s, oil revenues had broadly generated enough resources for the government to disguise unemployment among Saudi nationals through a tacit social contract under which they were guaranteed jobs in the civil service. Many of the jobs created through this process were effectively sinecures. As a result, the state sector has accounted for a sizeable proportion of employment among Saudi nationals (KSA-CDS 2005).

In 2002, the government for the first time released employment and labour force data. Based on figures gathered at the end of 1999, overall unemployment (male and female) was estimated at 8.1 per cent, with Saudi male unemployment at 6.8 per cent and female unemployment at 15.8 per cent (SAMBA 2002: 1). In July 2004, based on figures gathered in 2002, the total number of unemployed was given as 300,000, representing 9.6 per cent of the available labour force. Saudi male unemployment stood at 7.6 per cent, and female unemployment at 21.7 per cent (KSA-CDS 2005).

The figures just given, however, do not provide an accurate picture of employment and unemployment among the Saudi population. The 'available labour force', to which the figures relate, covers a relatively small part of the Saudi population. According to the figures of the Saudi Central

Department of Statistics, only 19 per cent of the Saudi population (35.3 per cent of the working age population) forms part of the labour force. This ranks among the lowest labour force participation rates of any country in the world, against an average 33 per cent in the rest of the Middle East and 45 per cent in Europe. The phenomenon is in part accounted for by the low level of female employment. The 2002 figures show that only 6.6 per cent of Saudi females above the age of 15 were employed (KSA-CDS 2005). The same figures, however, also indicate that significant numbers of men did not form part of the available labour force due to being unable to work, whether on grounds of disablement or for other unspecified reasons. Some 308,389 men were in this category, constituting some 6.7 per cent of all Saudi men over 15 (KSA-CDS 2005).

The low level of labour force participation suggests that, among those who are not counted as 'available for work' (and who therefore appear in the employment/unemployment tables), there may well be many who would wish to work – or could usefully be employed – if the conditions were right and the work was available. A variety of factors explain why Saudis may choose not to put themselves forward for participation in the labour force. The cultural factors discouraging women from entering the labour market are well-known. Even when women do gain access to employment, their salaries are on average approximately half those of men with the same level of education. The extent to which men's salaries exceeds those of women with the same educational qualifications in practice varies substantially according to the educational level. For those with university first degrees, the difference is 1:3. For those with postgraduate degrees, there is little difference between male/female remuneration (KSA-CDS 2005).

A substantial proportion of the jobs currently available in the Kingdom, moreover, are ones which Saudi citizens are either reluctant or unqualified to perform. With a non-Saudi labour force estimated at between 5 and 6 million (WMO 2003: 305), there would appear to be sufficient jobs for Saudis to take up. However, about one-half of the non-Saudis in the labour force work in domestic jobs (maids, drivers etc.) which are shunned by Saudis. Many of the remaining jobs require technical or professional specialisations for which few Saudis have been trained (in part due to their reluctance). At the end of 2004, for example, there were 54,000 nursing jobs in the country, but only 1,000 of these were filled by Saudis (Migration Policy Institute 2005). The schools and universities are now producing large numbers of Saudis, both men and women, with academic qualifications, but this is not necessarily what is required in the economy – especially the private sector.

Even when Saudis hold the formal qualifications and are prepared to accept available jobs, moreover, they do not necessarily obtain employment. Saudi labour is substantially more expensive than migrant/ expatriate labour. This comes about not through legal regulation but through understandings that Saudi labour employed in the private sector should benefit from similar conditions to that employed in the public sector. The 2002 employment statistics indicate that the average monthly wage/income of Saudis in jobs requiring qualifications up to secondary school level was approximately three times greater than that of non-Saudis with the same qualifications; for those with university qualifications, Saudis were earning about twice that of non-Saudis (SAMBA 2002: 5). Saudi labour also benefits from stronger contractual regulations on dismissal and redundancy and is regarded as being more difficult to manage than migrant/expatriate labour. Government policies which dictate the replacement of expatriate by Saudi labour in the private sector, then, are undermined by practical realities. Saudisation programmes have been pursued with some determination in recent years, with private companies being required to increase the share of Saudis employed in their labour forces by 5 per cent per year and instructions that some fields of economic activity should be free of foreign labour (e.g. travel agencies and gold markets). Yet in practice this strategy conflicts with the economic interests of employers; its failure to achieve results is not surprising.

It is for reasons such as this that some commentators have put significantly higher figures on Saudi unemployment than those provided by the government. Given that estimates of those who might ideally like to work are bound to be vague, however, these figures inevitably vary widely. The US Energy Information Administration estimated unemployment in Saudi Arabia at 15–20 per cent (US-EIA 2004a); the CIA World Fact Book 2003 placed the figure at 25 per cent (US-CIA 2004); and some Saudi sources have suggested that the figure may be as high as 30 per cent (EIU 2004: 22). A figure between 15 per cent and 20 per cent would probably be reasonably realistic.

Long-term trends of population and labour force growth indicate that the problem of unemployment is destined to become increasingly critical. The Saudi population through the decades of the 1980s and 1990s was growing at a rate of 3.9 per cent per annum – one of the highest population growth rates in the world (World Bank 2004: 40). Although the rate of increase is expected to fall to 2.6 per cent over the 2002–15 period, the rise in population numbers will still be substantial. The US Census Bureau estimates that Saudi Arabia's population will double between 2003 and 2050, rising from 24 million to 50 million (US-CB 2004). These figures include non-Saudis resident in the country, but both the absolute numbers and the proportion of non-Saudis in the population are expected to fall. As may be expected, the major expansion in the Saudi population is among the young, with some 70 per cent of the population now being below 30. The available Saudi labour force, therefore, is growing at an even higher rate than the population. The Seventh Development Plan estimated that the available labour force will grow at about 4.7 per cent per annum in the period through to 2020 (255,000 new workers annually). Over the 2000–02 period employment in the public and private sectors combined was expanding by less than 90,000 jobs annually, absorbing about one-half of the job-seekers coming on to the labour market at that time (SAMBA 2002: 3). The estimates in the Seventh Development Plan, moreover, may well be an underestimate, given that women are likely to become more demanding in seeking employment. The economy, therefore, will need to be functioning at a significantly higher level if it is to satisfy the employment needs of the population.

The high unemployment level is one of the key stress points in Saudi Arabia's political as well as economic development. Although a relatively young and growing population is potentially a great economic asset, this is only the case if these new recruits to the labour market can find employment. Otherwise, political discontent will ensue. At the level of macro-economics, high unemployment will subdue private consumption, limiting overall real GDP growth. High unemployment and falling per capita income will further limit savings in the economy, which is vital for investment levels. The negative impact of foreign labour remittances on the Saudi balance of payments currently comes to some $16 billion annually (US-E 2004: 15). The latter feature, furthermore, reduces private consumption within the country and lessens the multiplier effects following from development spending.

Equitability in the distribution of rewards from the economic process

The importance of considerations of equity lies in perceptions: whether the population sees the distribution as fair. There is at present a wide-spread perception among the Saudi population, expressed through both religious and secular discourse, that the distribution is inequitable. The existence of real poverty in a country with such substantial oil revenues appears anomalous. It is significant that the first three points in the National Reform petition presented by reformers to Crown Prince 'Abdallah in 2003 covered issues of corruption and economic inequity.

The petition called on the government to

1 implement the concept of fairness in economical plans and distribute the wealth between different regions,
2 put in place restrictions to control public spending, and determine spending priorities, while fighting corruption and preventing the spreading of bribery and expropriation of public land and
3 strengthen and empower oversight and accountability institutions, such as the Public Supervision Directorate, and connect it with the *Majlis al-Shurah* (*Arab Gateway* 2004).

The issue is in part one of simple inequality: the gap between those who benefit most and those who gain least is unacceptably wide. There is no statistical evidence to document such inequalities, but the existence of a wide gap is clear from casual observation. The demands made in the reform petition, however, make it clear that the problem goes beyond this. There is the perception that inequalities at all levels stem from unequal and unfair access to the centres of governmental decision-making. Those who are close to the centres of power (especially the royal family) are seen as making the major economic gains, using their positions to prevent others from benefiting. Such patterns of behaviour are hardly surprising, given that political decision-making tends to be governed by association rather than accountability. The phenomenon of the royal family taking an increasingly dominant role in the private sector has been referred to by Daryl Champion as a distinct form of crony capitalism, which he calls *'asabiyah* capitalism (Champion 2003: 10–12). The extent of the royal family's private economic activities has been documented by Sharaf Sabri (Sabri 2001).

Claims of unequal access tend to be linked to allegations of corruption, where crucial economic decisions stem from pay-offs to those who hold administrative or executive office. The figures on corruption in Saudi Arabia, as published in Transparency International's *Corruption Perceptions Index 2004* (TI 2004), are in fact reasonably reassuring. Although the Kingdom ranks as more corrupt than other states within the Gulf Cooperation Council (GCC), its overall global ranking puts it in the middle of the table, close to Poland and China and well ahead of many other Arab countries (e.g. Egypt, Algeria and Morocco). Nonetheless, the role played by agency commissions in the Saudi system is often difficult to separate from bribery, and although agency commissions are limited by law to 5 per cent of the value of any contract, there are known to be cases which have exceeded that limit and which have not led to prosecution. The pressures to which Saudi government officials are subject should also be recognised. Transparency International reports that the areas of activity in which bribery is most common internationally are public works, defence, and oil and gas. These are the main areas where Saudi governmental contracts have been focused. On Transparency International's (TI) Bribery Payers' Index, moreover, a number of Saudi Arabia's main trading partners rank high in terms of hosting companies which are perceived as 'likely to pay or offer bribes' (TI 2002).

Development of the social and physical infrastructure

Given the substantial funding which the Saudi government has put into the development of the country's social and physical infrastructure over the past 3 decades, it may seem surprising that deficiencies still exist in this field. Yet this is the reality. Some of the investment in infrastructure in the past has been misdirected, leaving significant areas where investment has been insufficient. New investment is also needed to meet the requirements of a growing population and economy.

On the side of physical infrastructure, a recent report has suggested that, over the next 20 years, a total of $267 billion of investment will be needed to cover the development of the power, telecommunications, petrochemical, oil and gas, and water and sewage sectors (NCB 2004). The current level of public expenditure on infrastructure could only finance a small part of this. Allocations for infrastructural development in the 2004 budget only come to SR 15.1 billion ($4.0 billion), constituting 6.5 per cent of total expenditure (SR 230 billion or $61.3 billion).

Funding of the country's social infrastructure (health, education and welfare services) also needs to increase. Government expenditure on education appears to have been generous with an allocation of SR 63.7 billion ($17 billion) in the 2004 budget. This constitutes about 25 per cent of the total budget. Nonetheless, private sector sources continue to insist that Saudi graduates do not meet the needs of the sector. Moreover, the greatest need may be for training (both prior to, and during, employment) rather than general education. Providing governmental support (in training, facilities and regulation) to enable more women to enter the employment market is also critical if dependence on foreign labour is to be reduced. In the health sector, despite substantial expenditure the levels of child and adult mortality are significantly higher than in most states of the GCC – and are approximately on a par with those in less well-endowed Arab states such as Jordan and Syria (WHO 2005). As for the provision of welfare, much of this is currently through general subsidies which do not target those elements in society most in need of assistance.

To meet these needs, the government will need both to attract substantially more private investment than is currently entering the country and to increase significantly public sector expenditure in critical developmental fields. The former requires policies which attract foreign investment, while at the same time providing an incentive for Saudi citizens to invest within their own country rather than holding their assets overseas. The increase in public investment needs to come from the re-direction of existing public funding and the raising of new revenue through taxation (which currently does not exist). In recent years, between 45 per cent and 50 per cent (48.2 per cent in 2004) of the overall budget has been allocated to 'direct government operations' – a rather opaque element in the Saudi budget which is largely made up of defence expenditure. The government should not count on rising oil revenues providing the funds needed for the new investment, both because this source is uncertain and because a substantial part of new oil earnings need to be put into a 'fund for future generations' for the country's non-oil future (see later).

Economic structures which safeguard the long-term viability of the economy

There are two respects in which current policies are not achieving this objective. Both of these relate to the need to make provision for the period when oil production begins to decline. First, the country requires substantial holdings of foreign assets to provide a long-term investment income, constituting a buffer for when income from oil production declines. The reserves held at the end of 2004 were lower than they were in the second half of the 1970s and through the 1980s. They reached a peak of $120 billion in the earlier period, declining substantially during and after the First Gulf War, and standing in 2004 at approximately $68 billion (US-E 2004: 2). Although the latter figure is substantially greater than the *c.*$30 billion to which reserves sank in the mid-1990s, there has been no sustained progress towards developing a 'fund for future generations' capable of supporting development in the post-oil era. It has, in fact, been private Saudi sources which have been ensuring their long-term economic position by investing abroad. At the end of 2004, it was estimated that private Saudi sources held at least $650 billion in investments outside of the country. While the latter sums are useful to the individuals concerned, the investment of so much private money outside of the country means that domestic investment has been weakened.

Second, despite governmental attempts to diversify the economy, progress made has been inadequate. The oil sector remains dominant, just as it was in the mid-1970s. Oil and oil derivatives account for 90–95 per cent of export earnings, 75 per cent of budget revenues and 35–40 per cent of GDP (US-E 2004: 3). One effect of this has been a decline in per capita income: the expansion of the GDP has not kept pace with population growth. Per capita income reached a peak of $28,600 in 1981, but in 2004 stood at about $9,000 (US-E 2004: 3). The centrality of hydrocarbon-based exports, besides putting in doubt the economy's long-term viability, implies a lack of employment opportunities. The hydrocarbon sector requires relatively few workers – only 2 per cent of the labour force. A significant part of oil revenues, in fact, is being used to employ Saudis in the public sector, often at rates which are not justified by the work performed. Diversification of the economy would also help to limit the economic downturn in times of weak global oil prices.

The record of reform before 2000

Since the oil boom in the 1970s, the government has dominated the Saudi Arabian economy; the main engines behind economic growth in Saudi Arabia are oil revenues and the government spending of those revenues. However, with the fall in the oil price in the 1980s, the Saudi government began to promote economic liberalisation, aiming in particular to reduce the role of the state in the economy. The actual pace of reform, however, was very slow: the measures were mostly insubstantial, and their implementation tended to be piecemeal.

Three different areas in which economic liberalisation was initiated, or at least where the intention to reduce the role of the state was mooted, can be identified: the reduction of subsidies, moves towards the privatisation of state corporations, and an application for membership of the World Trade Organisation. First, then, was the attempt to cut back the level of subsidies. Some reduction in subsidies did occur, although only at the end of the period covered here (Malik 1999: 132). The International Monetary Fund (IMF) noted that between 1981/82 and 1993 subsidies and transfers accounted for 2.9 per cent of GDP, whereas the average between 1994–97 amounted to 1.2 per cent of GDP (*MEED*: 15.1.1999). The 1995 budget introduced new measures to raise revenues and cut subsidies, with the raising of charges for visas, permits, petroleum products, water, electricity, air tickets and telephones (*MEED*: 15.1.1999). This was the first sizeable increase in charges for services for Saudi citizens and seemed to constitute the first stage in eliminating state subsidies as advised by the World Bank and the IMF. However, the budgets which followed this in the late 1990s did not introduce any new measures to reduce costs or increase revenues, to the disappointment of the IMF (IMF 2001). In 1998 modest measures were introduced increasing the prices of first and business class airfares on domestic routes, bringing in departure taxes on international travel, and restructuring the electricity tariffs (*MEED*: 15.1.1999).

Second, the government moved slowly towards the privatisation of state corporations. The main development took the form of creating an appropriate framework for privatisation rather than actually privatising state corporations. This was initiated on 6 August 1997, when the Council of Ministers issued a 'decision' identifying eight objectives for privatisation aimed at improving the efficiency of the national economy and enhancing its competitive ability. The objectives were: encouraging private sector investment, enlarging the productive assets of Saudi citizens, encouraging domestic and foreign capital to invest locally, increasing employment opportunities, providing services to citizens and investors, rationalising public expenditure and reducing the burden of the government budget, and increasing government revenues (KSA-CM 1997). These, and the description given of the policies needed to achieve them, were clearly well-conceived. However, the elaboration of the detailed legal framework which was needed to make these statements of principle operational was slow in coming. The IMF noted at the end of 1999 that the legal framework for privatisation, and the elaboration of the steps needed to implement the process, were still being developed (IMF 1999: 26).

Some practical measures towards loosening state control of the economy were nonetheless taken. The Public Investment Fund (PIF), the government investment arm, was entrusted with the task of preparing case studies for privatisation, undertaking the evaluation of assets and the formulation of restructuring programmes (Malik 1999: 130). Among the major corporations which were investigated and assessed were Saudi Arabian Airlines (SAUDIA) and the Saudi Arabian Mining Company (MAADEN).

As a first stage towards privatisation, some previously publicly managed operations were converted into private companies – albeit with the shares still owned 100 per cent by the government. In December 1997 the Council of Ministers determined that all of the activities of the Ministry of Posts and Telecommunications, except for those relating to the Ministry's regulatory role and its operation of the partly subsidised postal services, should be hived off to form a separate company which would in due course be sold to private investors (*FT*: 8.5.98). In the same year, the management of the Saudi Port Authority was turned over to a private company (Malik 1999: 131). In 1998 the Council of Ministers passed a decree establishing the Saudi Telecommunications Company (STC), which would take over the running of the Saudi telephone and telegraph system (SAMA 1998: 65). The government also announced plans to unify the ten regional electricity companies into the Saudi Electricity Company (SEC) as a first step towards privatising the sector (*Arab News*: 1.12.98). Local authorities were also turning their attention towards privatisation, contracting out the operation of some of their facilities – largely so as to contain costs (*MEED*: 27.11.98). Jeddah municipality, for example, contracted out the management of its wholesale fruit and vegetable market.

Third, the government indicated that Saudi Arabia would be interested in membership of the World Trade Organisation. The Saudi application for membership first reached the General Agreement on Tariffs and Trade (GATT) (prior to the WTO's formation) in 1993, and a Working Party on Saudi membership was formed in the same year. The initial round of discussions in the Working Party (involving both sides), however, did not take place until May 1996. The latter discussions covered trade in goods. A second round was held in November 1996, focusing on trade in services and intellectual property rights (Malik 1999: 133). Over the three years which followed, a further five meetings of the Working Party were held. These meetings seem to have been directed at defining the conditions on which Saudi membership would be possible. The major changes in Saudi economic policies and practices needed to satisfy the conditions, however, were not being made.

Economic reform since 2000: the dynamics and the administrative structures

The sections which follow will focus on the reforms which the Saudi government has sought to carry out since 2000, within the framework of Washington Consensus prescriptions. Over these years, the move towards economic reform has been particularly strong. The central issue is whether these measures will be effective in resolving the problems outlined earlier in the section on *Areas of existing economic inadequacy*, creating a solid basis for development.

The paradox of recent reform measures in Saudi Arabia is that they have been put forward at a time when the immediate financial pressures are less than before. The higher oil price since 2000, and especially since the beginning of 2003, has meant that the immediate financial imperative driving economic reform – the need to reduce costs so as to balance the budget – has been weakened. With oil prices reaching $60 dollars per barrel of Brent crude in June 2005, against a low point of $10 dollars per barrel in 1996, the Saudi government has had the resources to stave off structural reform. Growth in real GDP rose to 7.2 per cent in 2003 and is expected to have achieved a still higher level in 2004 (IMF 2005). Yet it has been precisely over this period that the pace of reform has quickened. These reforms may well change the relationship between the Saudi state, the private sector and the wider society. Whether they are sufficient to resolve the underlying problems, however, is not so clear.

A number of reasons may be put forward as to why reform has advanced just when the immediate financial pressures have eased. First, domestic political unrest has become more open and explicit than before, such that the government has felt impelled to re-shape its policies. Even though the government may be earning more from oil revenues, the problems facing the population have not necessarily eased. Unemployment levels have continued to rise, in part through the high population growth, and living standards have fallen. These are key factors behind the growing political discontent in the country.

Second, Saudi Arabia has been subject to much greater international pressure since 9/11 2001, where the United States has identified Saudi Arabia's domestic conditions as feeding the forces of international terrorism. The domestic and international pressures relate as much to political as to economic issues, yet there is a rationale for prioritising economic reform. It is less controversial and problematic for the Saudi government and indeed to some extent provides a cover for the failure to pursue radical political reform.

Of critical importance in the new dynamic towards economic reform has been Saudi Arabia's application for membership of the WTO. As noted earlier, the Saudi Arabian government entered into negotiations in 1996. It was, however, not until 2002 that the critical issues impeding membership began to be seriously addressed. The issue of WTO member-ship has in practice become one of the main drivers of economic reform in the Kingdom. The issue has been used by those intent on reform to provide a rationale for forcing the pace, and many of the legal changes which are discussed in the section on *Reforming the legal framework to encourage foreign investment* later stem directly from the need to satisfy WTO conditions of membership. Admission to the WTO would certainly ensure greater transparency in the trade regime and make the economic environment more accommodating to non-resident business. Saudi Arabia has constituted one of the largest economies outside of the WTO.

The need to undertake economic reform has led to the creation of new administrative structures to carry the process forward. The development of these new institutions began in August 1999 with the creation of the Supreme Economic Council (KSA-SEC), which was given responsibility for evaluating economic, industrial, agricultural and labour policies so as to assess their effectiveness. The focus of the KSA-SEC has been on opening up Saudi markets and attracting investment.

The year 2000 saw the creation of a series of organisations covering economic policy in areas which were critical to the process of economic reform. In January of that year the Supreme Council for Petroleum and Minerals (SCPM) was established, with responsibility for policymaking on the exploitation of the Kingdom's hydrocarbon resources. The Council was to give particular attention to the attraction of international investment into this field, starting with the natural gas sector. In April 2000 the establishment of the Supreme Council of Tourism (SCT) was announced, with responsibility for fostering tourism and encouraging investment in this sector. The notion that the Kingdom should actively encourage tourism in different parts of the country and encourage international investment in new projects, rather than simply respond to the annual flood of pilgrims to the holy places, marked a significant new departure for the Kingdom. The Secretary General of the new Council announced a 20-year plan for the development of tourism in September 2003, which envisaged that by 2020 there could be as many as 2.3 million Saudis employed in tourism (AMEINFO 2003). April 2000 also saw the establishment of the Saudi Arabian General Investment Authority (SAGIA), which was given the task of promoting foreign investment and serving the interests of the business community as a 'one-stop shop' for licences, permits and other administrative procedures relevant to business. SAGIA was to work closely with the KSA-SEC and the SCT, playing a mediating role between investors and the government (SA-IR 2005b).

Reforming the legal framework to encourage foreign investment

Central to the government's plans for economic reform – and to the perceptions of international financial institutions about the requirements for sustainable development in Saudi Arabia – have been measures to promote foreign investment. The latter is seen as being necessary if the needs of Saudi Arabia's rapidly rising population and workforce are to be met. The law on foreign direct investment provides the main framework for governmental attempts to boost foreign investment, but legal changes affecting taxation, capital markets, intellectual property rights and insurance are also important.

The law on foreign direct investment

Prior to April 2000, foreign investment was only permitted in the Kingdom if it fulfilled three conditions: undertakings had to be 'development projects'; investments had to generate technology transfer and there had to be a Saudi partner with at least 25 per cent equity. Applications for licences tended to take a long time, except for those where the government was a partner. Foreign companies and individuals, apart from other GCC citizens, could not own land or engage in internal trading and distribution activities.

The new law was endorsed by the Council of Ministers in April 2000 and became effective in June of that year (SAGIA 2004e). A framework for future legislative and regulatory activities was established by the law, intended to enhance the country's investment climate and attract capital. Critical elements of the new law, and of the executive rules of the law which were enacted at the same time, were

- Companies could now be 100 per cent foreign owned (except in certain specified sectors), and foreign and Saudi companies were to be treated on an equal basis. Previously, the Foreign Capital Investment Committee had usually demanded 51 per cent Saudi ownership. Under the new law, foreign companies could apply for low-cost loans from the Saudi Industrial Development Fund (SIDF), on the same terms as Saudi companies. These could cover up to 50 per cent of a venture.
- Foreign companies were now allowed to own land for licensed activities and for housing employees. Previously, the Saudi partner had been required to hold the land.

Perhaps most significant of all, however, was the role given to SAGIA as a facilitator for foreign investment, speeding up investment decisions and reducing bureaucracy. SAGIA was mandated under the new law to make a decision on all investment applications within 30 days, and in the event of failing to meet that deadline was required to issue the licence forthwith. The basis on which decisions on issuing licences were taken, moreover, were made very explicit, with investment being permitted in all areas except for those specified on a 'negative list'. The minimum investments for licences to be issued were also specified: SR 25 million for agricultural projects, SR 5 million for industrial projects and SR 2 million for service projects.

Guarantees against the full or partial confiscation of investments were made more explicit than they had been before, as also were the arrangements for foreign investors to repatriate funds and transfer money so as to fulfil contractual obligations. For the first time, foreign companies were given authority to act as sponsors for non-Saudi staff.

As a corollary to the Foreign Direct Investment Law, the Council of Ministers enacted a Real Estate Law later in the same year (SAGIA 2004g). The law was sub-titled 'The System of Real Estate Ownership and

Investment of Non-Saudis', and gave the entitlement to non-Saudis to own real estate for their private residence.

Tax reform

Attracting more foreign investment also required changes to the taxation levied on such investment. Prior to 2000 the main rate of corporate tax for foreign investors stood at 45 per cent. In the light of the low rates of corporate tax in the smaller states of the Gulf, this acted as a strong disincentive for foreign investors. The comparison with tax regulations covering Saudi companies, moreover, emphasised the disadvantage to foreign investors. For Saudi companies there was no corporate tax but simply an obligation to pay the 2.5 per cent *zakat* contribution, which in practice was not rigorously or consistently enforced.

In 2000 the overall rate for foreign investors was reduced to 30 per cent, and with the introduction of a new Corporate Tax Law in July 2004 the rate fell further to 20 per cent (SAGIA 2004d). For investments in the hydrocarbons sectors, however, a higher rate was payable: 30 per cent in natural gas investment activities, and 85 per cent in oil and hydrocarbons production. In practice foreign investors could still only enter the latter field in conjunction with ARAMCO.

Although the taxation changes improved the environment for investors, the level of taxation on foreign businesses was still substantially more than in other Gulf countries. In the United Arab Emirates (UAE) and Bahrain, for example, no corporate tax is levied. The decision to reduce corporate tax, therefore, was unlikely to lead investors to shift investment from the smaller Gulf states to Saudi Arabia. There was some danger that it would cut the government's non-oil income without necessarily leading to a major boost to foreign investment. Nonetheless, the new law did clarify the regulations and procedures with regard to tax, and as such could be expected to increase confidence among potential investors.

Regulating the capital markets

Foreign investment can also be conceived in terms of investments, currently held outside of the country by Saudi citizens, returning to the country. The reform of the capital markets was intended to encourage such a capital movement and to encourage Saudis with money to invest to look to domestic rather than foreign investment. It has been estimated that Saudi citizens in 2004 held some $650 billion in holdings outside of the country (with some estimates putting the figure as high as $1 trillion).

Prior to the adoption by the Council of Ministers of the Capital Markets Law in June 2003 (SAGIA 2004b), Saudi Arabia did not have a stock exchange. It had been possible to trade shares through the national securities depository centre, but there was no regulatory framework facilitating such trading or protecting the interests of investors. The Law formally established the Saudi Arabian Stock Exchange (SASE), whose activities were to be regulated by a Saudi Arabian Securities and Exchange Commission. The latter, now named the Capital Markets Authority, was duly set up in June 2004. It was made responsible for organising the capital market, protecting investors from unfair practices, achieving efficiency and transparency in securities transactions, and developing and monitoring all aspects of the trade in securities (SACMA 2005). Trading in the SASE was limited to GCC nationals, but non-GCC nationals could participate through investing in mutual funds offered by Saudi Arabian banks.

With a well-regulated market, it was believed that capitalisation would increase. It would be easier to float companies, and the latter would in turn have more incentive to gain a listing on the stock market. They would also benefit through being able to issue corporate bonds. International banks would be able to win licences for investment banking in the country. However, these benefits may not come quickly. Even with the full implementation of the law, Saudi Arabia's capital markets will remain weak. A range of institutions are needed if a capital market is to constitute an effective financial instrument, channelling funds from those who wish to invest and putting it in the hands of those who are developing economic projects. The potential impact of the SASE is limited by the absence of investment banks, independent brokerage firms, asset management firms etc. and by the inadequacy of venture capital (Zahid 2004). At the end of 2004, there were still only 71 companies listed on the Saudi stock exchange, and in some sectors only one company was represented.

Nonetheless there was a marked increase in share dealings in 2002–03, even before the detailed procedures of the new law had become effective. The value of share dealings grew by some three-fold over the period between end-December 2002 and end-December 2004 (AMEINFO 2004).

Intellectual property rights

Foreign investors need to know that they are operating in a market where copyrights on their products are respected. In June 2003, the Council of Ministers approved a new Copyright Law (SAGIA 2004c), replacing the previous 1990 law. The 2003 law, which came into effect six months after publication in the official gazette, protected intellectual property rights in the fields of literature, arts and sciences, computer programmes, audio recordings and visual displays. The legal change was consistent with the requirements of the WTO's Agreement on Trade Related Aspects of Intellectual Property Rights (TRIPS).

There remain doubts, however, as to whether the Saudi government will enforce the law effectively enough to meet external requirements. In 1995 Saudi Arabia was placed on the US's 301 Priority Watch List, and at the time of writing the country remains on the list despite the new law. The List comprises the countries which in the view of the US Trade Representative 'do not provide an adequate level of Intellectual Property Rights protection or enforcement' and are pursuing 'the most onerous or egregious policies that have an adverse impact on US right holders' (US-TRO 2004).

A new Patent Law was passed by the Council of Ministers in July 2004 (KSA-CM 2004), covering integrated circuits, plant varieties and industrial designs. Formulated with a view to meeting the requirements of TRIPS, the law may improve Saudi Arabia's position with regard to the 301 Priority Watch List.

Regulating the insurance sector

In July 2003 the Council of Ministers approved a new Insurance Law to regulate the insurance sector in the Kingdom (*MEES*: 6.12.2004). The law opened the sector to foreign investors and created a legal framework for the many insurance companies operating in the Kingdom.

The impact of legislation on actual investment

As has already been indicated, the passage of the new legislation will not necessarily have the effect of increasing the level of investment in Saudi Arabia. Much depends on the way in which government bodies handle the new legal frameworks and on how the new investment structures compare with those in surrounding countries.

Up to March 2004 SAGIA had issued some 2,220 licences, for projects whose total value came to $15 billion (*MEES*: 6.12.2004). About three-quarters of these were wholly foreign-owned. If this were followed by actual investment on a similar scale, Saudi Arabia would be benefiting from a major boost in foreign investment. A company obtaining a licence, however, does not necessarily proceed into invest-ment. Through to the end of 2003 there was little hard evidence that Saudi Arabia was attracting a substantial scale of investment. UNCTAD's *World Investment Report 2004* ranked Saudi Arabia as

31st in the world rankings for investment potential, but 138th for actual investment performance (UNCTAD 2004a: A.1.5 and A.1.7). The performance indicator measures the extent of foreign direct investment relative to the size of the economy. One hundred and forty countries were compared, with only Indonesia and Suriname ranking below Saudi Arabia. A wide gap exists, therefore, between potential and performance. Over the period between 2001 and 2003, in fact, the flow of inward investment into Saudi Arabia registered a negative figure of $387 million. More funds were leaving Saudi Arabia through the repatriation of profits on investment, then, than were entering the country in new investment. Although a positive figure of $208 million was registered for the year 2003 by itself, suggesting that the trend may be changing, it is too early to draw such a conclusion (UNCTAD 2004a).

The extent to which the Saudi investment law can be seen as attractive to investors is, of course, greatly dependent on the scope of the 'negative list' referred to earlier – that is, the sectors where foreign investment is barred. In February 2001, in the immediate aftermath of the law's promulgation, the Supreme Economic Council produced a negative list of 22 sectors in which 100 per cent foreign ownership was not allowed (SAGIA 2005b). These included oil exploration and production, fisheries, electricity distribution, insurance, telecommunications, printing and publishing services, education, trade, and land and air transportation. The list was extensive and initially gave the impression that the scope for foreign investors was narrow – at least for those wanting 100 per cent ownership of any scheme. The council seems to have been under pressure, from parts of the private sector supported by some elements within the government, to restrict the scope of foreign investment. SAGIA itself, however, favoured the shortening of the negative list. In February 2003 the Supreme Economic Council duly removed six sectors from the list, either fully or partially (SAGIA 2005b). The bans on foreign investment in education, transmission and distribution of electrical power within the public network, and pipeline transmission services were totally removed. The fields of printing and publishing services, telecommunications and insurance services were partially opened up. In February 2004, more areas (including mobile phone services) were removed from the partially-restricted list, and insurance was removed totally, which still left 3 industrial and 15 service sectors on the list (SAGIA 2005b). Some of the restricted fields which remain relate to defence and to the provision of services in the holy cities, where the exclusion of foreign companies is to be expected. The restrictions on foreign investment in oil exploration and production, trade, and land and air transportation are, however, significant – cutting important parts of the economy off from foreign investment. Nonetheless, the areas which are now open to foreign investors are extensive.

An instructive case showing the problems which foreign investment still encounters, despite the new law, is the Saudi Integrated Gas Initiative (SGI). The gas sector did not fall within the ambit of the negative list, and indeed the development of this sector was planned around the attraction of foreign investment on a massive scale. The initiative was critical to the country's ability to meet its future energy requirements. The SGI included projects in a range of industrial undertakings which were dependent on gas either as a power supply or a feedstock: electricity generation plants, water desalination facilities and petrochemical plants.

Both the international oil companies and the Saudi government appeared eager for a major partnership to exploit the country's gas resources within the framework of the SGI (US-EIA 2004b). The conception, announced in December 2000, was that ten international oil companies would form a consortium to carry through the huge projects which were envisaged under an arrangement coordinated with ARAMCO. It was expected that the international oil companies would inject some $30–$40 billion of investment into the Saudi economy over a 20-year period. This would constitute the first major reopening of Saudi Arabia's upstream hydrocarbons sector to foreign investment since the sector was nationalised in the 1970s, and the centrepiece of the country's whole foreign investment strategy. With new discoveries having raised Saudi Arabia's gas reserves to the fourth largest in the world (after those of Russia, Iran and Qatar) there was much at stake in this initiative. It was expected, moreover, that the gas initiative would prompt wider reforms in the economic system, given that it would force the government to review the tariff rates for power and water, removing subsidies in these sectors.

Negotiations with the international oil companies proceeded through 2001, 2002 and the first half of 2003, but in June 2003 the Saudi Oil Minister announced the termination of negotiations (US-EIA 2004b). The SGI, as originally conceived, was abandoned. It appears that there had been two major stumbling blocks causing the breakdown of negotiations. First, the companies were dissatisfied with the extent of the gas reserves to be opened up for foreign investment and specifically the exclusion of the Saudi ARAMCO Reserve Area. Second, they found the rate of return which was being offered unattractive.

The abandonment of the SGI constituted a major setback for hopes of attracting substantial foreign investment into the development of this crucial sector. The project has now been re-packaged as a number of smaller and more limited undertakings. The new scheme is less ambitious than the original and relies substantially less on foreign investment. The first major contract (and the largest so far) was signed in November 2003. This was worth some $2 billion and involved a consortium between Shell, Total and ARAMCO. The three companies would undertake gas exploration and develop gas production in a 209,160 square kilometre area of the Empty Quarter. Not all of the $2 billion constituted foreign investment: 30 per cent was ARAMCO's share of the total cost.

Saudi Arabia also signed three more agreements under the relaunched gas development package in early 2004, with Lukol (Russia), Sinopec (China) and a consortium of Eni (Italy) and Repsol YPF (Spain), to explore and develop gas reserves in the northern zone of the Empty Quarter. ARAMCO was a 20 per cent partner in each of the three joint ventures. The three companies' initial investment in the first exploration phase was expected to come to less than $1 billion (SAGIA 2005a).

Some foreign investment may be attracted into the banking sector as a result of the foreign investment law. In October 2003, the Saudi Arabian Monetary Agency (SAMA) announced that it would allow Deutsche Bank AG to begin independent operations in the Kingdom, and in the course of 2004 similar announcements were made with regard to the American bank JP Morgan Chase and the French BNP Paribas. This was the first time such banks had been allowed in since the 1970s, when the banking industry was nationalized (Dun and Bradstreet 2004: 50).

The WTO and trade liberalisation

Negotiations for Saudi Arabia to join the WTO are clearly important to the process of economic reform in the country. The measures discussed in the previous section were all influenced by the requirements of the WTO. Trade liberalisation has been another key requirement. Attention needs to be given, therefore, to the issues raised in the negotiations and the extent to which these have been resolved.

As noted earlier, negotiations with the WTO have been under way since 1996. By the end of 1999 it was possible to identify where the main problems lay. On the Saudi side, there was an insistence that the United States and the European Union lift customs duties on Saudi petrochemical products as a condition for Saudi Arabia opening its own markets. On the WTO side, there were requirements that the Saudi government place upper limits on tariffs, remove protective barriers to trade, open service sectors (such as banking) to greater foreign participation, liberalise regulations on foreign investment and improve the business climate in such areas as the protection of intellectual property rights.

The legal changes outlined in the section on *Economic reform since 2000: the dynamics and the administrative structures* have satisfied many of the WTO's requirements for structural reform. To some extent they were designed specifically to meet these requirements, but they were also responses to a wider need for reform. Either way, they brought about economic changes of the kind envisaged by the WTO.

Saudi Arabia has also pressed ahead with another measure necessary if membership is to be agreed. WTO rules require that a country seeking membership must agree arrangements with its main trading partners on market access and cutting customs duties. These are then to be widened to all other WTO countries. Saudi Arabia's main trading partners in recent years have been the European Union and the United States. A trade agreement with the European Union (the Kingdom's leading trade partner) was reached in August 2003 (EUbusiness 2003a). This required Saudi Arabia to reduce import tariffs on most EU agricultural and industrial products, although 165 items in the agricultural, dairy and poultry sectors were given a greater degree of protection (EUbusiness 2003b). The Saudi agreement with the European Union stipulated that the Saudi Arabian service sector would be further opened up, including the banking, insurance, construction and telecommunications sectors. Saudi Arabia would end the practice of selling gas cheaper on the domestic market than on the international market (Dun and Bradstreet 2004: 50). The one major trading partner with which an agreement had not been reached by the end of 2004 was the United States. Although it was clear since mid-2003 that the US government was intent on Saudi Arabia joining the WTO, seeing this as integral to President Bush's Greater Middle East project (AMEINFO 2005), the US government seems to have been more demanding in its requirements than was the European Union. The United States was said to be seeking greater concessions from Saudi Arabia in areas such as intellectual property rights, fuel price discounts, non-tariff measures and financial service sector reform.

Once the US–Saudi trade agreement is reached, most of the obstacles which have hindered Saudi accession to the WTO will have been resolved – given the changes to Saudi law and economic policies which have already occurred. Among the critical elements which remain, is Saudi Arabia's current practice of giving certain merchants sole right to serve as agents of foreign companies. To change the law on this may not be easy, in the light of the politically powerful lobby of merchants who will resist it. It is unlikely, however, that the WTO would accept the continuation of the practice as it does significantly constrain competition. Changes to the labour law (to increase labour mobility) and the introduction of a new competition law (enabling foreign companies to compete on an equal basis with local firms), may also be required.

Membership of the WTO will enable the Kingdom to expand the market for its petrochemicals exports – a necessary move in the light of the investment which the government has put into this sector. Membership, however, also presents a number of challenges. Saudi companies will have to improve their productive efficiency in the face of greater international competition.

Privatisation

Privatisation moves are closely linked to two dimensions of economic reform which have already been discussed: the attraction of foreign investment and the satisfaction of conditions for WTO membership. The Washington Consensus regards privatisation as holding two major benefits for economies. First, it increases productivity through reducing the role of the 'bureaucratic' public sector. Second, it encourages the growth of private sector-led investment growth, a significant proportion of which will be from foreign sources. The latter, it is contended, will increase efficiency and introduce new technology. Both of the latter arguments have been used in justifying an extensive privatisation policy in Saudi Arabia.

Following years in which only limited privatisation occurred, a new push towards privatisation was initiated in 2001. The new phase was marked by the decision, in February 2001, to give the Supreme Economic Council responsibility for supervising the privatisation programme, determining which activities were to be privatised, developing a strategic plan and timetable for the privatisations, and monitoring the implementation. In August 2001 the Supreme Economic Council created a Privatisation Committee to take charge of the process, with members representing relevant ministries and economic bodies (KSA-SEC 2005).

In June 2002 the Supreme Economic Council accepted the privatisation strategy which had been drawn up by its privatisation committee, and in November of that year the Council of Ministers approved the listing of public utilities and activities which were targeted for privatisation (SAGIA 2004h). The latter listing was extensive: water supply and drainage, water desalination, telecommunications, air transportation, railways, some roads (expressways), airport services, postal services, flour mills and silos, seaport services, industrial city services, government shares in some government corporations (including the Saudi Electric Company, banks, the Saudi Arabian Basic Industries Corporation (SABIC), the Saudi Arabian Mining Company, the Saudi Telecommunications Company and local oil refineries), government shares in paid-up capitals of joint venture companies in Arab and Islamic countries, hotels, sports clubs and a wide range of municipal, educational, social, agricultural and health services. The scope of what was being proposed was impressive.

Close consideration appears to have been given to devising a framework for privatisation which would ensure that the economy benefited fully. In a document entitled 'Basic Issues to be Dealt with in the Privatisation Process', which formed part of the privatisation strategy, stress was laid on creating a proper regulatory framework for the privatised sectors with the establishment of regulatory agencies, devising a systematic method for setting tariffs for services which were previously subsidised through government corporations, creating procedures for some public enterprises to be restructured prior to sale, bringing in strategic partners to cope with the largest privatisation projects, and fostering the correct business environment for privatisation by ensuring the proper functioning of capital markets and promoting human resource development among the Saudi population (SAGIA 2004a). Privatisation, then, was not being regarded primarily as an easy way for the government to meet its budget deficit, but as a process involving structural transformation.

The main measures of privatisation were initiated in the later part of 2002, after the guidelines had been laid down. The most important such measure so far has been the initial public offering for 30 per cent of STC (the country's sole fixed line and GSM service provider), which was held between 17 December 2002 and 6 January 2003. This was the first major government sell-off since the part privatisation of SABIC in the early 1980s. There was strong demand for the sale: according to the finance ministry, the government generated a net $4 billion from the sale of 90 million shares. Around one-third of the shares were sold to two state-run pension funds, the Retirement Pension Directorate (RPD) and the General Organisation for Social Insurance (GOSI), which together hold some 65 per cent of total government debt. The remainder of the shares were sold to Saudi citizens. With the public offering of shares, STC rapidly became the largest publicly traded company in Saudi Arabia (Zahid 2004). As the government retains majority control of the corporation, however, it seems unlikely that the broadening of the share ownership will change the way the corporation is run.

Two other two initial public offerings have been announced, both involving companies playing substantial roles in the economy. In May 2004 the Supreme Economic Council approved the long-awaited sale of the government's stake in the National Company for Co-operative Insurance (NCCI). The initial public offering duly took place in December 2004 and January 2005, with 7 million NCCI shares being put on the market at SR 205 each. This was equivalent to about 70 per cent of the company's total capital. The offering was over-subscribed by 11.5 times (Zawya 2005). The Supreme Economic Council also approved in May

2004 the privatisation of the Saudi Arabian Mining Company (MAADEN). Wide-ranging re-structuring of the latter company has already begun, so as to sell it off in different parts. According to the company, the precious metals business will be the first to be sold off. There is also expected to be an initial public offering for the 50 per cent of shares in the National Commercial Bank held by the government (Dun and Bradstreet 2004: 25).

Privatisation of services in a number of fields has been advancing. The privatisation of the management and operation of local and international airports has been announced; the postal services are being operated now by private operators and plans for the privatisation of urban transport systems and of some medical care facilities are being discussed.

Elsewhere, the privatisation remains more a matter of conjecture and discussion than of practical planning. Long-standing candidates for sale, where detailed discussions are now said to be underway, include the petrochemical and steel producer SABIC, which is still 70 per cent owned by the state, and SAUDIA. In both cases, the discussions still relate to partial rather than total privatisation. The sale of more of the government shares in SABIC would be particularly significant. The company accounts for about 10 per cent of world petrochemical production, and with the new projects which it has in hand that percentage will continue to increase (US-E 2004).

Perhaps of greater importance than privatisation, however, has been the evidence that the opening up of fields of investment to private investors is actually being effected. In other words, government policies do seem to be expanding the private sector even in the absence of significant privatisation. Governmental plans at present, for example, envisage that capital investment of $117 billion in power and $80 billion in water is needed before 2020, with most of the money coming from the private sector (US-E 2004: 16). Power projects worth $15 billion were put up for offer in January 2004, to private investors inside and outside the Kingdom. In August 2004 the Council of Ministers licensed a foreign company (the UAE-based Etisalat) to establish and operate the second mobile phone network in the country. In June 2003 the Supreme Economic Council opened up the Saudi aviation sector to private enterprise, making it possible for Saudi-owned private companies to operate domestic airline services. Private health clinics, hospitals and educational facilities are also developing.

Measuring the reforms against the needs

Despite the progress which has been made in some dimensions of economic reform, there remain substantial inadequacies in what has been achieved. Critical areas in which further reform is needed are covered in this section.

Completing accession procedures for WTO membership

This is required not simply because of the benefits which Saudi Arabia could draw through greater access to international markets for its petrochemicals, but to provide the impetus for legal and policy changes needed for the long-term viability of the economy. Membership will increase transparency and predictability in the commercial environment. WTO membership will also enable Saudi Arabia to pool its strength with that of other developing and industrialising countries within the WTO (led at present by Brazil, India and China) seeking to shift the advantage of international trading practices away from the interests of the developed industrialised countries.

Developing further the legal framework affecting private investment

The investment environment in Saudi Arabia remains less favourable than that in the other GCC states. The latter, for example, have lower tax regimes; Bahrain and the UAE levy no corporate tax on either domestic or foreign investment. This in itself may not be decisive: companies could accept a higher tax regime if it is accompanied by other advantages. Saudi Arabia has a larger domestic market, Saudi hydrocarbon resources are considerably larger, and the overseas holdings of its citizens are much more substantial. However, some of the other aspects of the commercial environment emphasise, rather than diminish, the disparity. Despite the setting up of SAGIA to act as a one-stop shop for foreign investment, establishing a business in the Kingdom remains time-consuming and bureaucratic. A recent report co-sponsored by the World Bank and the International Finance Corporation (IFC) notes that the minimum capital requirement for setting up a business in Saudi Arabia is 15 times the average income, there are 15 procedures which need to be completed, and the average time needed to complete the process is 64 days (World Bank 2005). Even by the standards of the bureaucratically heavy Middle East, these figures are unusually high.

Undertaking a more far-reaching privatisation of state corporations and services

As noted earlier, the pace at which privatisation has been carried forward so far has been slow. To some extent this has been justified by the absence of regulatory frameworks for the sectors concerned. These frameworks certainly need to be in place before privatisation is undertaken, in order to ensure that the process does not involve the stripping of state assets, the establishment of privately owned monopolies and the exploitation of consumers. The creation of competitive markets is essential. However, the elaboration of the regulatory frameworks has itself not been given sufficiently urgent attention.

A number of public corporations (e.g. those in the electricity, mining and insurance sectors) have now spent several years awaiting privatisation. Even if the government continues to hold a majority stake in the companies, it could allow the corporations to be run on a commercial basis. A further problem is that the government has sometimes indicated that jobs should not be cut following privatisation (Malik 1999: 258). This, however, removes one of the major benefits of the privatisation process – to eliminate unproductive jobs and to improve efficiency.

Reshaping government finances: re-directing expenditure and generating new revenue

The Saudi economy requires substantial new public investment. However successful the government may be in attracting private investment, the promotion of economic development and social welfare will still depend on the state playing a strong and effective role in the economy. Contrary to the view put forward by many economists, spending on the country's social infrastructure (health, education and welfare services) needs to increase. Only with improved educational standards and the provision of social support for those currently in unproductive or uncompetitive employment (see later) can an internationally competitive labour market be created.

While rising oil revenues may provide some of the funds needed for new investment, this can not resolve the underlying problem. Dependence on a rising price of oil is risky. The country should, moreover, be putting its short-term gains into a fund to sustain development in the post-oil era.

Money for new investment, therefore, will have to be raised in two ways: redirecting existing expenditure and finding new sources of revenue. On the expenditure side, there are three areas where expenditure can be reduced. First, military expenditure is currently excessive, making up about 40 per cent of central government expenditure. Even by Middle Eastern standards, this is very high. The regional average in the Middle East is 21.5 per cent, as against 14.5 per cent for the developing world, and a global average of 10 per cent (Cordesman 2003b: 391). There is little evidence that the high expenditure has brought security. On the contrary, the major threat to security appears currently to come from the domestic environment and is perhaps better treated by effective socio-economic policies and political understanding than by sophisticated weaponry. Second, there is widespread acknowledgement that resources are being wasted partly through expenditure which has no formal controls and partly through corruption. A strict system of financial accountability for all monies engendered and disbursed would help to limit the wastage. At present not all the revenue from oil sales appears in the budget. National accounts need to document the whole revenue and expenditure process. Third, general subsidies which do not target the specific parts of the population in particular need should be curtailed. Although such expenditure has been reduced in recent years, significant spending continues.

On the revenue side, new sources of revenue need to be developed. Pressure on the Saudi government to 'diversify fiscal revenues' has recently been exerted by the IMF (IMF 2005), and there is good reason for this to be done as membership of the WTO will reduce customs revenues. The IMF has suggested the introduction of value-added tax (VAT) on certain goods, which other GCC states have also discussed, and the introduction of income tax for Saudi citizens and corporate tax for Saudi companies. Currently, as noted earlier, Saudi companies only pay *zakat*, and Saudi citizens do not pay income tax.

Making Saudi labour competitive

Government policy at present seeks to impose Saudi labour on private employers. While the intentions behind this policy are commendable, it is (under current conditions) incompatible with moves towards increasing the international competitiveness of the Saudi private sector. This incompatibility will become increasingly apparent with Saudi Arabia's incorporation into the WTO framework. As noted earlier, the operation of the Saudi labour market in effect guarantees Saudi labour higher wages/salaries than those offered to expatriate/migrant labour – except at the highest levels of technical-professional expertise. Given that Saudi labour also benefits from stronger contractual regulations on dismissal and redundancy, and often lacks the experience and technical/educational training of migrant labour, the freeing of the labour market (as favoured by the WTO) would reduce the employment of Saudis in the private sector.

Current regulations forcing the private sector to employ more Saudis, therefore, may have short-term benefits but will not be viable or effective in the long term. The long-term resolution of the problem must be to enable Saudi and non-Saudi labour to compete on an equal basis. On the one hand, this entails raising the competitiveness of Saudi labour. There are, in turn, two dimensions to this: improving the quality of Saudi labour through training and reducing the extra costs to employers of employing Saudis (in effect, lowering salaries and expectations). On the other hand, the cost of migrant labour to employers needs to be increased through improving their wages and labour conditions (or, if necessary, imposing taxes on companies for every non-Saudi employed). This need not necessarily follow from government *diktat* (apart from, perhaps setting and enforcing a minimum wage). Better conditions of employment for foreign labour in the private sector may emerge naturally from allowing more scope for labour organisation. Any reduction in international competitiveness resulting from this needs to be met by increased governmental support for private sector operations and by encouraging service and industrial sectors to adopt higher levels of technology (thereby also reducing the need for migrant labour).

Conclusion

The debate on economic reform in Saudi Arabia, both within the country and in international circles, has been governed too much by the limited concerns of the Washington Consensus. The reform measures which have been proposed in such circles are no doubt useful. The creation of a viable economy for the long term, however, requires more profound structural changes, focused most crucially on making Saudi labour competitive nationally and internationally. The Saudi state will need to relax its control over some economic activities, but greatly expand its role in others. A new social contract is needed between the state and the population to bring this about, encompassing political as well as economic dimensions.

The need to reform the economy and provide productive employment has an urgency which requires a radical approach. The reforms undertaken to date suffer from three problems. The first is that they have been implemented slowly and partially. Economic reform will become more difficult the longer it is left. Rising unemployment and deteriorating social conditions, fed by one of the highest rates of population growth in the world (almost 4 per cent during the 1980s and 1990s), will intensify political unrest and social disruption.

Second, the content of the reforms is inadequate. The wider reforms which are needed are in many ways the most difficult, requiring a more far-reaching social and political transformation than has so far been envisaged. Central to the needed reform is the issue of labour and employment. Saudi labour must be as productive and cost-effective as migrant labour. While the problem of unemployment may gain temporary redress through the imposition of Saudi labour on unwilling employers, this will not create a productive economy for the long term. Saudi labour needs to be able to compete with expatriate/migrant manpower, such that employers see the economic gain of employing Saudis. The balance needs to be re-adjusted on both sides: making Saudi labour more productive and less expensive to employers, and improving the working conditions of migrant labour (and/or imposing taxes on employers of migrant labour), thereby making it more expensive.

Third, a massive redirection of governmental finances is needed so as to provide the resources for the Saudi state to re-structure the economy and the social structure. In addition to freeing up the regulations and bottle-necks which are currently discouraging investment, the state needs to be investing in areas which will shape development so as to ensure more employment for Saudis, greater equity, better social conditions and a viable economy for the long term. The character of the role played by the state needs to be different from the past. The state needs to divest itself of the ownership of most of the productive processes, so as both to save/raise money and to allow competitive forces to run companies and corporations more effectively. The resources (both financial and administrative) freed by these measures must then be used to improve the country's physical and social infrastructure. On the basis of improved educational and health services, and better welfare provision (such that the impact of making Saudis redundant from existing sinecure positions can be softened), the productive potential of the population can be released.

A radical agenda of the kind proposed requires, as stated earlier, a new social contract between the state and the population. A significant level of trust is needed, built on governmental transparency and a stronger com-mitment to socio-economic equity and greater popular accountability. Privileged access to the resources of the state must be limited. Taxation will need to be used to reduce inequalities. A clear dividing line must be drawn between the state and the private sector, such that private sector gain is not dependent on governmental favour.

6 Foreign policy

Dilemmas of the alliance with the United States and the challenge of international terrorism

Overall perspective

Considerations of domestic and external security have been critical in determining the direction of Saudi foreign policy. Both sets of concerns have interacted closely with two key elements impinging on and conditioning policy: the relationship with the United States and the impact which Saudi Arabia's religious ideology has on the country's role in the world.

Even more clearly than in earlier times, the years since 1990 have thrown into relief the dilemmas faced by the Saudi government in balancing the different concerns and elements underpinning its foreign policy. The central dilemmas have arisen in four main areas: coping with international terrorism, fostering security and stability in the Gulf region, playing a leadership role in the context of the wider Arab world and confronting pressures to cohere with international human rights conventions and uphold democratic freedoms. The interplay between the dynamics of the US–Saudi informal alliance, domestic and external security threats, and the country's Wahhabi religious structures and ideology, has undermined the coherence of policy in all of these areas. Whether the Kingdom can continue balancing its policy between factors which appear increasingly incompatible constitutes an important quandary for the country's future.

The dimensions of potential incompatibility relate to the very core of Saudi foreign policy. The informal alliance with the United States both strengthens and weakens the Saudi position on most key issues. The Kingdom's ability to defend itself against terrorism and external security threats, to project its importance in the Arab world and to avoid international condemnation for human rights abuse, is strengthened by the support which it receives from the United States. At the same time, however, the close relationship with the United States intensifies the security challenges facing the Kingdom, and deepens its political vulnerability. As will be shown later in this chapter, the relationship was critical in making the Kingdom a target of Islamist violence and (at times) of Iranian and Iraqi antagonism. It also undermined the credibility of Saudi attempts to resolve the Palestine problem. On human rights issues, the relationship – at least up to 9/11 – gave the Saudi government the ability to treat lightly pressures from international bodies to improve its human rights record.

The religious ideology projected through Saudi foreign policy has thrown up similar paradoxes. It has, on the one hand, enabled the regime to mobilise the population against external threats. The latter have been portrayed as emanating from sources hostile to Islam, or purveying distorted or schismatic interpretations of Islam. The projection of the Islamic role, moreover, enables the Saudi government to advance claims to leadership in the Arab and Islamic worlds, as well as to rebut allegations of human rights abuse through proclaiming an alternative interpretation of human rights. On the other hand, the emphasis on religious legitimacy weakens both the coherence and the flexibility of foreign policy. The regime's close links with the United States, widely seen as Israel's core ally, provide a weapon for domestic and external critics to attack and discount the proclaimed religious legitimacy. The preparedness of the government to allow non-Muslim military forces to use Saudi territory in attacking other Muslim countries similarly undermines the credibility of religious claims. Saudi governments find themselves caught in an acute dilemma. Either they pursue policies which are necessary for the country's security, but which compromise their claims to religious legitimacy, or else they avoid compromising their religious claims, but thereby undermine the security of the state.

The approach taken in this chapter is to focus on the origins and development of one particular dimension of Saudi Arabia's foreign relations. This dimension is formed by a dynamic of interaction: that between the Saudi–US relationship and the challenge of international terrorism. It is contended that the interaction has been central to the major changes which Saudi Arabia's position in the regional and global orders has undergone. Other dimensions of policy can be fitted around this central dynamic. Much of this chapter, then, takes the form of a narrative, with attention focused on the critical developments in Afghanistan during the 1980s and 1990s. These were to have a critical impact on the growth of international terrorism, the US–Saudi relationship and Saudi Arabia's role in the global order. A detailed account of how events unfolded, and what was driving them, is crucial – given that some of the allegations of Saudi governmental responsibility for international terrorism rest on mistaken perceptions of the train of developments.

'Terrorism' is used here to refer to the deliberate targeting of civilians by non-government groups employing violence to forward a political or ideological cause.

1979–82: deepening the basis of the alliance with the United States following the Iranian revolution

Over the decade which followed 1979 the relationship between Saudi Arabia and the United States deepened. The Iranian pillar in the US Twin-Pillar Policy had fallen away, leaving Saudi Arabia with added strategic significance to the United States. The United States was now building up its potential for direct military action in the region (initially through the Rapid Deployment Force), but needed a strong local partner to provide diplomatic and strategic support. In the perception of both the US and Saudi governments, moreover, the region was now subject to a wider threat. Following the entry of Soviet troops into Afghanistan in December 1979, the Gulf region and its vital oil reserves were seen as threatened by an 'arc of crisis' encircling the Gulf. The increase in Soviet military involvement in South Yemen, the growing strength of the Soviet naval presence in the Indian Ocean and the existence of regimes favourable to the Soviet Union in the Horn of Africa, all buttressed the latter perception. Saudi Arabia and the United States saw themselves as engaged in a common struggle, where the security of Saudi Arabia and the survival of its regime were necessary for the economic stability of the Western world.

The common struggle, moreover, was not confined to the Gulf region. The Saudi government had, in effect, become a partner of the United States in a worldwide campaign against radical and leftist governments and movements. Saudi financial support was given to a wide range of pro-Western or anti-Soviet governments and movements. On occasions such support went to causes which the US administration itself could not openly support. Saudi assistance to the anti-Sandinista forces in Nicaragua, for example, was arranged secretly through US presidential channels – a move which circumvented the US Congress's refusal to permit US resources to be used for such purposes. In Africa, Saudi financial support helped to replace the dependence which some African countries (such as Somalia) previously had on the Soviet Union. Coordination of policy in Afghanistan was also taking shape at this time. The major developments there, however, are covered in the next section.

The coordinated US–Saudi strategy was complemented by massive increases in Saudi expenditure on weaponry and military training, and close military cooperation between the United States and Saudi Arabia. Saudi defence spending had come to less than $5 billion annually in the early 1970s, but by the end of the decade had reached $20 billion and in 1984 exceeded $30 billion (Cordesman 1987: 127; 2003a: 72). Arms imports, of which slightly less than half were from the United States, doubled between 1979 and 1981 (Cordesman 1987: 128).

The attempt to undermine Soviet-supported movements and govern-ments, and to confront the radicalism emanating from Shiite Iran, cohered well with Saudi domestic policy at this time. These policies were portrayed as expressing the Islamic identity of the Kingdom, guided by a re-assertion of Wahhabi principles. The security threat to the Kingdom, and the need to act decisively in protecting the country's security, were also easy to convey to the Saudi public. The outbreak of the Iran–Iraq War in September 1980 brought open military conflict close to Saudi Arabia. There was a widespread perception that if Iraq were to suffer defeat, the Kingdom would be the next domino to fall, with a tide of Iranian Shiite expansionism covering the region. Some $25 billion of Saudi grants and low-interest loans went to Iraq in the course of the war.

The formation of the Gulf Cooperation Council in 1981 stemmed directly from the perceived security threat. The Council's objective was described as cooperation in economic, social, cultural and administrative fields, yet in practice collective defence was a key part of the agenda (Peterson, 1987: 194). The perceived threat also affected Saudi policies in the wider Arab world. The need to reach consensus within the Arab world on the basis for a negotiated settlement with Israel was greater than before. The exclusion of Egypt (still, at that time, the most militarily powerful Arab state) from the Arab League following the Camp David agreement now carried more negative effects than before. Moreover, the close relationship with the United States required some gesture of flexibility over Israel's acceptability as a legitimate state actor. The Fahd Plan of 1981, followed by the Fez Plan of 1982 (which effectively followed the same framework), gave expression to these new policy concerns. Both plans recognised the need for 'peace between all states of the region' – a phrase which signified acceptance of Israel's right to exist, subject to Israeli withdrawal from all territories occupied in 1967. By the middle of the 1980s, however, the focus of Arab concerns had, for the first time since the creation of Israel, moved away from Palestine. With Israel rejecting the plans, the United States unwilling to exert decisive pressure on Israel, and the security concerns in the Gulf and Indian Ocean gradually becoming more urgent, Saudi Arabia's strategic focus was increasingly close to that of the United States.

Over this period, as for the remainder of the 1980s, the issue of human rights did not seriously impinge on the Saudi–US relationship. The greater profile given to human rights in US foreign policy under President Carter (1976–80) was followed by a different approach under President Reagan (1980–88). A distinction was now made between totalitarian and authoritarian governments; and the focus of pressure was on the former.

The Communist countries were defined as totalitarian, whereas Saudi Arabia fell within the authoritarian bracket (Cohen 1979: 233).

1982–90: global partnership with the United States and the Afghan struggle

While the Saudi–US partnership during the 1980s was global in scope, it was in Afghanistan that the developments most critical to Saudi Arabia's future – both domestic and international – took place. This section traces how US and Saudi involvement in Afghanistan provided the setting for the development of armed Islamist activity there, with activists drawn from the wider Islamic world and espousing increasingly radical global objectives. The three sections after that cover the processes whereby this armed Islamist militancy fed into international terrorism and the impact which this had on the US–Saudi relationship and Saudi Arabia's domestic environment and global role.

The use of international terrorism by Islamists, then, emerged from the groupings which came together in Pakistan and Afghanistan in the early 1980s, to engage in a guerrilla war against the Soviet-backed regime in Afghanistan. A key figure in organising Arab support – human and financial – for the Afghan Islamists during the 1980s was 'Abdallah 'Azzam. 'Azzam was of Palestinian origin and had studied jurisprudence in Damascus and al-Azhar universities. During his time in Egypt he had identified politically with the Muslim Brotherhood, although he also had some contacts with leaders of the radical Islamist *al-Jama'a al-Islamiyyah* (Islamic Group) movement. In 1978 he was appointed to teach Islamic law at King 'Abd al-'Aziz University in Jiddah, where he came into contact with the bloc of exiled Muslim Brothers and Saudi *salafi* preachers which had been working in close coordination since the late 1960s. He also developed close links in Saudi society, both at the official level and among wealthy individuals in the private sector. These contacts were to serve him well in the years ahead. In 1980 he moved to Pakistan, gaining appointment at the Saudi-financed International Islamic University in Islamabad. His decision to move stemmed from an encounter with a delegation of Afghans who had come to Saudi Arabia seeking support, and his objective was to use his presence in Pakistan, and his links in Saudi Arabia, to bring effective aid to the cause of the Afghan Islamists (Kepel 2004: 84–85).

In 1984 'Azzam opened an office in Peshawar close to the Afghan border. The organisation which he was now running was known as the *Maktab al-Khidamat al-Mujahidin* (Services Office for the *Mujahidin*), and its mission was to facilitate the reception and organisation of the Arab volunteers who had come to support the struggle against the Afghan government and its Soviet backers. The operation made use of funding which was raised externally, largely from Saudi sources. 'Azzam's role in assisting and organising the Arab volunteers went beyond simple material provision. He was erudite in his religious knowledge and an articulate and inspiring speaker, able to shape the volunteers into a coherent body with a common vision – at least in the early part of the 1980s. His longer-term objective was to use the Afghan experience to create an international Islamic force, fighting for Islamic causes in different parts of the world. Initially most of the volunteers were employed in providing humanitarian and logistical back-up for the Afghan fighters, but after 1986 they became more directly involved in the fighting. Nonetheless, they never accounted for a major part of the overall conflict (Ruthven 2002: 202–206).

In the later part of the 1980s, the Arab volunteers no longer constituted so cohesive a grouping. Those who had come within the framework of the *Maktab al-Khidamat* had, in any case, only constituted part of the whole body of Arab volunteers – albeit the most organised and effective part. The growth of discord reflected differences among the Afghan movements, but it also stemmed from the variety of Islamist trends which were now represented among the expanding body of Arab volunteers. 'Azzam had sought to focus the immediate struggle on defeating the Soviet enemy and its perceived Afghan collaborators. This required downplaying differences with the governments in power in the Islamic world and at least postponing any confrontation with the United States. Volunteers coming from other backgrounds did not necessarily share these priorities. The Egyptian Islamists, for example, had a rather different agenda. *Al-Jama'a al-Islamiyyah*, conducting a campaign of violence against the Mubarak regime in Egypt, sought to retain the link between the two struggles. *Al-Jihad al-Islami* (Islamic Jihad), meanwhile, was increasingly focusing on the global struggle against the United States. The bitter in-fighting among the different groups was probably responsible for the assassination of 'Azzam in 1989 (Burke 2003: 82).

'Usama bin Ladin visited Afghanistan for the first time in 1980 and soon established a close working relationship with 'Azzam. His personal wealth, and his links in Saudi Arabia with other individuals and organisations able and willing to support the Afghan cause, provided the resources which 'Azzam needed to develop an effective organisation. 'Usama also contributed his own charisma, earned through an ascetic lifestyle and a reputation for taking a human and personal interest in the welfare of the Arab volunteers. After 1986, his reputation grew further when reports of his bravery and resilience in military engagements began to circulate. When 'Azzam was assassinated, 'Usama took on the leading role in supervising the *Maktab al-Khidamat*. At the end of the 1980s, his thinking was increasingly influenced by another powerful Islamist strategist and ideologue: 'Ayman al-Zawahiri, the leader of *al-Jihad al-Islami*. Al-Zawahiri's focus was on a wider international struggle against both Communism and the United States, and 'Usama's attention gradually moved in the same direction (Ruthven 2002: 208–210). The inner core of those involved in the *Maktab al-Khidamat* at this time sometimes referred to their network as 'the base' (*al-qa'idah*). The term became more common when they left Afghanistan and sought a wider international role.

'Usama left Afghanistan and returned to Saudi Arabia in the later part of 1989, after the withdrawal of Soviet troops. Much of the infrastructure which had been built up for the support of the volunteers remained in place. Increasing numbers of volunteers arrived, intending to take part in the final push to remove the Najibullah regime. Although the regime proved stronger than had been envisaged, it finally collapsed in 1992. Both the Afghan Islamist movements and the Arab volunteers, however, had now become divided into disparate and often antagonistic groupings. US and Saudi governmental funding for the Afghan movements, through Pakistani channels, was no longer available, weakening the dynamic which had made them work together within a coordinated framework. Many of the Arab volunteers were linked to Islamist organisations within their countries of origin, from which they took direction – often in conjunction with one or other Afghan faction (Burke 2003: 103–104). Neither 'Usama nor his inner group were in a position to exert effective influence over them. It was from this maelstrom of division and extremism that much of the international terrorism of the early 1990s stemmed.

Through the 1980s, the role played by 'Abdallah 'Azzam, 'Usama bin Ladin and the Arab volunteers cohered well with Saudi and US policies. The addition of Arab human and material resources in the struggle against the Soviet presence in Afghanistan buttressed the United States' own efforts to this end. A Soviet withdrawal from Afghanistan would damage Soviet credibility, perhaps causing its regional allies to re-position themselves. The arc of crisis supposedly threatening Gulf oil would cease to cause such immediate concern. As for Saudi policy-makers, support for the Afghan struggle enabled the regime to project its Islamic/Wahhabi credentials – fighting Communism and promoting active Wahhabi/*salafi* proselytism – while at the same time proving to the United States its value as a strategic partner. The support for a struggle which moved public opinion in many parts of the Islamic world buttressed the Saudi regime's claim to global Islamic leadership, highlighting the contrast between Saudi commitment and Iranian diffidence. Specific benefits to domestic policy also accrued: the radical *salafi* elements in Saudi society which had begun to threaten the establishment were provided with an external outlet.

The two governments were not just seeking to achieve a common goal in Afghanistan, but were pursuing complementary policies, closely coordinated. The government of Pakistan was the third element in the collaborative enterprise. The United States was bound by an agreement with the Pakistan government to fund only the Afghan groups and to channel its funding and military training through the Pakistani military intelligence organisation, Inter-Services Intelligence (ISI). US funding through this channel was matched dollar-for-dollar by Saudi governmental funding. The groups which the ISI chose to support, led by individuals who were seen as being closest to Pakistan, were in practice the more extreme Islamist groupings: the *Hizb-e-Islami* led by Gulbuddin Hekmatyar and the *Ittehad-e-Islami* led by 'Abd al-Rab al-Rasul al-Sayyaf. Support for the two groupings cohered well with Saudi religious inclinations. Al-Sayyaf and his group followed Wahhabi precepts and Hekmatyar also upheld a strongly *salafi* line. They attracted most of the governmental and private funding coming direct from Saudi sources, and most of the Arab volunteers assisted by the *Maktab al-Khidamat* within Afghanistan were associated with one or other of them (Burke 2003: 59–60, 68–70).

While the United States provided training for the fighters from the *Ittehad-e-Islami* and the *Hizb-e-Islami*, the latter groupings in turn oversaw the training of the Arab volunteers – using facilities and resources provided by Saudi and other Gulf sources. Saudi Arabia, therefore, was financing the struggle in two different ways: through the Pakistani channel and direct to the Afghans and Arabs who were engaged in combat. Some of the latter funding was governmental and some from private sources, but both were distributed through arrangements orchestrated by the Saudi General Directorate of Intelligence. The supply of US shoulder-launched surface-to-air Stinger missiles to the *Ittehad-e-Islami* and the *Hizb-e-Islami* was ultimately critical to the outcome of the struggle. Once the Soviet troops had lost the security of air support, the balance of the conflict shifted (Bergen 2001: 77–82).

When 'Usama returned to Saudi Arabia in 1989 he enjoyed the respect of significant numbers of Saudis – especially in those circles committed to international Islamic activism. Neither the government nor the press gave public recognition to the role which he had played, but the talks he gave in mosques and elsewhere were well attended. Some of the inner group from Afghanistan, including 'Ayman al-Zawahiri, had accompanied him to Saudi Arabia and remained with him. 'Usama was not at this stage seen as an opponent of the regime. His political activism was directed against the United States rather than the Saudi regime, and he initially remained within the limits of what was permitted by the regime. He organised a boycott of US goods in protest against US policy in Palestine.

Tapes of his talks began to be circulated and were not forbidden. He was given responsibilities in his family's business, but remained living simply (Burke 2003: 136–140).

1990–96: restructuring the relationship following the Iraqi occupation of Kuwait

In the course of 1990–91, two developments occurred which were to change the dynamics of the US–Saudi relationship: the Iraqi occupation of Kuwait in August 1990 (leading to the Gulf War of 1991) and the disintegration of the Soviet Union. The latter brought to an end the perceived Soviet security threat to the region.

The confrontation with Iraq deepened the military and political cooperation between Saudi Arabia and the United States. The Saudi decision to invite US military forces onto Saudi territory, taken within 10 days of the Iraqi invasion, was unprecedented in Saudi history. For the first time, substantial numbers of non-Muslim troops were stationed on Saudi territory, with a major regional war launched from this territory. Most of the 500,000 troops deployed by the United States in the Gulf during the war were based in Saudi Arabia. While most of the US military forces had left the country by the end of 1991, some 5,000 US military personnel remained in the country through the decade. In addition to the military, there were some 30,000 US civilians living in Saudi Arabia at this time. The US Combat Air Operations Center, coordinating US military operations in the Gulf region (stretching as far as Afghanistan), was established at an air force base in Eastern Province and remained there through to August 2003. The monitoring of military developments in Iraq through the 1990s by the airborne warning and control system (AWACS) and other planes overflying the country was carried out largely from Saudi territory. Some of the bombing of Iraqi installations, when Saddam was held to be in breach of UN resolutions, also appears to have been carried out by US planes operating from bases in Saudi Arabia. The Kingdom was at the same time buying increased quantities of weaponry from the United States, for the use of its own defence forces. Of the $71 billion worth of arms agreements agreed between the United States and Saudi Arabia from 1950 to 1993, $17 billion worth were concluded between 1991 and 1993 (CRS 1996: 8).

The heavy US military presence in Saudi Arabia changed the character of the relationship. While this was still portrayed as one between equal partners, the reality was different. The United States was now intimately involved in political and strategic developments in the Gulf region, using Saudi territory and resources to pursue its objectives there. The Saudi government was expected to bear much of the cost of the US military presence. The US Department of Defence estimated the cost of the 1991 Gulf War to the United States at $61 billion, but of this $54 billion was offset by contributions from 'other members of the Coalition' (US Dept. of Defence 1992: Appendix P). The actual burden of cost, therefore, was only $7 billion. Saudi Arabia was responsible for some $30 billion of the contributions to the United States, in addition to its own expenditure on the war. The total cost of the war to Saudi Arabia came to about $60 billion. The continuing US military presence in Saudi Arabia through the decade was also largely financed by the Kingdom. This financial support did not translate into a significant ability to influence US actions in the region. Saudi security interests *vis-à-vis* Iraq may have been served, but new grounds were provided for radical Islamists to mobilise domestic and international Islamic opinion against the regime.

The second development was the disintegration of the Soviet Union and the end of the Cold War. The United States was now no longer in need of Saudi support in the confrontation with Soviet communism. This had immediate significance for developments in Afghanistan, which in turn reflected back on the US–Saudi relationship. Following the departure of Soviet troops from the country in February 1989, the Soviet-backed regime of Mohammed Najibullah gradually lost control. Islamist factions finally took over power in April 1992. In the course of the decade which followed, the security threat to the United States coming from Afghanistan was from radical Islamists – especially after the Taliban took power in Kabul in September 1996. 'Usama bin Ladin moved his base to the country in that same year.

Some basis for Saudi–US cooperation on the global level still existed. Saudi Arabia's Islamic role had three possible uses to the United States, within the New World Order. The first was as a counter to Russian influence in the Caucasus and Central Asia. Saudi funding of new mosques and religious foundations in those regions served US strategic interests by strengthening Islamic consciousness and thereby blocking the chances that Russia would be able to regain its position of power in the newly independent republics. The second was to prevent the expansion of Iranian religious influence (again, mainly in the Caucasus and Central Asia), given that Iran was also seeking to use religious channels to strengthen its political position. The third was to bring the excesses of radical Islam under control, through spreading a more conservative vision of Islam.

In practice, however, a cooperative strategy based on Saudi Arabia's religious role among Muslims was awkward. Some of the religious movements benefiting from Saudi support were antipathetic to the United States. The

Saudi government's ability to control the excesses of radical Islam, moreover, proved to be limited. Some of the Saudi religious establishment was itself supportive of radical Islamist ideas and was intent on using the opening up of Central Asia and the Caucasus to spread this approach. The link with the United States, furthermore, weakened the regime's credibility in Islamist circles, drawing new converts to the radical cause.

The course of developments is best followed by tracing how radical Islamism developed through the 1990s, paying particular attention to the individual whose activities were to have a critical impact both on Saudi Arabia's domestic stability and on Saudi–US relations: 'Usama bin Ladin.

An abrupt turning point in 'Usama's relationship with the Saudi regime came after the Iraqi occupation of Kuwait in August 1990. While he had for long been militantly antagonistic to the secular Ba'thist regime in Iraq regime, he was outraged at the Saudi government's preparedness to allow US troops on to Saudi soil. Other radical Islamic circles in the Kingdom shared this sense of outrage, as also did some of the radical Afghan Islamists who had benefited most from Saudi support in Afghanistan. Al-Sayyaf, leader of the *Ittehad-e-Islami*, was particularly militant on this issue, strongly denouncing the Saudi government's position. The positions taken by 'Usama and al-Sayyaf at this time reflected the change of perspective occurring within *salafi* circles. Radical Islamist movements which had been funded by Saudi money, and shaped by Wahhabi precepts, were now directing their critique at the Saudi regime. In September, 'Usama secured a hearing with the Minister of Defence, Prince Sultan, and put to him an alternative: he would assemble an international force of *mujahidin* (fighters for a religious cause), of a similar kind to that which had fought in Afghanistan, to defend the Kingdom. The proposal was rejected by Prince Sultan, who nonetheless paid respect to the Bin Ladin family's role as 'loyal friends of the Al Saud' (Burke 2003: 136–137).

'Usama now became more strident in the articulation of his views. His speeches to gatherings in mosques and elsewhere were now more explicit in denouncing those political leaders in the Islamic world who cooperated with the United States and who acted on a basis of *kufr* (unbelief). In May 1991 he issued a private communiqué to 'members of al-Qa'ida' calling for the formation of a 'single pure and Muslim army ... of 10,000 soldiers who would be ready, at a moment's notice, to march to liberate the land of the two holy places' (Burke 2003: 140). However, the political signifi-cance of this appeal at the time was not substantial. There was no identi-fiable organisation known as al-Qa'ida, beyond the small inner network which had worked with 'Usama in Afghanistan. The political activity which was attracting attention within Saudi Arabia then was that centred around the petitions to the government. Despite his being in Saudi Arabia at the time, 'Usama was not a signatory to the Letter of Demands signed by leading religious figures and academics in May 1991 (see p. 80). The central target of 'Usama's anger, moreover, was the United States, and the sought-for 'liberation' was from the US military presence in Saudi territory.

The Saudi authorities placed him under a loose form of 'city arrest' in the middle of 1991, forbidding him to leave Jiddah without permission. In the later part of 1991 he obtained authority to travel to Pakistan, on the pretext of settling some of his financial arrangements there. He never returned to Saudi Arabia, but in due course moved on to Sudan, where he took up residence (Bergen 2001: 85–86). His failure to return, and his decision to base himself in Sudan – whose Islamist regime was inimical to Saudi Arabia – made clear his alienation from the Saudi system. It was, however, not until April 1994 that the Saudi government stripped him of his nationality, seeking at the same time to freeze the limited funds of his still remaining in the country (*Guardian*: 11.4.94). The timing of the latter move was linked to 'Usama's explicit alignment with the radical Saudi Islamists whose domestic confrontation with the government reached a peak in that year and the establishment in London of an office through which he could spread his critique of the regime and articulate his support for the opposition. The short-lived office in London operated under the title of Committee for Advice and Reform in Saudi Arabia, issuing communiqués which mixed practical and religious grievances. Among these grievances were the rising unemployment, the lavish expenditure on royal palaces, the issuing of legislation which was not based on Islamic law and the waste of money on the Gulf War. One communiqué called for the resignation of King Fahd (Bergen 2001: 96).

'Usama's years in Sudan, through to his effective expulsion in 1996, were ambiguous in character. The welcome which was given to him by the Sudanese regime was motivated largely by economic considerations, and 'Usama himself appears to have seen his primary role there as an investor who could bring development and improved conditions to this poor and Islamist-governed country. Over the five years which followed his arrival, he had brought some \$2 billion of investment into the country – from his own resources and those of other individuals and institutions who were encouraged to come into partnership with him. His projects ranged from road-building to trading companies, agricultural schemes, banking, manufacturing projects and a bakery (Bergen 2001: 87). At the same time, however, he remained engaged with international Islamic causes and was developing, with 'Ayman al-Zawahiri, his strategy for an international force of *mujahidin* to fight for Islamic causes – increasingly seen in terms of confronting the United States, especially in the context of its military presence in Saudi territory. He financed the establishment of camps in

Sudan where Arab *mujahidin* who had fought in Afghanistan were settled, and in some of these military training was provided. He sought to play a role in the fight against US military involvement in Somalia, although the significance of his role there may be questioned (Bergen 2001: 87–90).

Over the early- and mid-1990s, international terrorism was becoming an increasing phenomenon in the international system. Among the key incidents which occurred were the bombing of the World Trade Centre in 1993, the attempt to assassinate President Mubarak of Egypt while on a visit to Ethiopia in July 1995 and the bombing of the US-run facility in al-Khobar (Saudi Arabia) in 1996. Allegations are often made about 'Usama's involvement in these. It is, however, doubtful that he directly instigated any of them. The two earlier incidents appear to have been the work of *al-Jama'a al-Islamiyyah*, while the latter was probably carried out by Saudi Shiites with links to elements in Iran. To some extent it was the very diffuse nature of the groupings which made it difficult to confront the problem: they were not coordinated under one organisation, and the problem could not be dealt with by dealing with one organisation. 'Usama's activities in, and pronouncements from, Sudan did, nonetheless, add to the ideological mind-set which encouraged such attacks, and some of the operatives involved in terrorist operations had passed through the camps in Sudan.

What can not be doubted is that most of the international terrorism occurring at this time stemmed from the networks of support which had been forged among Islamists in Afghanistan during the 1980s. From the early 1990s, therefore, the Saudi government was confronting a problem which it had itself helped to create – in conjunction with the governments of the United States and Pakistan. The problem, moreover, impinged directly on the most critical aspects of the Kingdom's political coherence: the dynamics of its domestic stability (resting on the accommodation of religious forces) and its close relationship with and dependence on the United States. The dilemmas posed in the domestic environment were themselves diverse, yet interlinked. The large number of Saudis among the Arab volunteers in Afghanistan, the prominence of Saudi nationals in terrorist operations and organisations, the support which radical Islamism (with its antipathy to the United States) enjoyed among substantial sectors of Saudi public opinion, and the preparedness of some private individuals to support charities with known links to Islamist radicalism, all constituted different dimensions of the problem facing the regime.

The dilemmas relating to the Saudi–US relationship were equally acute. On the one hand, Saudi involvement with the United States had itself become an incitement to terrorism, both towards the US and towards Saudi Arabia. This was fuelled by opposition to the US military presence on Saudi territory and to the Kingdom's close political cooperation with a power whose regional policies were perceived as being inimical to Arab/Islamic interests. On the other hand, the rising tide of international terrorism, with links to Saudi Arabia, increased the regime's sense of vulnerability and hence its inclination to seek protection from the United States.

In the course of 1996, 'Usama's presence in Sudan became problematic to the Sudanese regime. In March of that year UN sanctions had been imposed on Sudan, as a result of Sudan's failure to hand over to the Egyptian authorities two Islamists from the *al-Jama'a al-Islami* group who were accused of involvement in the assassination attempt on President Mubarak. The Sudanese government, at odds with all of its neighbours and with most major powers, badly needed to improve its international standing. Pressure was being exerted on Sudan by both the United States and Saudi Arabia to close down all of the *mujahidin* camps in the country and to expel 'Usama (Niblock 2000: 199–208). In May 1996 'Usama seems to have agreed to leave, returning to Afghanistan. He initially went to the areas which were controlled by his former Afghan ally, Gulbuddin Hekmatyar. Sudanese offers to supply the United States with information on 'Usama's activities while he had been in Sudan were not taken up (Kepel 2004: 91).

1996–98: intensification of the international terrorist threat to Saudi Arabia and the United States

The Saudi government clearly hoped that 'Usama's activities would be restrained or curtailed in Afghanistan. There was a realistic basis to this belief. The Taliban were gradually extending their control over the country, and 'Usama's links had previously been with groups who were now fighting the Taliban. The Taliban, supported by the Pakistani ISI, were intent on securing their undisputed control over Afghan territory, bringing the activities of diverse radical Islamist groups under control. Saudi Arabia, moreover, seemed assured of a privileged relationship with a unified Taliban-controlled Afghanistan. The Saudi government had provided financial support for the Taliban, in conjunction with the Pakistani government, and the new Afghan regime would require continuing support to survive. Besides Pakistan and Saudi Arabia, the only other country which extended recognition to the Taliban when they took over the reigns of power in Kabul in September 1996 was the United Arab Emirates. The remoteness of Afghanistan from the international scene also seemed to suit Saudi purposes. 'Usama would find it difficult to use this inhospitable terrain to project his ideas or to organise international terrorism. 'Usama's move to Afghanistan, then, would enable the Saudi regime to control

'Usama at arm's length – without having the embarrassment of prosecuting him in Saudi Arabia.

Religious considerations also suggested that the Taliban would work with the Saudi government. The more conservative circles of Saudi Wahhabism had for long perceived an affinity between Wahhabism and the Deobandi movement from which the Taliban sprung. Some Wahhabis, indeed, saw the Deobandis as their closest equivalent in South Asia. On this basis, Saudi private and charitable funding had flowed to the *madrasah*s run by the Deobandi movement in Pakistan since the 1970s. Between 'Usama and the Taliban, on the other hand, there was a wide divergence in mentality and ideology. The Taliban were isolationist and inward-looking, focusing on the control of Afghanistan. Their breed of religious revivalism, calling for a return to an earlier and more just form of society, was comparable to some of the Mahdist movements which had marked Islamic history. In their case the envisaged return was to a romanticised version of Pashtun village life (Burke 2003: 123–124). 'Usama's concerns and foci were in the international arena.

The Saudi government's assessment, however, was mistaken. Within a year of arriving in Afghanistan, 'Usama had established a workable relationship with the Taliban. Despite the differences in mentality and outlook, they also shared some common ground. Both took a literalist approach to Islam and saw themselves as constituting an island of Islamic purity in an ocean of *kufr* (unbelief) and misinterpretation (Burke 2003: 181–184). The Taliban were, moreover, attracted by the financial benefits which 'Usama could bring to their impoverished country and aware that his presence could be played-off against the Saudi government to ensure that support from the latter was also forthcoming.

The relationship between the Taliban and 'Usama over the four years which followed 1997, when they entered into formal cooperation, was marked both by tension and a sense of common struggle. The tension stemmed from the difficulty which the Taliban experienced in managing 'Usama and by their realisation that al-Qa'ida was making Afghanistan the target for external intervention. They did not accept doctrinally his authority to issue *fatwa*s and resented his making political pronouncements which undermined their quest for international recognition (Bergen 2001: 178–179). The sense of common struggle was based on a perception of shared victimhood and the need to face the external enemy together. Although the Taliban on occasions sought the expulsion of 'Usama from their territory, they moved steadily away from this option as their isolation increased. Their failure to gain international recognition was both the cause and the effect of 'Usama's continued presence in the country.

'Usama's intention to pursue his political objectives actively from Afghanistan was made explicit soon after his arrival there. In August 1996 he issued an 8,000 word 'Declaration of War Against Americans Occupying the Land of the Two Holy Places'. The Declaration was in part a denunciation of the Al Saud. The latter were were accused of straying from the correct Islamic way and inflicting injustice on the population. As the Al Su'ud had followed a pagan legal code, they could no longer be considered Muslims and must be resisted – a duty which all Muslims should uphold. On the other hand, it called for opposition to the 'Crusader–Zionist alliance' which was occupying the 'land of the two holy places' and massacring Muslims in many parts of the world. He called for the establishment of 'fast-moving light forces that work under complete secrecy' and which would 'hit the aggressor with an iron fist' (Burke 2003: 163).

The focus of immediate action was centred on the United States:

> The situation can not be rectified unless the root of the problem is tackled ... Hence it is essential to hit the main enemy who divided the *ummah* into small countries ... and pushed it for the last few decades into a state of confusion.
>
> (Burke 2003: 165)

The importance of this stark message is worth stressing. It marked a substantial break from the position which most Islamist movements had taken in the past, where the immediate targets were the governments of Islamic countries which were regarded as having reneged on Islam. 'Usama was, for the moment at least, turning the focus away from change within Islamic countries and directing it at what he regarded as the source of the woes experienced by contemporary Muslims. In an interview in October 1996 he repeated and emphasised the point: 'It is crucial to overlook many of the issues of bickering to unite our ranks so we can repel the greater *kufr*' (Burke 2003: 165). The message that Muslims should lay aside their differences so as to confront the United States and the Western world, and the violence of the threats against the United States, were made yet more explicit in the early part of 1998. In a statement in February 1998 announcing the establishment of a World Islamic Front, 'Usama called for the defeat of factionalism within the Islamic world and also justified the use of violence against the United States. The killing of Americans and their allies (both civilian and military), the statement said, was justified 'in order to liberate the al-Aqsa mosque and the Holy Mosque ... and in order for their armies to move out of all of the lands of Islam'. The latter perspectives were contained in a 'Declaration of *Jihad* against Jews and Crusaders' (Burke 2003: 176).

The international terrorism which developed in the late 1990s and through to September 2001 was increasingly linked to 'Usama and the al-Qa'ida group. Some of the inner group around 'Usama had travelled with him from Khartoum, while others (most notably al-Zawahiri) joined him in Afghanistan shortly after his arrival. At this stage, most of the major terrorist attacks, from the August 1998 bomb explosions at the US embassies in East Africa to the 9/11 attacks in Washington and New York, were geared specifically at the United States. There were some incidents within Saudi Arabia, but these were directed at US targets within the country.

Despite the links between Saudi nationals and the growth of international terrorism, there was at this stage no adverse effect on the Saudi–US relationship. The two governments saw themselves as joint targets of al-Qa'ida's terrorist campaign. Although the violence was mainly directed at US installations, 'Usama's militant denunciations of the Saudi regime posed a direct threat to the Kingdom's stability. His popularity among many Saudis gave these denunciations weight, feeding into the domestic unrest caused by Islamist activists within the country. Saudi Arabia, moreover, remained of pivotal importance to US military strategy in the region, providing both the military facilities and the operations centre from which Saddam's Iraq could be monitored and attacked, and from which Iran's activities could be checked.

The Saudi channel constituted one of the few avenues through which Taliban activities could be observed and perhaps influenced. There was still some reason to believe that Saudi influence might prove effective in eliminating the threat from al-Qa'ida. The intensification of 'Usama's militancy led the Saudi government to put pressure on the Taliban regime for 'Usama's expulsion and forcible return to Saudi Arabia. In June 1998, Prince Turki (head of the Saudi Directorate of Intelligence) reached agreement on this with Mullah Mohammad Omar, the Taliban leader. Mullah Omar had himself been angered by 'Usama's 'Declaration of *Jihad* against Jews and Crusaders', which had been issued without prior consultation with him. His only request was that a joint commission of Saudi and Afghan *'ulama* be convened to provide a fitting legal justification. When Prince Turki returned to Afghanistan with two planes and sufficient military personnel to take charge of 'Usama, however, events had moved on. The August 1998 bombing attacks on the US embassies in East Africa, and the US 'Operation Infinite Reach' involving missile strikes against al-Qa'ida training camps in Afghanistan, had driven the Taliban into a more entrenched position. The Taliban leader refused, in early September 1998, to hand 'Usama over, and the planes returned to Riyadh empty (*Guardian*: 5.9.01).

Even the dimension of human rights, which was given greater emphasis under President Clinton than under the two preceding presidents, failed to create division. The Department of State annual country reports on human rights practices were, in fact, explicit in detailing human rights abuses in Saudi Arabia: discrimination on grounds of sex and religion was described as 'legal and systemic'. The areas of human rights abuse included the repression of Shi'a Muslims, the mistreatment of foreign women working in domestic service, general discrimination against women, and the lack of civil liberties, political rights and workers' rights. The reports from 1995 and 1996 onwards, moreover, attributed blame for human rights abuses to the Saudi government, saying that the Saudi government 'commits and tolerates serious human rights abuses' (US-DOS 1995). Earlier reports had avoided any direct attribution of responsibility. However, US officials generally refrained from publicly stating concern over human rights abuses in Saudi Arabia. Even during congressional hearings on US weapons sales to Saudi Arabia, there was little mention of human rights. Nor is there any evidence that human rights figured significantly in diplomatic exchanges between the two countries. The policy seemed to be one of 'silence and inaction' (Labooncharoen: 45).

1998–2001: from the East Africa bombings to 9/11

The suicide attacks on the US embassies in Kenya and Tanzania on 7 August 1998, and the US response to them, were critical to the unfolding of events. The attacks were carried out on the anniversary of the day, 8 years earlier, when King Fahd had invited the United States to send troops to Saudi Arabia (Kepel 2004: 92). 'Usama denied responsibility for the attacks, perhaps to distance himself from an operation which had not been approved by the Taliban leadership. There is, however, substantive evidence that they were indeed instigated and implemented by al-Qa'ida. 'Usama, in any case, expressed his approval of what had been done. The United States responded, on 20 August, by carrying out missile strikes against facilities in Afghanistan associated with al-Qa'ida. The main target was the al-Badr complex of camps, near Khowst, where 'Usama was known to have had attended a meeting with senior al-Qa'ida leaders shortly before the attacks (US-NC 2004: 116). There was also a missile attack on a pharmaceuticals factory in Sudan which the US government claimed was linked to al-Qa'ida and was producing a precursor chemical for nerve gas (US-NC 2004: 117).

Despite the carnage caused to innocent civilians in East Africa, al-Qa'ida was strengthened by the events of August 1998. A new dimension had been added to the aura surrounding 'Usama. He had, in the eyes of radical Islamists, shown his seriousness in opposing the United States, and his practical ability to strike at United States interests in distant parts of the world (Burke 2003: 181). The US retaliation, intended to kill him and his close collaborators, had proved ineffective. The United States had at the same time bombed an innocent target in Sudan: the pharmaceuticals company was soon shown to have had no connection either with the production of chemical weapons or with 'Usama (*Observer*: 30.8.98). The lesson which appeared to come from these events was that the United States was an impotent superpower: unjustly lashing out at whatever target was convenient and incapable of punishing those who were determined to challenge it. No doubt this outcome was what the attacks in East Africa had sought to achieve.

The implications of these events for al-Qa'ida, the Taliban, Saudi Arabia and the United States were considerable. 'Usama had achieved a new cult status within the Islamic world – a symbol of resistance to the United States and to a global order deemed to be unjust. Many more adherents were attracted to the camps in Afghanistan run by al-Qa'ida. A dynamic had been created which spontaneously drew together an international army of Islamist militants. The members of this army were not dependent on a central leadership. Moved by their fervour, willing to sacrifice their own lives and confident that the United States was the main enemy, they could organise attacks independently. The presence of militants in the Afghan camps, in fact, was not strictly necessary – although no doubt useful so as to provide training and religious instruction. More important was the spread of an idea: militants could act directly against US interests, as and when they saw fit.

For the Taliban, the room for manoeuvre had narrowed. They could not now, without losing face in the Islamic world, expel 'Usama from their territories. They became increasingly dependent on al-Qa'ida. They were no longer in receipt of Saudi governmental finance, and the Pakistani authorities had cut off logistical military supplies. As a result of this, they were reliant on al-Qa'ida's militants to maintain control of the country, and on al-Qa'ida to bring in funding (mainly from private sources committed to radical Islamism). Over the three remaining years of Taliban rule in Afghanistan, the two movements became increasingly closely intertwined – to such an extent that their separate identities within Afghanistan were no longer clear (Bergen 2001: 175–178).

The long-term implications of these developments for Saudi Arabia were severe. The ability of the Saudi government to control 'Usama's activities in Afghanistan was now very limited. Any hope of securing his expulsion from the country had evaporated. Diplomatic relations with the

Taliban were, in any case, frozen – though not broken (US-NC 2004: 122). 'Usama's stature had grown among disaffected Saudis, and increasing numbers of young Saudis made their way to Afghanistan. This was to be reflected in the large numbers of Saudis who, after the US military action in Afghanistan in 2001, were captured by US troops and sent to Camp Delta in the US facility at Guantanamo Bay. In April 2004, some 25 per cent of all of the detainees at Guantanamo were Saudi (160 out of a total 650; *UPI*: 2.4.04), constituting by far the largest national contingent. These detainees, moreover, constituted only a small proportion of those Saudis who had been recruited into the al-Qa'ida forces in Afghanistan. Estimates of the total numbers of Saudi recruits in Afghanistan in 2001 put the figure at approximately 10,000. Some of the recruits became disillusioned by the Afghan experience, abandoning their militant stance. Many, however, returned to Saudi Arabia with a deepened disaffection towards the Saudi regime and possessing military training and experience. This was to shape the terrorist threat which Saudi Arabia faced after 2001.

While there was no immediate impact on the governmental relationship between Saudi Arabia and the United States, the sources of future crisis were developing quickly. Through to the al-Qa'ida attacks on New York and Washington in September 2001, neither the US nor Saudi governments adopted a coherent policy in confronting the threat facing them. The US government failed to recognise al-Qa'ida's ability to mount a large-scale operation against US interests, and to understand how US policy in the wider Middle East fed into the well-springs of Islamist terrorism. The Saudi government, for its part, was unable or unwilling to confront the domestic religious infrastructure which was promoting a favourable view of, and complicity in supporting, al-Qa'ida. Saudi private funding, furthermore, was helping to maintain the infrastructure of international terrorism which al-Qa'ida had created.

A gap was opening up between governmental policy and public opinion on both sides. As events unfolded, this was to constitute a critical factor restricting the room for manoeuvre of the two governments. The domestic environments were to attain a new significance in shaping the relationship. On the Saudi side, journalistic reports spoke of a spreading conviction that the United States was hostile to Arab and Islamic interests in the region (*NYT*: 4.12.00). This was fuelled by continuing resentment at the US military presence in the region, but it was deepened by ongoing events in the Middle East. Of particular importance here were the emotions stirred up by the outbreak of the second *intifadah* in Palestine in September 2000 and the impact which UN sanctions were having on the Iraqi population. Regional events, indeed, acted as a spur for young Saudi militants to travel for training and instruction to the al-Qa'ida camps in

Afghanistan (Kepel 2004: 102–103). The climate of public opinion would have made it difficult for the Saudi government to confront the orthodox religious leaders who, despite being close to the governing system, were purveying views which encouraged extremist attitudes among the population. There is, however, little evidence that such an option was given serious consideration.

Within the United States, the tenor of popular opinion was also becoming divorced from that of the inter-governmental relationship. There was growing public criticism of the Saudi government's record on human rights, its failure to curb Islamist extremism and the flow of Saudi money which was going to Palestinian sources to support resistance to the Israeli government. While these were also issues taken up through official channels, the governmental relationship still reflected the value to the United States of the two countries' strategic and economic cooperation (*FT*: 30.8.00). The strong personal links between some of the Saudi and US leaders, moreover, played a role in preventing confrontation. These links were particularly strong once a Republican President (George W. Bush) had returned to the White House in January 2001. Close contacts between senior Al Su'ud princes and senior members of the Republican Party had been in existence for some time, orchestrated in part through the good offices of the Saudi ambassador in Washington, Prince Bandar bin Sultan Al Saud. Interlocking financial interests buttressed the relationship among some of the individuals concerned (Moore 2003: 6–15). In 1998, during the long run-up to the US presidential election of 2000, reports circulated of meetings between senior Republicans and senior Al Su'ud princes, aimed at developing a common strategy on the Middle East. Promises of Saudi policies favourable to US business were, reportedly, traded against promises of a stronger US line on Palestine. When George Bush became President in 2001, then, there was on both sides a belief that Saudi–US relations would be strengthened further.

2001–05: the impact of 9/11

After the al-Qa'ida attacks on New York and Washington of 9/11 2001, it was no longer realistic to imagine that Saudi religious influence could be used to promote US security and political interests in the region. Within a day of the attacks, it was known that 15 of the 19 hijackers were of Saudi nationality. The presumption that 'Usama was behind the attacks was made almost immediately after the news of the events was broadcast. Unable to control the growth of Islamism among its own population, the Saudi government no longer appeared a useful instrument in combating the wider Islamist threat. The close personal relations between the two leaderships ensured that those Saudis who wanted to leave the

United States could do so immediately, aware that a popular backlash against them might be forthcoming. Within a week of the events, some 600 Saudis had left the United States. Among these were members of the Al Saud, and of leading commercial families in the Kingdom. One symbol of the changed relationship between the two countries in the period following 9/11 was Saudi Arabia's non-participation in the two major US military operations in the region at that time: those in Afghanistan (from November 2001) and in Iraq (from March 2003).

US policies towards Saudi Arabia were now coloured by the perception in the United States that the Saudi government carried an indirect responsibility for what had happened. This was expressed most explicitly in non-governmental circles. A very negative view of Saudi Arabia, and sometimes of Islam in general, was articulated in the US press and in a number of high-circulation books which captured and promoted the popular mood. Among the latter were *Hatred's Kingdom* (Gold 2003), *Sleeping with the Devil* (Baer 2003) and *The Two Faces of Islam: the House of Saud from Tradition to Terror* (Schwartz 2002). Think-tank reports added to the upsurge of criticism. A Rand Corporation report on Saudi Arabia in 2002 described Saudi Arabia as an enemy of the United States, while a Cato Institute report in 2004 catalogued all of the negative aspects for the United States stemming from its continued relationship with Saudi Arabia – calling for a pulling-away from the formerly close alliance (CATO 2004: 543). The change in US public attitudes to Saudi Arabia was documented by opinion polls. Whereas in January 2001, 58 per cent of those polled revealed a favourable attitude to Saudi Arabia, in December of that year only 24 per cent held a favourable view (Gause 2002).

The non-governmental reaction in the United States was of significance to US foreign policy in two ways. First, the impact of 9/11 on popular consciousness had placed the relationship with Saudi Arabia at the forefront of national debate. This element of the domestic environment could no longer be ignored. Second, the dividing line between informed public criticism and governmental attitudes was blurred. While some of the critique of Saudi Arabia came from those opposed to US governmental policy – alleging continued complicity between the two leaderships, based on their economic interests – other parts came from think tanks close to the centre of government decision-making (*Guardian*: 24.11.02). Neo-conservatives, within and outside government, straddled the divide between government policy and non-governmental opinion. Their views found expression in think-tank reports. The Cato Institute's report, for example, came from an organisation which articulated the views of neo-conservatives (within and outside government) on foreign policy issues.

There was, in any case, a significant overlap between governmental policy and think-tank criticism: the government line was put more diplomatically, but similar issues were covered. A common line among neo-conservatives was that Saudi Arabia was part of the problem in the Middle East, not part of the solution (Geoffrey Kemp in *al-Ittihad*: 23.6.02).

The elements of criticism which can be identified as coming from governmental sources, and on whose grounds pressure was exerted on the Saudi government, covered a wide range of issues. The significance of the criticism lay in the centrality of the policy-areas which were targeted. Key elements of Saudi Arabia's political and economic system were censured. The educational system was criticised for instilling in Saudis prejudicial attitudes towards Jews and Christians. It was also blamed for graduating large numbers of students with religious qualifications, who were unemployable within the economy and provided recruits for Islamist radicalism. The political system was seen as failing to offer avenues through which popular grievances could be openly discussed and articulated. Without such avenues, discontent was impelled to express itself in extreme and violent forms. Economic reform had, it was said, been insufficient, leading to socio-economic discontent. The country needed a major influx of foreign investment, so as to provide more employment, but entrenched interests within the system were frustrating the achievement of this objective – so as to maintain the corrupt practices which had brought them wealth. Besides the critique directed to these aspects of social and economic policy, and to the political structure, there was also continuing criticism of the perceived Saudi failure to staunch the flow of Saudi human and material resources going to al-Qa'ida operations (*Guardian*: 15.5.05).

Most of the criticisms were valid, as will be evident from other chapters of this book. Yet in practice they were no more valid in 2001 than they had been over the previous quarter-century. The political and economic shortcomings, moreover, were not simply attributable to Saudi governmental misgovernment but were closely related to the US–Saudi relationship itself. US support had enabled and encouraged the regime to ignore calls for political reform, and had created the context in which Saudi resources had been diverted away from socio-economic development and towards wasteful military expenditure. The defence contracts often incorporated substantial 'agency fees' going to individuals close to the centre of government.

The Saudi government's reaction to the events of 9/11 was also crucial to how the relationship with the United States developed. The initial response was to deny that Saudi nationals had played so large a part in the attacks. Once it had been established beyond question that 15 of the 19 hijackers were Saudi, however, the government was forced to give new attention to its domestic environment. The Saudi Islamists who were prepared to espouse terrorism were clearly drawing sustenance, whether through support or opposition, from aspects of state policy. On the one hand, their religious conceptions were rooted in a particular interpretation of Wahhabi thought, which had matured in the religious environment promoted by the state. On the other, social inequality and political exclusion underpinned the militancy. Many of the activists came from marginalized sections of the Saudi population, whose religious militancy was often associated with a harsh critique of Saudi government policy – especially as regards the US military presence in the country.

The Saudi governments' re-evaluation led to policy adaptations in two areas, both of which impinged on the US–Saudi relationship. First, the Saudi government gave renewed emphasis to the process of political and economic reform. This was, of course, consistent with US policy. In practice, however, it did not contribute greatly to improving the relationship and in some respects engendered new fields for dispute. The reality was that the Saudi polity remained distant from the democratic freedoms which the United States now claimed must constitute the cornerstone of a stable and prosperous Middle East. This became increasingly apparent with the rising stridency of US proclamations of an agenda for democratic change – from the initial generalised references to spreading democracy after the Iraq War, through to the rather more specific proposals put forward in the Middle East Partnership Initiative, the Middle East Free Trade Area proposal and the Greater Middle East Initiative, introduced respectively in March 2002, June 2002 and June 2003 (Niblock 2003: 47–58). Political and economic reform in the Kingdom had, as shown in previous chapters, been on the Saudi government's agenda since the early 1990s. The pace of change certainly quickened after 2001, with the introduction of municipal elections, hints of creating more opportunities for women (*Guardian*: 6.7.02) and new measures of economic liberalisation, but the system remained distinctly illiberal. The Saudi governmental response to the US Greater Middle East Initiative was negative and critical. In the economic sphere, moreover, the government showed reluctance to open the Saudi economy to the extent sought by the United States. The US conclusion of Free Trade Agreements with other members of the GCC was seen as a deliberate attempt to undermine Saudi economic policy. Also crucial to the US perception was the slow pace of educational reform – an area of policy where the '*ulama* proved effective in resisting change.

The second adaptation of policy was more directly problematic to the United States. Islamist radicalism had in part been provoked by the US military presence in Saudi Arabia. The government, therefore, began gradually to re-think its attitude towards this military presence. The change was probably encouraged by the shock felt within Saudi governing circles at evolving US attitudes: the Kingdom had moved within a few months from being a key friend and partner of the United States to the status of problem country. The movements of Saudi citizens in the United States were being monitored closely, Saudis were no longer able to gain easy entry into the United States, and many of the richest and most powerful people in the country (including the Minister of Defence, Prince Sultan) found themselves subject to private legal actions in the US courts (*Guardian*: 19.10.02). The latter case, brought by lawyers on behalf of US citizens who had lost relatives in the 9/11 attacks, accused them of indirect involvement in 9/11 through providing support to charities financing al-Qa'ida. A poll based on educated Saudis, conducted in September 2002, revealed that 87% of the sample held a negative view of the United States (Zogby 2002: 61).

A further factor encouraging the Saudi government to rethink its attitude to the US military presence after 9/11 stemmed from strategic developments in the Gulf. It became increasingly evident that the United States was poised to use military force within the region, initially in Afghanistan and then in Iraq. Saudi Arabia might then be seen as the springboard from which the United States attacked other Muslim countries, making the country a target for intensified Islamist anger. In the US attacks against the Taliban regime in Afghanistan in October 2001, there-fore, the Saudi government refused to allow Saudi airfields to be used by planes engaged in the operations. Nonetheless, the orchestration of the military action was managed from the US Combat Air Operations Centre in Dammam. With the focus of US attention switching to Iraq at the begin-ning of 2002, the issue of Saudi support for a land-based attack on Iraq arose. Saudi territory would have constituted the most convenient base from which to operate. In the course of January 2002, however, the first intimations were given that Saudi Arabia would ask the United States to withdraw its military forces from Saudi territory (*Guardian*: 19.1.02). The Saudi government was particularly reluctant to have Saudi territory used in attacking Iraq. As plans for the latter began developing, therefore, the United States gave attention to building-up alternative operating facilities in the Gulf (in particular in Qatar). The decision to withdraw all US troops was announced in April 2003 (*Guardian*: 4.4.03), and all the forces (except for 200 military training personnel) had been moved by August 2003. The Combat Air Operations Centre was shifted in the latter month to the al-Udaid camp in Qatar.

By the time the United States, in March 2003, launched its attack on Iraq, therefore, the close military coordination between the two sides had come to an end. The Kingdom did not participate in the war, whether by providing facilities or contributing forces or finance. Its non-involvement in an operation which was so critical to the United States was indicative of the extent to which the relationship had changed. Shortly after the war, a Republican member of the US Senate, Senator Arlen Specter, introduced the Saudi Arabia Accountability Act before both houses of the US Congress. The bill, tabled in November 2003, required the US President to provide certification that Saudi Arabia was making maximum efforts to fight terrorism. If such certification was not given, according to the bill, a series of measures would be taken against Saudi Arabia: prohibition of exports of defence items covered by the Arms Export Control Act and of any items (either economic or military material) on the Commerce Control List; and restriction of travel by Saudi diplomats in the United States to a 25-mile radius of Washington (*NYT*: 19.11.03). In mid-2005, the bill remained under discussion in Congress.

In the period following the Iraq war, the Saudi–US relationship was subjected to new pressures. Saudi Arabia was blamed for failing to stem the flow of Saudis joining the insurgency against the United States in Iraq. According to some estimates, approximately one-quarter of the foreign insurgents fighting in Iraq were Saudi nationals (although such foreign fighters made up only a small fraction of the overall insurgency). The ability of the Saudi government to prevent Saudis from joining the insurgency was, in practice, limited. Some of those who joined the insurgency had been outside of Saudi Arabia for a prolonged period, forming part of the international circle of al-Qa'ida militants who moved between different Islamist struggles. Their movements, were not within Saudi governmental control. Those who did travel from Saudi Arabia, moreover, could not easily be stopped – the land borders between the two countries were extensive, and there were in addition many indirect routes available. A new layer of distrust, however, had been laid. On the Saudi side, there were suspicions that the United States was intent on taking power away from the Sunni Arab community in Iraq, perhaps allowing a Shiite state to emerge in the country.

Saudi Arabia had itself become a primary target for terrorism, with attacks reaching a peak in the course of 2003 and 2004 (*Observer*: 9.11.03; *Guardian*: 24.6.04). The return to the Kingdom of fighters who had been in Afghanistan, and the new dynamic which was given to radical Islamism by the war in Iraq, help to account for this (*Guardian*: 21.11.02). A further factor was the developing characteristics of international terrorism: groups of radical Islamists were now operating more spontaneously in the international arena, rather than acting under specific instructions from the al-Qa'ida leadership. The departure of US troops from Saudi territory had won the regime support from some of the more established Islamist opponents (*MidEast Mirror*: 1.12.03), who now adopted a more moderate stance towards it, but the fringe of extremism stoked from outside had grown (*Observer*: 28.7.00). As for the reform measures, these could only achieve results in the long term. They brought no immediate change to the conditions faced by the most marginalized parts of the population.

Developments on the Palestine issue added to the discomfiture of Saudi policy-makers. The intensification of conflict there, and the feelings which this engendered among Saudis and other Arabs, were fostering domestic and regional instability. The developments stoked support for extremist movements. This led the Saudi government to table a new initiative aimed at achieving an Arab Israeli peace settlement. Besides securing regional peace, the initiative offered a means whereby the Kingdom could re-build its diplomatic position: re-asserting its claim to diplomatic leadership of the Arab world and winning appreciation from the United States for adopting a constructive and conciliatory approach to Israel. In February 2002 Crown Prince 'Abdallah floated the plan, which was then submitted to the summit of Arab League heads of state in Beirut on 27 March (CRS 2003: 10). The plan was significant. Unlike previous Arab peace plans (apart from the Israeli–Egyptian Camp David agreements) it envisaged a settlement under which the Arab states would establish 'normal relations' with Israel. The commitment, then, was not simply to the recognition of Israeli sovereignty and the maintenance of peace, but to the whole range of economic, cultural and political cooperation normally conducted between states. There was, however, a significant price to be paid by the Israeli side: withdrawal from all of the territories occupied in 1967. This latter stipulation was consistent with earlier Arab peace plans (indeed, it repeated the phrase used in the 1981 Fahd Plan), but its reiteration at this time was important. The Israeli government's insistence on retaining control of most of Jerusalem and substantial tracts of the West Bank had come to be accepted by US policy-makers.

The response from the United States and other Western powers failed to do justice to the delicacy of the plan's balance. The Saudi government was congratulated for its preparedness to maintain normal relations with Israel, but the condition which accompanied the offer was down-played. President Bush, during Crown Prince 'Abdallah's visit to Texas in April 2002, described the Prince's role as 'statesmanlike', while a White House spokesman referred to 'areas of disagreement' between US and Saudi plans (CRS 2003: 10). No major outcome ensued, and the diplomatic initiative soon became lost in the build-up to conflict in Iraq.

Despite the change in the dynamics of Saudi–US relations, there was still a basis of cooperation. Saudi Arabia's interests remained closely entwined with those of the United States in terms of commercial interaction and military supplies. Its foreign assets, and the private sector's overseas holdings, remained predominantly in the United States. The United States retained its position as the major source of the Kingdom's imports and the major destination of its exports. The majority of foreign investment in Saudi Arabia still came from US companies. The attraction of Saudi Arabia's resources, indeed, still underpinned some of the political contacts between the two sides: $613 billion worth of investment opportunities were made available to US firms when Crown Prince 'Abdallah visited the United States in May 2005 (*Arab News*: 6.5.05). The visit was intended to rebuild a relationship of trust between the two countries. The United States also remained reliant on Saudi Arabia to counter pressures within the Organisation of Petroleum Exporting Countries (OPEC) for higher prices and to defuse regional antagonism to US policy in Palestine and elsewhere. Close personal links continued between some senior princes and the US presidential circle. The withdrawal of US troops, moreover, did not detract from Saudi Arabia's strategic dependence on the US presence in the region. Reliance on US military sales indeed was cperhaps even more acute in the absence of US troops.

Conclusion

The dilemma in foreign policy faced by the Saudi government in the early part of the millennium, therefore, has been how to reconcile its domestic interests, its security needs and its global strategies. While the dilemma has, in different forms, been present ever since the foundation of the Saudi state, the acuteness of the dilemma today rests on the apparent incompatibility of the different interests. It has become increasingly difficult to maintain a reasonable balance between bolstering domestic support for the regime, countering international terrorism, playing a regional role which promotes harmony and security in the Gulf and the wider Middle East, and managing the relationship with the United States so as to secure support necessary for the survival of the regime. Questions are increasingly being asked, within the country as well as outside, as to the value of preserving the dependent relationship with the United States, given the cost in other dimensions of policy. Harmonious domestic conditions and constructive relations with other regional states could benefit from a re-focusing of Saudi foreign policy. The regime would, however, need to reform its own structures and dynamics to survive the change. In the long term, Saudi Arabia's interests may well be best served by shifting its international cooperation towards the countries of South Asia and the Far East, whose rapidly growing economies and increasing political weight make them viable partners.

Conclusion

Crisis, reform and stability

The dynamics shaping developments in the different historical phases of the contemporary Saudi state have been explained. The task now is to assess whether a state ruled by the Al Su'ud will survive into the future, and if so in what form. The ascension of King 'Abdallah to the throne makes this an apposite time to take stock of the regime's strengths and weaknesses, using this as a basis to identify the factors likely to determine the regime's survival or downfall.

The assessment is best put in the context of earlier crises facing the Saudi state. As the analysis has shown, the Saudi state has passed through three periods of acute crisis since oil production began. 'Acute crisis' is one where the coherence of the state is threatened by challenges coming from the domestic or international environments. The three crisis-periods are: 1958–62, 1979–80 and the years since the mid-1990s (and especially since 2001). In each case, the threats have arisen through the failure of state policies to resolve the problems faced by, or meet the concerns of, significant parts of the population. In practice, the policies pursued by the state have themselves created the problems, as a side effect in the pursuit of other objectives.

In both of the earlier periods, there were widespread expectations in the outside world that the Saudi regime was doomed to gradual or sudden collapse. Between 1958 and 1962, the spread of Arab nationalism in the region (which had swept away the monarchies in Egypt and Iraq) seemed poised to add an Arabian Republic to the galaxy of regional republics. The Saudi monarchy seemed yet more outdated and ill-fitted to modern conditions than were those of Egypt and Iraq. In the 1979–80 period, there was among some an assumption – albeit never very realistic – that Saudi Arabia would be subject to the same process of change as Iran had been. As another pro-Western monarchy, deemed to be serving US interests and wasting money on inoperable US military equipment, the tide of Islamic radicalism would undermine the credibility of the system – prompted by guidance and encouragement from Iran – and lead to its demise. So also today, especially since 9/11 2001, forecasts of the regime's collapse have been frequent. These tend now to be centred on the perception that the regime is confronted by problems which are insuperable and will sooner or later destroy it.

A comparison with the outcome of the earlier crises may be instructive. In the 1958–62 period, the challenges faced by the regime could not have been met without a structural transformation in the Saudi state. The problems of King Saud's rule, in other words, were not simply attributable to incompetent government but to the dynamics of the state. Resources allocated according to these dynamics were not resolving the problems which were arising, but aggravating them. A strong centralised state leadership and administration was needed, capable of resolving problems directly rather than working through intermediaries. A new basis of legitimacy – complementing the existing ones – developed out of the state's direct provision of welfare, improved facilities, and development to the population. Eudaemonic legitimacy was now critical in projecting the regime's right to rule. The problems facing the state, therefore, were resolved through structural change.

In the 1979–80 crisis-period, the challenges were met by re-ordering the existing system, rather than transforming the state's processes of government. The key to the re-ordering was the renewed emphasis given to the religious circle of cooperation. The religious leaders now regained some of the direct authority, and hence intermediary role, they had lost in the 1962–79 period. They constituted once again a basis of support and not simply a source of advice and influence. At the same time, policies promoting social welfare, economic development and social infrastructure were intensified. The objective here was clearly to reinforce the regime's eudaemonic legitimacy and ensure the quiescence of the population. It has been the contention of this book that the government's decision to eschew structural political reform following the events of 1979 was a major miscalculation. Rather than moving towards greater pluralism, the regime moved towards greater rigidity – and placed a key instrument for enforcing that rigidity in the hands of the Wahhabi *'ulama*. Instead of laying the basis for a democratic/structural element in the regime's legitimacy, the regime gave strength to religious leaders intent on maintaining strict limits both on conduct and discourse. When some of the religious elements nurtured within this framework turned their criticism on the actions of the state, following the 1991 Gulf War, the state was unable to project effectively the basis of legitimacy underpinning its policy decisions.

The problems faced by the Saudi regime in its current crisis are ones which can only be remedied through structural change. A simple tampering with the existing system, as happened in 1979–80, will not suffice. The situation is more akin to that of 1958–62, although the kind of transformation required is very different. The analysis in this book has brought out three major problems facing the Saudi state today: how to make Saudi labour competitive internationally and reduce the need for migrant labour, how to maintain regime security and national security (when insecurities are in part engendered by the alliance on which security depends), and how to bring within the system some of the groupings currently alienated from it. All of these problems are already acknowledged by the Saudi regime, and some of the policies pursued by the government are intended to resolve them. Yet each of the problems, as will be shown below, is linked to characteristics intrinsic to the current structure of the Saudi state. Their resolution requires the regime to develop a new strand to its legitimacy basis, a democratic/structural one. The survival of the regime depends on its ability to do this.

First, the labour problem. The essence of this is that Saudi Arabia's further integration into the global economy, to which the government is committed for both political and economic reasons, will require labour to be employed at internationally competitive rates. The government's commitment to such integration is represented by its application for WTO membership, and a corollary is for the private sector to play an increasingly prominent role in the economy. In practice, migrant labour within the Kingdom is already employed at internationally competitive rates, whereas the remuneration and conditions of Saudi labour are above these rates. The problem can be resolved in one of two ways: either allowing the continued (and probably increased) use of migrant labour, or else reducing the levels of remuneration and protection provided for Saudi labour. The former is unacceptable to most Saudis and would undermine stability by creating an ever-increasing rate of Saudi unemployment. The latter would weaken the regime's eudaemonic basis of legitimacy, given that the regime draws support from the provision of favoured conditions to large parts of the population.

Some element of the solution can be found in strengthening eudaemonic support in other ways, through improved welfare provision and an enhanced social infrastructure from which the whole population can benefit. It would be unwise, however, to rely on this alone. The move requires developing a democratic/structural element to the legitimacy basis, if only to spread responsibility for the effects of economic restructuring. Even the improvement of welfare provision and social infrastructure necessary for eudaemonic objectives, moreover, is most effective when the population itself can take responsibility for expressing its needs and ensuring their satisfaction.

Second, the security problem. The close relationship with the United States has been a key element in maintaining the security of the regime and the state, whether from domestic or external threats. Yet the relationship also engenders some of the security threats, associating the Saudi regime with regional and global policies which significant numbers of Saudis and others in the region regard as antagonistic to Arab and Muslim interests. The domestic threat faced by the regime in the 1990s was given a focus by the presence of US troops on Saudi territory. The regime, therefore, finds itself caught in a dilemma: the satisfaction of its perceived need for US support itself increases the need for support.

The reasons for the close relationship with the United States requires some consideration. No doubt the feeling of need for US support is partially grounded in the regional balance of power and the attraction which Saudi hydrocarbon resources hold for external predatory powers. Many of the regional powers surrounding Saudi Arabia certainly have substantially larger populations and therefore the manpower to maintain larger armies (although the most powerful regional state, Israel, has a population of only a little more than a quarter that of Saudi Arabia). The regime's apparent lack of confidence in its ability to defend itself and the Saudi state unaided is, however, difficult to understand fully without taking account of the structure of the state. With up to 40 per cent of its massive budget spent on defence, and some of the most up-to-date weaponry in the world, Saudi Arabia should have the ability to operate as an effective guarantor of regional security – as well as safeguarding its own security interests.

Part of the problem may lie with the regime's reliance on legitimacy bases which are partial. As shown in Chapter 1, legitimacy which rests on religious/ideological or traditional bases is inevitably partial. Those who are not encompassed by the identity on which the legitimacy is grounded (e.g. non-Wahhabis, when the state is framed around a Wahhabi ideology) are liable to be alienated from the state. Their allegiance may be attracted through the channels of personal or eudaemonic legitimacy, but that depends on how effective the state leadership is and the extent to which it can create a shared sense of economic justice. In situations where legitimacy is partial, therefore, the opportunity exists for regime-change through the mobilisation of alienated parts of the population – presumably initiated or accompanied by a military coup. Where there are outside powers which might provide support to the alienated elements, whether through religious ethnic common feeling or political manoeuvring, the threat becomes especially acute. Although the Saudi regime has clearly sought to ensure that its military forces are grounded on parts of the population whose support is assured, and keeps the National Guard as a counterweight to the regular military forces, the edge of uncertainty remains. The outside guarantor, therefore, remains useful.

The solution to the security problem would, again, be to develop a new basis of legitimacy. What is needed is similar to that which exists in most democratic states: a conviction among all major sections of the population that the government has the right to govern, whether or not the policies it pursues are well regarded. Any attempt at military-backed change will then be met by the passive and perhaps active resistance of the population. In today's global order, moreover, resistance to the military-backed removal of democratic governments also comes from the international system, especially in countries with the regional and international importance of Saudi Arabia. The resolution of the security issue, therefore, is for the regime to develop a coherent democratic/structural basis to its legitimacy. The foreign policy options open to the government would be substantially widened.

Third, the problem of giving currently alienated groupings an incentive to abandon non-constitutional avenues of change and to work within the system. This leads directly to the need for a democratic/structural basis of legitimacy. There is here, however, a problem which needs to be recognised. As a result of the political dynamics in place since 1979, the only effective social mobilisation at the popular level has been that conducted by Islamist groupings. Such groupings have generally not overtly sought democratisation, but rather the full implementation of Islamic codes of practice. The opening of the political system to elections would almost certainly bring elements with Islamist credentials into positions of authority – as happened to a limited extent in the municipal elections. This, however, is a necessary part of a truly representative system: the outcome of popular choice must be accepted. It does not constitute a reason for delaying the process. In the longer term, there may come to be a different balance. What is important to ensure is that no grouping which wins an election can restrict the scope or character of future elections. This could be achieved by creating a strong constitution with guaranteed rights, where the royal family would act as guarantor. Introducing a framework of rights, and clear legitimation processes, then, are in the interests of the regime itself. Much of the Saudi Islamist discourse in recent times, moreover, has itself focused on issues of political legitimation: the basis on which governments in Islamic countries acquire rights to govern and the rights which individual Muslims should enjoy. The notion of an agreed framework for the conduct of government, therefore, is not alien to them.

All of the major problem-areas confronting Saudi decision-makers today, therefore, lead to a common conclusion: that the problems can only be resolved through structural reform and that the development of a democratic/structural basis of legitimacy is a necessary part of this. A simple re-ordering of the existing system will not be sufficient. The long-term survival of the Al Su'ud monarchy, then, is dependent on its ability and willingness to move back from direct political power, becoming simply a royal (rather than a ruling) family. It would remain, however, as the ultimate guarantor of the system, no doubt wielding powerful influence. Such a change is already well advanced in some other Arab monarchies, such as in Jordan and Morocco. Without a transition to democratic/structural legitimacy, the problems outlined earlier will not be resolved and will continue to create instabilities nationally, regionally and internationally.

Some may conclude from this that the Saudi regime is on the verge of collapse. It is not. The regime retains immense strengths. The vast economic resources at its disposal enable it still to defuse major short-term discontents, binding key sectors to the interests of the state. Large parts of the population retain a deep loyalty to the Al Su'ud and their rule. The armed and security forces are strong (relative to any domestic threat) and there has been no serious sign of disaffection. There is, moreover, no widely acceptable alternative to the current rulers. Unless political conflict stems from conflict within the ruling family, therefore, the collapse of the regime is highly unlikely. The instabilities referred to in the last paragraph, therefore, are ones which the system can contain and control. The danger, rather, is that the instabilities will affect the wider regional and international environments, feeding into conflict situations elsewhere. Problems of political exclusion, lack of productive employment and opposition to foreign involvement can achieve external impact through individuals taking their causes abroad, as has already happened in the case of Saudi Arabia. A simple re-ordering of the existing system will not be sufficient.

The ability of the Saudi regime to control such instabilities as may exist within the country should not be taken as an argument for gradualism. No doubt there is reason to prepare the basis for change carefully and avoid unnecessary disarray. Yet a preference for gradualism may indicate a disinclination to envisage structural change. Some of the changes which have been occurring in Saudi Arabia over the past five years have been very encouraging. The room for debate and discussion within the Kingdom has been substantially widened, such that a genuine discourse over the future development of the state is now possible. The different trends of opinion are identifiable and acknowledged, as was evident in the government's institution of a National Dialogue. Opinions critical of government policy can find expression in newspapers. But it remains true that this remains distant from a form of accountability where decisions are made by elected representatives.

The ascension of King 'Abdallah to the throne may provide the means and the incentive to change the pace of reform. While he was Crown Prince 'Abdallah showed commitment to reform, and frustration with those who delayed it. He may now feel himself in a strong enough position to carry it through. The popular respect which he enjoys, based on his considerable personal integrity, adds to the potential. Ultimately, however, the transformation of political power in Saudi Arabia can not be done only from the top, but requires the active involvement of the population – whose views need to be articulated through legitimised political organisation.

Bibliographical survey of the existing literature

The bibliographical survey provided here covers only English-language works. The practice in using references in the text has also, where possible, been restricted to English-language texts. The objective has been to present references which are easily accessible to English-medium readers. Only where there is no alternative, and a reference is deemed essential, has an Arabic-language reference been used.

The historical development of the state of Saudi Arabia during the twentieth century is now quite well covered. The expansion of Saudi control over the Arabian peninsula, the strategies which 'Abd al-'Aziz used in establishing his authority, and the relations which he forged with outside powers during the first four decades of the century were well covered in books published in the 1970s and 1980s. Among these were Helms (1981), Troeller (1976), Goldberg (1986), Habib (1978) and Leatherdale (1983). Documentary information on the same period was made available in the books produced by al-Rashid (1979–85). Some of the writings of early European travellers and visitors to the area also contained useful information on the social and economic conditions which existed in Saudi Arabia before the discovery of oil. Among these were Doughty (1888), Howarth (1964), Philby (1955), Rihani (1928), Twitchell (1953) and Wahba (1964).

More recently, and providing an excellent coverage of Saudi history, is al-Rasheed (2002). The latter brings together, and gives more analysis on, much of the earlier material, and takes the account on into the 1990s. Also important a general history is Vassiliev (1998). A specific part of the historical background, relating to the role of 'Ibn 'Abd al-Wahhab, is covered in great detail by DeLong-Bas (2004). McLoughlin (1993) has added to the knowledge about 'Abd al-'Aziz's reign, as also have Kostiner (1993) and al-Damer (2003).

General information on social, economic and political developments in Saudi Arabia since the discovery of oil was first brought together in a comprehensive way in the insightful book of Holden and Johns (1981). A more limited selection of material was presented at about the same time in the works by Lacey (1981) and Niblock (1981). Other more recent work which has taken a comprehensive look at the country are Cordesman (2003a), Champion (2003), Aarts and Nonneman (2005), Long (1997) and Abir (1988 and 1993).

A number of useful (but sometimes short) works in the late 1970s and the 1980s analysed aspects of the contemporary political system and political economy: Al-Yassini (1985) covered the role of religion in the state; Bligh (1984) the struggles for power within the Al Su'ud; Heller and Safran (1985) the role of the new middle class; Huyette (1985) the development of the Council of Ministers; Koury (1978) the decision-making system; and Lackner (1979) the economic substructure of political power. This areas of interest has attracted much more extensive writing in recent years. Some of this is from an explicitly critical viewpoint, such as the books by Aburish (1994), Jerichow (1997 and 1998), Abulkhalil (2004) and Simons (1998). Other works have been more academic studies of the political processes, as with Kechichian (2001) and Fandy (1999).

Strategic and international relations aspects have attracted considerable attention – not surprisingly in view both of Saudi Arabia's strategic significance and of the importance of these aspects to the contemporary Saudi state. Early works in this field were those by Halliday (1974), Safran (1985) and Quandt (1981). The most detailed and comprehensive information is found in the works of Cordesman (1984, 1987 and 2003b). There is now a considerable book publishing industry centred on 'Usama bin Ladin's activities, and many of these cover the Saudi background and links of 'Usama. Some of the works are sensationalist and one-dimensional, such as Bergen (2001), Gold (2003) and Schwartz (2002). Others are high-quality works which paint a well-balanced picture. Foremost among the latter are Burke (2003) and Kepel (2004).

The economy was, initially, not well covered. Some partial coverage was provided in the works by Knauerhase (1975), Carter (1977), Turner and Bedore (1979), and Moliver and Abbondante (1980). Another early work was that of El Mallakh (1982), which gave a thorough overview of the economy as it was at the turn of the 1970s/80s. This was followed by the works by Abdeen and Shook (1984), Johany *et al.* (1986), Presley and Westaway (1989) and Young (1983). More recently there have been some important works on aspects of the political economy, such as Chaudry (1997), and Wilson (2004), and a number of books looking at particular aspects of the economy. Among the latter are Azzam (1998) and Kanovsky (1994).

The social and political dimensions of the process of economic development are examined in a number of books. Abdel-Rahman (1987) and Shaw and Long (1982) looked at the general character of the development which has occurred; Birks and Sinclair (1980), Ibrahim (1982), Sirageldin *et al.* (1984) and Woodward (1988) focused on the labour market. Ibrahim and Cole (1978) and Katakura (1975) examined the impact of development policies on the bedouin. There has been surprisingly little socially based literature in recent years, but one such is Yamani (2000).

What has been covered here has been published books. There has, however, also been a large number of worthwhile and significant articles, whose titles can be accessed in the bibliography which follows. The references found in the text of this book, moreover, reveal another very important source of material: unpublished PhD theses. There are probably more unpublished theses on Saudi Arabia than on any other Arab country, and many of them are of high quality. Material on Saudi Arabia on the internet is becoming ever more essential to researchers. Most important here are the statistics which are found on the web-site of the Saudi Ministry of Planning.

Glossary

'Aqidah	belief, faith or creed
'Asabiyah **capitalism**	crony capitalism based on family connections
'Ashurah	Shiite mourning ritual
Bay'ah	pledge of allegiance
Bida'ah	innovation
Da'wah	literally, call. Used to signify a message put across by a religious teacher
Dhimmi	protected people
Diwan	court (of a ruler)
Du'ah	preachers
Fatwa	religious edict
Fiqh al-waqi'a	application of Islamic law to an actual situation
Hajj	pilgrimage
Hijra **(plural** *hujar***)**	literally meaning migration. In this text, the agricultural settlements to which the *Ikhwan* migrated.
Hizb-e-Islami	party of Islam (Afghan political party)
'Id al-adha	festival marking Abraham's willingness to obey God by sacrificing his son
Ijtihad	interpretation (of Islamic texts)
Ikhwan	literally, brothers. In this text, the brotherhood of ex-bedouin settled in the *hujar* and playing a military role in the expansion of the Saudi state
Intifadah	uprising
Al-Jama'a al-Islamiyyah	Islamic Group
Jihad	the struggle to establish the law of God on earth, interpreted by some to mean holy war
Al-Jihad al-Islami	Islamic Jihad

Kufr	unbelief
Madrasah	school
Mahdi	one sent by God to guide the Muslim community
Majlis al-Shurah	Consultative Assembly
Maktab al-Khidamat al-Mujahidin	Services Office for the *Mujahidin*
Mujahidin	fighters for a religious cause
Muwahhid (**plur:** *muwahhidun)*	upholder of the one-ness (of God)
Al-qa'idah	the base
Salaf al-Salih	the 'pious forefathers', comprising the prophet's companions and the first three generations of the Muslim *ummah*
Shari'ah	Islamic law
Shirk	idolatry or polytheism
Shurah	consultation
Sunnah	the reported sayings and deeds of the prophet
Taqlid	tradition
Tawhid	one-ness (of God)
'Ulama	religious leaders/scholars
Ummah	the Muslim community
Zakat	taxation based on Islamic precepts

Bibliography

Books, reports and theses

Aarts, Paul and Nonneman, Gerd. (2005) *Saudi Arabia in the Balance: Political Economy, Society, Foreign Relations*. London: Hurst.

Abdeen, Adnan M. and Shook, Dale N. (1984) *The Saudi Financial System*. New York: John Wiley.

Abdel-Rahman, Osama. (1987) *The Dilemma of Development in the Arabian Peninsula*. London: Croom Helm.

Abir, Mordechai. (1974) *Oil, Power and Politics: Conflict in Arabia, the Red Sea and the Gulf*. London: Frank Cass.

—— (1988) *Saudi Arabia in the Oil Era: Regime and Elites: Conflict and Collaboration*. London: Croom Helm.

—— (1993) *Saudi Arabia: Government, Society and the Gulf Crisis*. London: Routledge.

Abukhalil, As'ad. (2004) *The Battle for Saudi Arabia: Royalty, Fundamentalism, and Global Power*. New York: Seven Stories.

Aburish, Saïd K. (1994) *The Rise, Corruption and Coming Fall of the House of Saud*. London: Bloomsbury.

Al-Ajmi, Khaled M. (2003) *Quality and Employability in Higher Education: The Case of Saudi Arabia*. PhD Dissertation, Middlesex University.

Albers, Henry Herman. (1989) *Saudi Arabia: Technocrats in a Traditional Society*. New York: Peter Lang.

Algosaibi, Ghazi. (2002) *Al-'Awlamah wa al-Huwiyah al-Wataniyah* (Globalisation and National Identity). Al-Riyadh: Maktabat al-'Ubayk.

Almana, Mohammed. (1980) *Arabia Unified: A Portrait of Ibn Saud*. London: Hutchinson Benham.

Almutlaq, Mohamed. (1995) *The Role of Foreign Aid in Saudi Arabia's Foreign Policy with Sub-Saharan African Countries as a Case Study (1975–1992)*. PhD Dissertation, University of Exeter.

Alshamsi, Mansoor J. (2003) *The Discourse and Performance of the Saudi Sunni Islamic Reformist Leadership 1981–2003*. PhD Dissertation, University of Exeter.

Anderson, I. (1981) *ARAMCO, The United States, and Saudi Arabia: A Study of the Dynamics of Foreign Oil Policy, 1933–50*. Princeton, NJ: Princeton University Press.

Al-Angari, AbdulRaman N. (2002) *The Palestine Issue in Saudi Arabian Foreign Policy*. Riyadh: Alangari.

Al-Awaji, Ibrahim M. (1971) *Bureaucracy and Society in Saudi Arabia*. PhD Dissertation, University of Virginia.

Al-Azma, Talal S.M. (1999) *The Role of the Ikhwan under 'Abdul-'Aziz Al Sa'ud 1916–1934*. PhD Dissertation, University of Durham.

Al-Damer, Shafi. (2003) *Saudi Arabia and Britain, 1939–1953*. Reading, PA: Ithaca.

Azzam, Henry. (1988) *The Gulf Economies in Transition*. London: Macmillan.

—— (1997) *The Emerging Arab Capital Markets: Investment Opportunities in Relatively Underplayed Markets*. London: Kegan Paul.

Baer, Robert. (2003) *Sleeping with the Devil*. New York: Crown.

Bakr, Mohammed A. (2001) *A Model in Privatization: Successful Change Management in the Ports of Saudi Arabia*. London: London Centre of Arab Studies.

Bangash, Zafar. (1988) *The Makkah Massacre and Future of the Haramain*. London: Open Press.

Barsalou, Judith M. (1985) *Foreign Labor in Sa'udi Arabia: The Creation of a Plural Society*. PhD Dissertation, Columbia University.

Basbous, Antoine. (2002) *L'Arabie Saoudite en Question*. Paris: Perrin.

Beling, Willard A. (1980) *King Faisal and the Modernisation of Saudi Arabia*. Boulder, CO: Westview.

Benoist-Méchin, Jacques. (1975) *Fayçal, Roi d'Arabie: l'Homme, le Souverain, sa Place dans le Monde (1906–1975)*. Albin Michel: Paris.

Bergen, Peter L. (2001) *Holy War Inc: Inside the Secret World of Osama bin Laden*, London: Weidenfeld and Nicolson.

Birks, J.S. and Sinclair, C.A. (1980a) *Arab Manpower: The Crisis of Development*. London: Croom Helm.

Bligh, Alexander. (1984) *From Prince to King: Royal Succession in the House of Saud*. New York: New York University Press.

Burke, James. (2003) *Al-Qaeda: The True Story of Radical Islam*. London: Penguin.

Carter, John R.L. (1977) *Leading Merchant Families of Saudi Arabia*. London: Scorpion.

CATO Institute. (2004) *CATO Handbook for Congress*. Washington, DC: CATO Institute.

Champion, Daryl. (2003) *The Paradoxical Kingdom*. New York: Columbia University Press.

Chaudry, Kiren A. (1997) *The Price of Wealth: Economies and Institutions in the Middle East*. Ithaca, NY: Cornell University Press.

Chubin, Shahram, ed. (1980) *Security in the Gulf. Vol 1: Domestic Political Factors*. London: International Institute for Strategic Studies.

Cobban, Helena. (1985) *The Making of Modern Lebanon*. London: Hutchinson.

Cole, Donald P. (1975) *Nomads of the Nomads: The Al-Murrah of the Empty Quarter*. Chicago, IL: Aldine.

Congressional Research Service (CRS). (1996) *Saudi Arabia: Post-War Issues and US Relations*. Washington, DC: Library of Congress.

—— (2003) *Saudi Arabia: Current Issues and US Relations*. Washington, DC: Library of Congress.

Cordesman, Anthony. (1984) *The Gulf and the Search for Strategic Security: Saudi Arabia, the Military Balance in the Gulf, and Trends in the Arab–Israeli Military Balance*. London: Mansell.

—— (1987) *Western Strategic Interests in Saudi Arabia*, London: Croom Helm.

—— (1988) *The Gulf and the West: Strategic Relations and Military Realities*. London: Mansell.

—— (2003a) *Saudi Arabia Enters the Twenty-First Century: The Military and International Security Dimensions*. London: Praeger.

—— (2003b) *Saudi Arabia Enters the Twenty-First Century: The Political, Foreign Policy, Economic, and Energy Dimensions*. London: Praeger.

Dahlan, Ahmed H. (1990) *Politics, Administration and Development in Saudi Arabia*. Brentwood: Amana.

De Corancez, Louis. (1995) *The History of the Wahabis from their Origin until the End of 1809*. Reading, PA: Ithaca.

Deffeyes, Kenneth S. (2001) *Hubbert's Peak: The Impending World Oil Shortage*. Princeton, NJ: Princeton University Press.

De Gaury, Gerald. (1966) *Faisal: King of Saudi Arabia*. London: Barker.

DeLong-Bas, Natana. (2004) *Wahhabi Islam: From Revival and Reform to Global Jihad*. New York: Oxford University Press.

Dequin, Horst. (1967) *The Challenge of Saudi Arabia: The Regional Setting and Economic Development as a Result of the Conquest of the Arabian Peninsula by King 'Abdul 'Aziz Al Sa'ud*. Hamburg: D.R.Gotze.

Doughty, Charles M. (1964) *Travels in Arabia Deserta*. London: Jonathan Cape. First published in 1888.

Dresch, Paul and Piscatori, James, eds. (2005) *Monarchies and Nations: Globalisation and Identity in the Arab States of the Gulf*. London: I.B.Tauris.

Dun and Bradstreet. (2004) *Country Report: Saudi Arabia*. London: Dun and Bradstreet.

Economist Intelligence Unit. (2004) *Country Report: Saudi Arabia*. London: EIU. May.

Elmadani, Abdulla. (2003) *Indo-Saudi Relations 1947–1997: Domestic Concerns and Foreign Relations*. PhD Dissertation, University of Exeter.

El Mallakh, Ragaei. (1982) *Saudi Arabia: Rush to Development; Profile of an Energy Economy and Investment*. London: Croom Helm.

Fandy, Mamoun. (1999) *Saudi Arabia and the Politics of Dissent*. New York: St Martin's Press.

Al-Farsy, Fouad. (1980) *Saudi Arabia: A Case Study in Development*. London: Stacey International.

Field, Michael. (1984) *The Merchants: The Big Business Families of Arabia*. London: John Murray.

Galindo-Marines, Alejandra. (2001) *The Relationship Between the Ulama and the Government in the Contemporary Saudi Arabian Kingdom: An Interdependent Relationship?* PhD Dissertation, University of Durham.

Gold, Dore. (2003) *Hatred's Kingdom: How Saudi Arabia Supports the New Global Terrorism*. Washington, DC: Regenery.

Goldberg, Jacob. (1986) *The Foreign Policy of Saudi Arabia: The Formative Years, 1902–18*. Cambridge, MA: Harvard University Press.

Graham, Douglas F. (1991) *Saudi Arabia Unveiled*. Dubuque: Kendall/Hunt.

Grayson, Benson Lee. (1982) *Saudi–American Relations*. Washington, DC: University Press of America.

Gros, Marcel. (1976) *Feisal of Arabia: The Ten Years of a Reign*. London: Emgé-Sepix.

Gunaratna, Rohan. (2002) *Inside Al Qaeda: Global Network of Terror*. London: Hurst.

Habib, John S. (1978) *Ibn Saud's Warriors of Islam: The Ikhwan of Najd and their Role in the Creation of the Saudi Kingdom, 1910–30*. Leiden: Brill.

Hajrah, Hassan Hamza. (1982) *Public Land Distribution in Saudi Arabia*. London: Longman.

Halliday, Fred. (1974) *Arabia without Sultans*. Harmondsworth: Pelican.

—— (1982) *Threat from the East*. Harmondsworth: Penguin.

Al-Hamid, 'Abdallah. (1995) *Huquq al-Islam bayn al-Adl al-Islam wa Jawr al-Hukum* (Human Rights between the Justice of Islam and the Oppression of Governments). London: Committee for the Defence of Legitimate Rights in Saudi Arabia.

Al-Harthi, Mohammed A. (2000) *The Political Economy of Labor in Saudi Arabia: The Causes of Labor Shortage*. PhD Dissertation, State University of New York.

Heikal, Mohamed. (1975) *The Road to Ramadan*. London: Collins.

Heinberg, Richard. (2003) *The Party's Over: Oil, War and the Fate of Industrial Societies*. East Sussex: Clairview.

Heller, Mark and Safran, Nadav. (1985) *The New Middle Class and Regime Stability in Saudi Arabia*. Cambridge, MA: Centre for Middle Eastern Studies, Harvard University.

Helms, Christine Moss. (1981) *The Cohesion of Saudi Arabia: Evolution of Political Identity*. London: Croom Helm.

Henderson, Simon. (1994) *After King Fahd: Succession in Saudi Arabia*. Washington, DC: Washington Institute for Near East Policy.

Holden, David and Johns, Richard. (1981) *The House of Saud*. London: Sidgwick and Jackson.

Hopwood, Derek, ed. (1972) *The Arabian Peninsula: Society and Politics*. London: Allen and Unwin.

Howarth, David Armine. (1964) *The Desert King: A Life of Ibn Saud*. London: Collins.

Hudson, Michael C. (1977) *Arab Politics: The Search for Legitimacy*. New Haven, CT: Yale University Press.

Al-Humaid, Mohammed, I.A. (2003) *The Factors Affecting the Process of Saudization in the Private Sector in the Kingdom of Saudi Arabia: A Case Study of Riyadh City*. PhD Dissertation, University of Exeter.

Hussein, Abdul-Rahman A. (1995) *Alliance Behavior and the Foreign Policy of Saudi Arabia, 1979–1991*. PhD Dissertation, George Washington University.

Huyette, Summer Scott. (1985) *Political Adaptation in Saudi Arabia: A Study of the Council of Ministers*. Boulder, CO: Westview.

Ibrahim, Saad Eddin. (1982) *The New Arab Social Order: A Study of the Social Impact of Oil Wealth*. Boulder, CO: Westview.

Ibrahim, Saad Eddin and Cole, Donald P. (1978) *Saudi Arabian Bedouin: An Assessment of their Needs*. Cairo: American University Cairo.

Islami, A., Reza S. and Kavoussi, Rostam Mehraban. (1984) *The Political Economy of Saudi Arabia*. Seattle, DC: University of Washington Press.

Jerichow, Anders. (1997) *Saudi Arabia: Outside Global Law and Order*. London: Curzon.

—— (1998) *The Saudi File: People, Power, Politics*. New York: St Martin's Press.

Johany, Ali D. (1980) *The Myth of the OPEC Cartel: The Role of Saudi Arabia*. New York: John Wiley.

Johany, Ali D., Berne, Michele and Mixon J. Wilson. (1986) *The Saudi Arabian Economy*. London: Croom Helm.

Al Juhany, Uwaidah M. (2002) *Najd Before the Salafi Reform Movement*. Reading, PA: Ithaca.

Kanovsky, Eliyahu. (1994) *The Economy of Saudi Arabia: Troubled Present, Grim Future*. Washington, DC: Washington Institute for Near East Policy.

Katakura, Motoko. (1977) *Bedouin Village: A Study of Saudi Arabian People in Transition*. Tokyo: University of Tokyo Press.

Kechichian, Joseph A. (2001) *Succession in Saudi Arabia*. New York: Palgrave.

Kepel, Gilles. (2004) *The War for Muslim Minds: Islam and the West*. Cambridge, MA: Harvard University Press.

Kerr, Malcolm H. and Yassin, El-Sayed. (1982) *Rich and Poor States in the Middle East*. Boulder, CO: Westview.

Khashoggi, Hani. (1979) *Local Administration in Saudi Arabia*. PhD dissertation, Claremont Graduate School.

Kingdom of Saudi Arabia, Central Planning Organisation (KSA-CPO). (1970) *First Development Plan, 1970–75*. Riyadh: Central Planning Organisation.

Kingdom of Saudi Arabia, Ministry of Planning (KSA-MP). (1975) *Second Development Plan, 1975–80*. Riyadh: Ministry of Planning.

—— (1980) *Third Development Plan, 1980–85*. Riyadh: Ministry of Planning.

—— (2000) *Seventh Development Plan, 2000–2004*. Riyadh: Ministry of Planning Press.

Knauerhase, Ramon. (1975) *The Saudi Arabian Economy*. New York: Praeger.

Kostiner, Joseph. (1993) *The Making of Saudi Arabia 1916–1936*. Oxford: Oxford University Press.

Koury, Enver M. (1978) *The Saudi Decision-Making Body: The House of Saud*. Washington, DC: Institute of Middle Eastern and North African Affairs.

Labooncharoen, Nontaporn. (1997) *The United States and Human Rights in Saudi Arabia* MA thesis, University of Durham.

Lacey, Robert. (1981) *The Kingdom: Arabia and the House of Saud*. London: Hutchinson.

Lackner, Helen. (1978) *House Built on Sand: A Political Economy of Saudi Arabia*. London: Ithaca.

League of Arab States (LAS). (1985) *Al-Qararat al-Siyasiyyat al-Khassah bi Qadiyah Falastin* (The Political Resolutions of the Arab League). Tunis: League of Arab States.

Leatherdale, Clive. (1983) *Britain and Saudi Arabia, 1925–39: The Imperial Oasis*. London: Frank Cass.

Lees, Brian M. (1980) *A Handbook of the Al Sa'ud Ruling Family of Saudi Arabia*. London: Royal Genealogies.

Lippman, Thomas W. (2004) *Inside the Mirage: America's Fragile Partnership with Saudi Arabia*. Boulder, CO: Westview.

Lipset, Seymour. (1960) *Political Man*. New York: Doubleday.

Long, David E. (1997) *The Kingdom of Saudi Arabia*. Gainesville, FL: University Press of Florida.

Looney, Robert E. (1982) *Saudi Arabia's Development Potential: An Application of an Islamic Growth Model*. Lexington, KY: Lexington Books.

Al-Mabrouk, Saud A. (1991) *'Dutch Disease' in a 'Small' Open Economy: The Case of Oil in Saudi Arabia*. PhD Dissertation, Colorado State University.

Mackey, Sandra. (2002) *The Saudis: Inside the Desert Kingdom*. New York: Norton.

McKillop, Andrew and Sheila Newman, eds. (2005) *The Final Energy Crisis*. London: Pluto.

McLoughlin, Leslie. (1993) *Ibn Saud: Founder of a Kingdom*. London: Macmillan.

Madani, Nizar O. (1977) *The Islamic Content of the Foreign Policy of Saudi Arabia; King Faisal's Call for Islamic Solidarity 1965–1975*. PhD Dissertation, The American University, Washington DC.

Malik, Monica. (1999) *Private Sector and the State in Saudi Arabia*. PhD Dissertation, University of Durham.

Marchand, Stéphane (2003) *Arabie Saoudite: La Menace*. Paris: Fayard.

Metz, Helen. (1993) *Saudi Arabia: A Country Study*. Washington, DC: Library of Congress.

Miller, Aaron David. (1980) *Search for Security: Saudi Arabian Oil and American Foreign Policy, 1939–49*. Chapel Hill, NC: University of North Carolina Press.

Moliver, D. and Abbondante, P. (1980) *The Saudi Arabian Economy*. New York: Praeger.

Moore, Michael. (2003) *Dude, Where's my Country?* London: Penguin.

Nahedh, Munira. (1989) *The Sedentarisation of a Bedouin Community in Saudi Arabia*. PhD Dissertation, University of Leeds.

Al-Naqeeb, Khaldoun Hasan. (1990) *Society and State in the Gulf and Arab Peninsula: A Different Perspective*. London: Routledge.

Niblock, Tim ed. (1980) *Social and Economic Development in the Arab Gulf*. London: Croom Helm.

Niblock, Tim ed. (1981) *State, Society and Economy in Saudi Arabia*. London: Croom Helm.

—— ed. (1982) *Iraq: The Contemporary State*. London: Croom Helm.

—— (2000) *'Pariah States' and Sanctions in the Middle East: Iraq, Libya and Sudan*. London: Lynne Rienner.

Nyrop, Richard F. (1985) *Area Handbook for Saudi Arabia, 4th. Edition*. Washington, DC: Government Printing Office.

Okruhlik, Mary G. (1992) *Debating Profits and Political Power: Private Business and Government in Saudi Arabia*. PhD Dissertation, University of Texas.

Oliver, Haneef J. (2002) *The 'Wahhabi' Myth: Dispelling Prevalent Fallacies and the Fictitious Link with Bin Laden*. Victoria: Trafford.

Al-Osaimi, Mohammed. (2000) *The Politics of Persuasion: The Islamic Oratory of King Faisal Ibn Abdul Aziz*. Riyadh: King Faisal Center for Research and Islamic Studies.

Philby, Harry St John Bridger. (1955) *Sa'udi Arabia*. London: Benn.

Population Reference Bureau. (2004) *2004 World Population Data Sheet*. Washington, DC: PRB.

Presley, John R. and Westaway, A.J. (1989) *A Guide to the Saudi Arabian Economy*. London: Macmillan.

Quandt, William B. (1981) *Saudi Arabia in the 1980s: Foreign Policy, Security and Oil*. Washington, DC: Brookings Institution.

—— (1982) *Saudi Arabia's Oil Policy*. Washington, DC: Brookings Institution.

Al-Rasheed, Madawi. (2002) *A History of Saudi Arabia*. Cambridge: Cambridge University Press.

Al-Rashid, Ibrahim, ed. (1976–85) *Documents on the History of Arabia. Vol.1: The Unification of Central Arabia under Ibn Saud; Vol.2: The Consolidation of Power in Central Arabia, 1925–28; Vol.3: The Establishment of the Kingdom of Saudi Arabia under Ibn Saud, 1928–35; Vol.4: Saudi Arabia Enters the Modern World: 1936–49(i); Vol.5: Saudi Arabia Enters the Modern World: 1936–49(ii); Vol.8: The Struggle between the Two Princes: The Kingdom of Saudi Arabia in the Final Days of Ibn Saud*. Chapel Hill, NC: Documentary Publications.

Rashid, Nasser I. and Shaheen, Esber I. (1987) *King Fahd and Saudi Arabia's Great Evolution*. Missouri, MO: International Institute of Technology.

Al-Rawaf, Othman. (1980) *The Concept of Five Crises in Political Development: Relevance to the Kingdom of Saudi Arabia*. PhD dissertation, Duke University.

Rihani, Ameen. (1928) *Ibn Sa'oud of Arabia: His Land and People*. London: Constable.

Robinson, Jeffrey. (1988) *Yamani: The Inside Story*. London: Simon & Schuster.

Ruthven, Malise. (2002) *A Fury for God: The Islamist Attack on America*. London: Granta.

Sabini, John. (1981) *Armies in the Sand*. London: Thames and Hudson.

Sabri, Sharaf. (2001) *The House of Saud in Commerce*. New Delhi: I.S. Publications.

Safran, Nadav. (1985) *Saudi Arabia: The Ceaseless Quest for Security*. Cambridge, MA: Harvard University Press.

Saif, Ahmed A. (2004a) *Constitutionalism in the Arab Gulf States*. Dubai: Gulf Research Center.

Saif, Ahmed A. (2004b) *Arab Gulf Judicial Structures*. Dubai: Gulf Research Center.

Salamé, Ghassan. (1987) *The Foundations of the Arab State*. London: Croom Helm.

Samore, Gary S. (1984) *Royal Family Politics in Saudi Arabia (1953–1982)*. PhD Dissertation, Harvard University.

Sandwick, John A., ed. (1987) *The Gulf Cooperation Council: Moderation and Stability in an Interdependent World*. Boulder, CO: Westview.

Al-Saud, Faisal bin M. (1988) *The Democratic Experience in the Saudi 'Open Meeting'*. PhD Dissertation, State University of California.

Al-Saud, Faisal bin S. (2003) *Iran, Saudi Arabia and the Gulf: Power Politics in Transition*. London: I.B. Tauris.

Saudi-American Bank (SAMBA). (2002) *Saudi Arabia's Employment Profile*. Riyadh: SAMBA.

Saudi Arabian Monetary Agency (SAMA). (1998) *Thirty-Fourth Annual Report*. Riyadh: Saudi Arabia.

Schwartz, Stephen. (2002) *The Two Faces of Islam: The House of Saud from Tradition to Terror*. New York: Doubleday.

Scoville, Sheila A., ed. (1979–95) *Gazetteer of Arabia: A Geographical and Tribal History of the Arabian Peninsula*. 3 Vols. Graz: Akademische Druck.

Al-Seflan, Ali M. (1981) *The Essence of Tribal Leaders' Participation, Responsibilities, and Decisions in Some Local Government Activities in Saudi Arabia: A Case Study of the Ghamid and Zahran Tribes*. PhD Dissertation, Claremont Graduate School.

Shaw, John A. and Long, David E. (1982) *Saudi Arabian Modernisation: The Impact of Change on Stability*. New York: Praeger.

Sheean, Vincent. (1975) *Faisal: The King and his Kingdom*. Tavistock: University Press of Arabia.

Simons, Geoff. (1998) *Saudi Arabia: The Shape of a Client Feudalism*. New York: St Martin's Press.

Sirageldin, Ismail A., Sherbiny, Naim A. and Ismail Sirageldin, M. (1984) *Saudis in Transition: The Challenges of a Changing Labour Market*. Oxford: Oxford University Press.

Spitaels, Guy. (2005) *La Triple Insurrection Islamiste*. Paris: Fayard.

Sultan, Khaled bin. (1995) *Desert Warrior: A Personal View of the Gulf War by the Joint Forces Commander*. London: HarperCollins.

Tbeileh, Faisal H. (1991) *The Political Economy of Legitimacy in Rentier States: A Comparative Study of Saudi Arabia and Libya*. PhD Dissertation, University of California.

Transparency International. (2004) *Background Paper to the 2004 Corruption Perceptions Index: Framework Document*. Berlin: Transparency International.

Troeller, Gary. (1976) *The Birth of Saudi Arabia: Britain and the Rise of the House of Sa'ud*. London: Frank Cass.

Turner, Louis and Bedore, James M. (1979) *Middle East Industrialisation: A Study of Saudi and Iranian Downstream Investments*. London: Royal Institute for International Affairs.

Twitchell, Karl S. (1953) *Saudi Arabia, with an Account of the Development of its Natural Resources*. Princeton, NJ: Princeton University Press.

United Nations Conference on Trade and Development (UNCTAD). (2004a) *World Investment Report*. Geneva: UNCTAD.

United States Department of Defence. (1992) *Conduct of the Persian Gulf War: The Final Report to the US Congress by the US Department of Defence*, Washington, DC: Department of Defence.

United States Department of State. (1995) *Country Report on Saudi Arabia Human Rights Practices*. Washington, DC: Department of State.

United States National Commission on Terrorist Attacks upon the United States (US-NC). (2004) *The 9/11 Commission Report: The Full Final Report of the National Commission on Terrorist Attacks upon the United States*. Washington, DC: US Government.

Vassiliev, Alexei. (1998) *The History of Saudi Arabia*. London: Saqi Books.

Vogel, Frank. (2000) *Islamic Law and Legal System: Studies of Saudi Arabia*. Leiden: Brill.

Wahba, Hafiz. (1964) *Arabian Days*. London: Barker.

Wilson, Rodney, Al-Rajhi, Ahmed, Al-Salamah, Abdullah and Malik, Monica. (2004) *Economic Development in Saudi Arabia*. London: RoutledgeCurzon.

Winder, Richard B. (1965) *Saudi Arabia in the Nineteenth Century*. New York: St Martin's Press.

Woodward, Peter. (1988) *Oil and Labour in the Middle East: Saudi Arabia and the Oil Boom*. New York: Praeger.

World Bank. (2004) *World Bank Indicators*. Washington, DC: World Bank.

World Migration Organisation (WMO). (2003) *World Migration 2003: Managing Migration*. Geneva: WMO.

Yamani, Mai. (2000) *Changed Identities: The Challenge of the New Generation in Saudi Arabia*. London: Royal Institute of International Affairs.

—— (2004) *Cradle of Islam: The Hijaz and the Quest for an Arabian Identity*. London: I.B. Tauris.

Al-Yassini, Ayman. (1985) *Religion and State in the Kingdom of Saudi Arabia*. Boulder, CO: Westview.

Young, Arthur N. (1983) *Saudi Arabia: The Making of a Financial Giant*. New York: New York University Press.

Zogby, James. (2002) *What Arabs Think: Values, Beliefs and Concerns*. Utica: Zogby International.

Articles, chapters in books and conference papers

Birks, J.S. and Sinclair, C.A. (1980b) 'The Oriental Connection', in Tim Niblock, ed., *Social and Economic Development in the Arab Gulf*. London: Croom Helm, pp. 135–160.

Bligh, Alexander. (1985) 'The Saudi Religious Elite (ulama) as Participant in the Political System of the Kingdom', *International Journal of Middle East Studies*, v. 17, n. 1, February, pp. 37–50.

Buchan, James. (1981) 'Secular and Religious Opposition in Saudi Arabia', in Tim Niblock, ed., *State, Society and Economy in Saudi Arabia*. London: Croom Helm, pp. 106–124.

Butterworth, Charles. (1982) 'Prudence against Legitimacy: The Persistent Theme in Islamic Political Thought', in Ali E. Hillal Dessouki, ed., *Islamic Resurgence in the Arab World*. New York and London: Praeger, pp. 84–115.

Cohen, R. (1979) 'Human Rights and Decision Making in the Executive Branch: Some Proposals for a Coordinated Strategy', in Donald Kommers and Loescher Gilbert, eds, *Human Rights and American Foreign Policy*. Notre Dame: Notre Dame Press, pp. 216–246.

Doumato, Eleanor. (1995) 'The Ambiguity of Shariah and the Politics of Rights', in Mahnaz Afkhami, ed., *Faith and Freedom*. London: I.B. Tauris, pp. 135–160.

Gause, Gregory. (2002) 'US-GCC Relations: The Coming Turning Point', Paper Presented to the Gulf Research Council (Dubai) Conference, 5 January.

Halliday, Fred. (1980) 'The Gulf Between Two Revolutions', in Tim Niblock, ed., *Social and Economic Development in the Arab Gulf*. London: Croom Helm, pp. 210–238.

International Monetary Fund. (1999) 'Saudi Arabia: Staff Report for the 1999 Article IV Consultation', Unpublished report, Washington, DC: IMF, 14 September.

——(2001) 'IMF Concludes 2001 Article IV Consultation with Saudi Arabia', Public Information Notice 01/119, Washington, DC: IMF.

——(2005) 'IMF Concludes 2004 Article IV Consultation with Saudi Arabia', Public Information Notice no. 05/3, Washington, DC: IMF, 12 January 2005.

Kechichian, Joseph A. (1986) 'The Role of the Ulama in the Politics of an Islamic State: The Case of Saudi Arabia', *International Journal of Middle Eastern Studies*, v. 18, n. 1, February, pp. 53–71.

Lacroix, Stephane. (2004) 'Between Islamists and Liberals: Saudi Arabia's New "Islamo-Liberal" Reformists', *Middle East Journal*. v. 58, n. 3, Summer, pp. 345–365.

Mejcher, Helmut. (2004) 'King Faisal Ibn Abdul Aziz Al Saud in the Arena of World Politics: A Glimpse from Washington, 1950 to 1971', *British Journal of Middle Eastern Studies*, v. 21, n. 1, May, pp. 5–24.

Naim, Moises. (1999) 'Fads and Fashions in Economic Reforms: Washington Consensus or Washington Confusion?' Paper prepared for the IMF Conference on Second Generation Reforms.

Niblock, Tim. (1985) 'Oil, Political and Social Dynamics of the Arab Gulf States', *The Arab Gulf Journal*, v. 5, n. 1, April, pp. 37–46.

—— (2003) 'Reform and Reconstruction in the Middle East: Room for EU–US Cooperation?' *The International Spectator*, n. 4, pp. 47–58.

Ochsenwald, William. (1981) 'Saudi Arabia and the Islamic Revival', *International Journal of Middle East Studies*, v. 13, n. 3, August, pp. 271–286.

Peterson, John. (1987) 'The GCC and Regional Security', in John Sandwick, ed., *The Gulf Cooperation Council: Moderation and Stability in an Interdependent World*. Boulder, CO: Westview, pp. 169–203.

Piscatori, James P. (1983) 'Islamic Values and National Interest: The Foreign Policy of Saudi Arabia', in Dawisha, Adeed, ed., *Islam in Foreign Policy*. Cambridge: Cambridge University Press, pp. 33–53.

Al-Rasheed, Madawi. (1998) 'The Sh'ia of Saudi Arabia: A Minority in Search of Cultural Authenticity', v. 25, n. 1, May, pp. 121–138.

Rugh, William A. (1973) 'The Emergence of a New Middle Class in Saudi Arabia', *Middle East Journal*, n. 27, Winter, pp. 7–20.

Salameh, Ghassan. (1980) 'Political Power and the Saudi State', *MERIP Reports*, n. 91, Spring, pp. 20–25.

—— (1981) 'Saudi Arabia: Development and Dependence', *Jerusalem Quarterly*, n. 20, Summer, pp. 109–122.

—— (1987) 'Islam and Politics in Saudi Arabia', *Arab Studies Quarterly*, Summer, pp. 306–326.

Stevens, Paul. (1981) 'Saudi Arabia's Oil Production', in Tim Niblock, ed., *State, Society and Economy in Saudi Arabia*. London: Croom Helm, pp. 214–234.

Wenner, Manfred W. (1975) 'Saudi Arabia: Survival of Traditional Elites', in Tachau, Frank, ed., *Political Elites and Political Development in the Middle East*. New York: Shenkman, pp. 157–192.

Zahid, Khan. (2004) 'Investment Challenges Facing Oil-Rich MENA Countries: The Case of Saudi Arabia', Paper presented to the OECD conference Mobilising Investment for Development in the Middle East and North Africa Region, held in Istanbul, 11–12 February.

Internet sources

AMEINFO. (2003) 'Prince Sultan bin Salman bin Abdulaziz Highlights Tourism Opportunities.' Accessed at www.ameinfo.com/28402.html, January 2005.

—— (2004) 'Saudi Arabia Stock Market Dealings.' Accessed at www.ameinfo.com.financial_markets/Saudi_Arabia, December 2004.

—— (2005) 'Can Saudi Arabia Ever Join the WTO?' Accessed at www.ame-info.com/ news/Detailed/42278.html, January 2005.

Arab Gateway. (2004) 'National Reform Document.' Accessed at www.al-bab.com/arab/docs/saudi/reform2003.htm, October 2004.

Al-Auda, Salman. (2003) *'Al-Shari'ah wa al-Hurriyah'* (Islamic Law and Freedom). Accessed at www.islamtoday.net/nprint.cfm?artid = 1549, July 2003.

EUbusiness. (2003a) 'EU backs Saudi Arabia Joining WTO.' Accessed at www.eubusiness. com/afp/030829173232.fnyapsil, December 2004.

—— (2003b) 'EU Trade Deal Brings Saudi Arabia Closer to WTO Membership.' Accessed at www.eubusiness.com/afp/030829173232.fnyapsil, December 2004.

Kingdom of Saudi Arabia, Central Department of Statistics (KSA-CDS). (2005) 'Social Statistics Labour Force Survey.' Accessed at www.planning.gov.sa/statistic/sindexe.htm, February 2005.

Kingdom of Saudi Arabia, Council of Ministers (KSA-CM). (1997) 'Privatisation Objectives and Policies.' Decision no. 60, August 1997. Accessed at www.sec.gov.sa/english/list.asp?s_contentid = 22&s_title+&ContentType = &Cat, February 2004.

—— (2004) 'The Patent Law 2004.' Decision no. 56, July 2004. Accessed at www.the-saudi.net/business-center/patentlaw.htm, October 2004.

Kingdom of Saudi Arabia, Ministry of Planning (KSA-MP). (2005) 'Achievements of the Development Plans, 1970–2000: Statistical Tables.' Accessed at www.planning.gov.sa/ PLANNING/INTROe.htm, July 2005.

Kingdom of Saudi Arabia, Supreme Economic Council (KSA-SEC). (2005) 'Privatisation Objectives and Policies.' Accessed at www.sec.gov.sa/english/list.asp?s_contentid = 22&s_title+&ContentType = &Cat, January 2005.

Migration Policy Institute. (2005) 'Saudi Arabia's Plan for Changing its Workforce.' Accessed at www.migrationinformation.org, January 2005.

National Commercial Bank (NCB). (2004) 'Saudi Arabia: Business and Economic Developments.' Accessed at www.saudieconomicsurvey.com/html/reports.html, January 2005.

Saudi Arabia Information Resource (SA-IR). (2005a) 'Kingdom's Population Figures.' Accessed at www.saudinf.com/main/y7651.htm, July 2005.

—— (2005b) 'Supreme Economic Council.' Accessed at www.saudinf.com/main/e111.htm, March 2005.

Saudi Arabian Capital Markets Authority (SACMA). (2005) 'About the Capital Markets Authority.' Accessed at www.cma.org.sa, January 2005.

Saudi Arabian General Investment Authority (SAGIA). (2004a) 'Basic Issues to be Dealt with in the Privatisation Process.' Accessed at www.sagia.gov.sa/innerpage.asp, December 2004.

—— (2004b) 'Capital Markets Law 2003.' Accessed at www.sagia.gov.sa, December 2004.

—— (2004c) 'Copyright Law 2003.' Accessed at www.sagia.gov.sa, December 2004.

—— (2004d) 'Corporate Tax Law 2004.' Accessed at www.sagia.gov.sa, December 2004.

—— (2004e) 'Foreign Direct Investment Law 2000.' Accessed at www.sagia.gov.sa, December 2004.

—— (2004f) 'Privatisation Announcements.' Accessed at www.sagia.gov.sa/innerpage.asp December 2004.

—— (2004g) 'Real Estate Law 2000.' Accessed at www.sagia.gov.sa, December 2004.

—— (2005a) 'Gas Projects.' Accessed at http://www.sagia.gov.sa/innerpage.asp?ContentID = 7&Lang = en&NewsID = 238, January 2005.

—— (2005b) 'Negative List.' Accessed at www.sagia.gov.sa/innerpage.asp, February 2005.

Saudi Constitutional and Civil Society Reform Advocates (SCCSRA). (2005) 'Urgent Appeal to Parliaments of Permanent Members of UN Security Council.' Accessed at www.metransparent.com/texts/saudi_constitutional_civil_society_advocates.htm, July 2005.

Transparency International (TI). (2002) 'Bribery Payers' Index.' Accessed at www.transparency.org/cpi/2002/bpi2002.en.html, December 2004.

United Nations Conference on Trade and Development (UNCTAD). (2004b) 'Country Fact Sheet: Saudi Arabia.' Accessed at www.unctad.org/fdstatistics, December 2004.

United States Census Bureau (US-CB). (2004) 'IDB Summary Demographic Data for Saudi Arabia.' Accessed at www.census.gov/cgi-bin/ipc/idbsum? cty = SA, December 2004.

United States Central Intelligence Agency (US-CIA). (2004) 'CIA Factbook.' Accessed at www.cia.gov/publications/factbook/geos/sa.html, November, 2004.

United States Embassy, Riyadh (US-E). (2004) 'Saudi Arabia: Economic Trends 2004.' Accessed at www.usembassy.state.gov/riyadh, December 2004.

United States Energy Information Administration (US-EIA) (2004a). 'Energy Topics: Historical Data.' Accessed at www.eia.doe.gov, November 2004.

—— (2004b) 'Saudi Arabian Gas Projects.' Accessed at www.eia.doe.gov/emeu/ cabs/saudi.html, December 2004.

United States Trade Representative Office (US-TRO). (2004) '2004 Special 301 Report: Watch List.' Accessed at www.ustr.gov/Documents_Library/ Reports_Publications/ 2004.html, December 2004.

World Bank. (2005) 'Doing Business in Saudi Arabia.' Washington, DC: World Bank, Accessed at www.rru.worldbank.org/doingbusiness, January 2005.

World Health Organisation (WHO). (2005) 'Child and Adult Mortality Statistics.' Accessed at www.who/int/countries, January 2005.

World Trade Organisation (WTO). (2005) 'Accessions: Saudi Arabia.' Accessed at www.wto.org/english/thewto_e/acc_e/al_arabie_saoudite_e.htm, January 2005.

Zawya. (2005) 'Saudi Arabian Equities.' Accessed at www.zawya.com/Equities. January 2005.

Newspaper and magazine references used

Arab News, Jiddah.
Financial Times (FT), London.
Guardian, London.
Al-Ittihad, Abu Dhabi.
Middle East Economic Digest (MEED), London.
Middle East Economic Survery (MEES), Cyprus.
MidEast Mirror, London.
New York Times (NYT), New York.
Saudi ARAMCO Dimensions.
United Press International (UPI).

Index